D0123026

# THE HUNT FOR KSM

Also by Terry McDermott

*101 Theory Drive*
*Perfect Soldiers*

# THE HUNT FOR KSM

INSIDE THE PURSUIT AND TAKEDOWN OF THE REAL 9/11 MASTERMIND, **KHALID SHEIKH MOHAMMED**

**TERRY McDERMOTT** and **JOSH MEYER**

Little, Brown and Company
*New York Boston London*

Little, Brown and Company
Hachette Book Group
237 Park Avenue, New York, NY 10017
www.hachettebookgroup.com

First Edition: March 2012

Little, Brown and Company is a division of Hachette Book Group, Inc., and is celebrating its 175th anniversary in 2012. The Little, Brown name and logo are trademarks of Hachette Book Group, Inc.



Map by Jessica Q. Chen

Library of Congress Cataloging-in-Publication Data
McDermott, Terry.
The hunt for KSM : inside the pursuit and takedown of the real 9/11 mastermind, Khalid Sheikh Mohammed / Terry McDermott and Josh Meyer.—1st ed.
p. cm.
Includes bibliographical references.
ISBN 978-0-316-18659-9
1. Mohammed, Khalid Shaikh, 1965– 2. Qaida (Organization)
3. Terrorists—Islamic countries. 4. September 11 Terrorist Attacks, 2001.
5. Terrorism—United States—Prevention. I. Meyer, Josh. II. Title.
HV6433.M52Q33144 2012
363.325092—dc23 2011041533

10 9 8 7 6 5 4 3 2 1

RRD-C

Printed in the United States of America

*To Mil*
*and*
*to Michael*

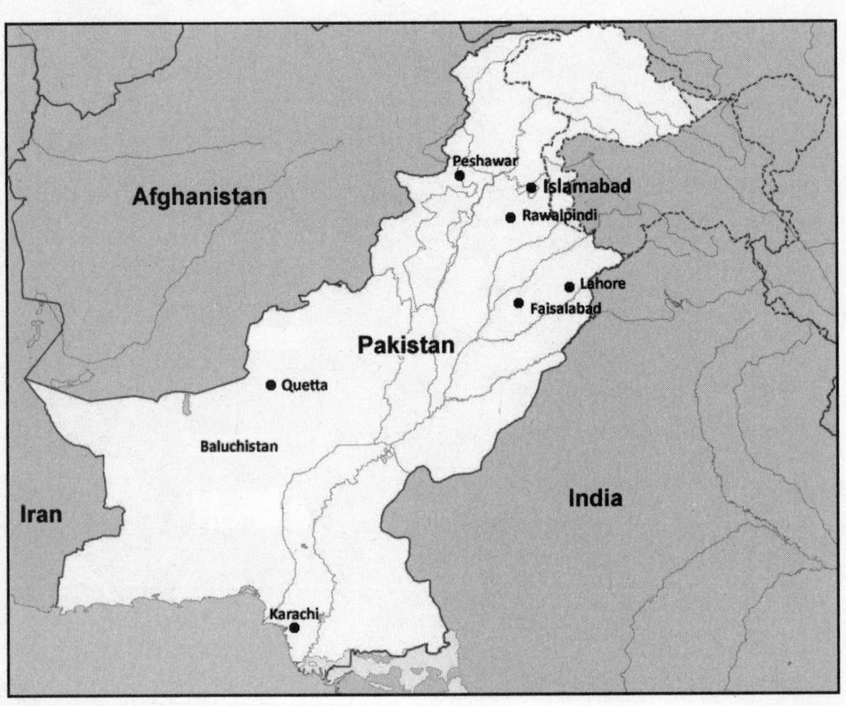

Peshawar
Islamabad
Afghanistan
Rawalpindi
Lahore
Faisalabad
Pakistan
Quetta
Baluchistan
India
Iran
Karachi

# CONTENTS

# PREFACE

Throughout the modern age of terror, Khalid Sheikh Mohammed has had the eerie ability to be at its center yet glimpsed only in the margins. He's been the ghost of our times.

In New York in 1993, he was nothing but a name at the other end of a modest contribution to a bomb maker's bank account. In Manila in 1994, he was again little more than a name, this time in a fax file buried in a laptop computer. In Qatar, he was the terror plotter who got away. In the months leading up to 9/11, he became an increasingly worrisome presence in the data raked into the nation's intelligence trough. He took on different names, different histories. None of it connected. None of it brought him out into the light. As time went on, he remained on the outside edge of anybody's ability to know quite who he was.

The art of investigation is in part the art of seeing, of finding a place to stand so that you *can* see. To see a ghost presents a special kind of problem. The American intelligence apparatus, under the right conditions and armed with the right information, can perform stunts Hollywood would be hard-pressed to imagine. It can zero in on a single man standing in front of a single cave in the farthest reaches of the Hindu Kush; it can extract a conversation from the back bedroom of a fourth-floor walk-up in old, crumbling

Cairo. It is a wondrous thing. Still, it is not magic; it needs a place to start, a place to stand. For six full months following the September 11 attacks on New York and Washington, half a year after four hijacked airliners had claimed nearly three thousand victims, the system had not yet found that point. The full and sustained efforts of the mighty American intelligence-gathering machine had yet to yield enough information to produce a single living man who was in any fundamental way responsible for the attacks.

It wasn't that the assumed perpetrators were unknown. The machine had identified a fairly long list of suspects. In fact, within minutes of the moment, 9:03:02 EDT, to be precise, when Marwan al-Shehhi, an anonymous young son of an Emirati prayer caller, plowed United 175 high into the World Trade Center's South Tower—the moment, that is, when it seemed certain the airline crashes on that sparkling lower Manhattan morning defied coincidence and almost certainly were not accidents—people in positions of power correctly suspected who was behind the assault: Osama bin Laden and his Al Qaeda organization.

Six months later, a war had been launched, a government toppled, and victory all but proclaimed. Yet the net remained empty of big fish. This was not for lack of clues or want of trying. An army had been unleashed. Agents from the Federal Bureau of Investigation chased tens of thousands of dead-end leads from coast to coast. The Central Intelligence Agency scoured the farthest reaches of the globe. And in the even darker reaches of space, the invisible web of satellites operated by the National Security Agency, National Reconnaissance Office, and the National Geospatial-Intelligence Agency caught and sifted billions of bits of data, telephone conversations, Internet chat, and e-mail, and captured thousands of images. Other friendly organizations spanning the planet churned out their own steady storms of data. No, there was no shortage of information. There was too much—a blizzard of it, a whiteout so complete investigators routinely lost their way within it.

The nation's leaders and its security agents were beside themselves in their ignorance. One investigator described it as overpowering: "The amount of intel that was coming through was immense, and it was raw intel. We'd been used to looking at the processed stuff. We'd get an overnight [cable] about a bomb plot at six a.m. from NSA, and then by eight a.m. it'd be processed and it'd be nothing. You were overwhelmed by it."[1] Everyone was petrified of the next attack, which they knew in their bones was imminent. They vowed to do whatever was necessary to stop it, but they really didn't know as much as they thought they did about who had produced the first assault. Al Qaeda, yes, about that all doubt had been obliterated. Bin Laden publicly crowed about his triumph. Between bin Laden at the top and the dead foot soldiers—the hijackers themselves—at the bottom, however, was a void.

We learned about the man who filled that void, Khalid Sheikh Mohammed, not long past the day that many 9/11 investigators had first learned themselves. There was an invitation from a source to attend the retirement dinner of an agent from the FBI's vaunted I-49 international terrorism squad in New York, which had spent the past eight years tracking Mohammed. The dinner adjourned to a raucous bar, where FBI, police, and firefighters had been gathering in the months since 9/11—to circle the wagons, to commiserate about setbacks, and to celebrate small victories. As the graybeards of the New York field office drank and laughed and toasted the newly liberated retiree, the doors of the bar swung open and in swaggered a group of about a dozen much younger agents. It was the PENTTBOM squad, the mostly inexperienced agents who had been given the daunting task of conducting the actual criminal investigation into the attacks on New York and Washington. There was an agreement between journalist and agents not to discuss the investigation that night. But a few hours of drinks later, an agent was asked for any crumb of information he could provide. A tip. A direction to go in. Maybe even a name. The agent thought about it for a minute, looked around to ensure that he was not being overheard, and said in a stage whisper, "Khalid Sheikh Mohammed."

In the ten years since, we followed those agents as they attempted to follow Mohammed. We soon learned that tracking the story of a ghost is not a great deal different from tracking the ghost himself. Khalid Sheikh Mohammed was the enigmatic empty center of every story he was in, always hidden behind the curtains, a wizard in his Oz.

Bringing KSM into focus—at least enough to learn who he was—took investigators years. Finding him took more time yet, and even after he had finally been run to ground he remained hidden. This time, his hiding places were furnished by the U.S. government. At the time of publication, KSM will have been in American custody for nine years, and still his story—and that of his pursuers—remains untold. There is a good chance his full story will never be told in an official venue. For reasons that perplex even its best friends, the United States has kept Mohammed in the shadows of its secret prisons for so long it seems likely he can now never be fully exposed to the light for fear of what he might say about what went on in the darkness. In the meantime, as myths tend to do when the truth is hidden, his legend has grown to mountainous heights and the sometimes heroic stories of those who pursued him have been banished.

We have attempted here to lure the ghost on stage, to dress him in his natural clothing, and to place him and those who fought him nearer the center of the events of the last two decades, many of which he set in motion.

## The Hunters and the Hunted

| THE HUNTERS | |
|---|---|
| Matthew Besheer | Former New York and New Jersey Port Authority detective and member of New York Joint Terrorism Task Force; currently police officer, Punta Gorda, Florida |
| Michael Garcia | Former assistant U.S. attorney, Southern District of New York; currently in private practice in New York City |
| Stephen Gaudin | FBI special agent; currently FBI legal attaché, overseas |
| Robert Grenier | CIA station chief, Islamabad, Pakistan; currently private security consultant, Washington, D.C. |
| Jennifer Keenan | Former FBI assistant legal attaché, Islamabad, Pakistan; currently assistant special agent in charge for national security, Minneapolis, Minnesota field office |
| John Kiriakou | Former CIA agent; currently private security consultant, Washington, D.C. |
| John O'Neill | Former head of counterterrorism, FBI; killed at World Trade Center on 9/11 |
| Francis J. "Frank" Pellegrino | FBI special agent; KSM case officer, New York City |
| Michael Scheuer | Former head of Alec Station, CIA; currently a writer living in Virginia |
| Dieter Snell | Former assistant U.S. attorney, currently in private practice in New York City |
| Ali Soufan | Former FBI special agent; currently private security consultant, New York City |
| Mary Jo White | Former U.S. attorney, Southern District of New York; currently in private practice in New York City |

| THE HUNTED | |
|---|---|
| Ali Abdul Aziz Ali (Ammar al-Baluchi) | KSM nephew, helped arrange financing for hijackers; Guantánamo prisoner |
| Mohamad Farik Amin | Senior member of Al Qaeda; currently imprisoned at Guantánamo |
| Ramzi bin al-Shibh (Omar) | Yemeni member of the Hamburg cell; volunteered as 9/11 pilot; never able to receive visa to enter U.S.; became KSM's contact to the hijackers; currently imprisoned at Guantánamo |
| Walid bin Attash (Khallad) | Veteran Yemeni Al Qaeda operative, nominated by Osama bin Laden to take part in 9/11 attacks; unable to participate due to difficulty obtaining visa; currently in Guantánamo |
| Iyman Faris | Pakistani American truck driver; KSM recruited to blow up bridges, other targets in U.S.; imprisoned in U.S. |
| Christian Ganczarski | German Al Qaeda recruit; helped KSM coordinate Djerba synagogue bombing; imprisoned in France |
| Mohammed Amin al-Ghafari | Associate of Mohammed Jamal Khalifa; active in Philippine charity organizations; managing director of Konsojaya shell company used by Manila conspirators; currently living in Australia |
| Rusman "Gun Gun" Gunawan | Brother of Jemaah Islamiyah leader Hambali; convicted of facilitating and aiding terrorism; currently imprisoned in Indonesia |

| | |
|---|---|
| Mustafa al-Hawsawi | 9/11 hijacker facilitator and Al Qaeda accountant; captured with KSM; currently imprisoned at Guantánamo |
| Nawaf al-Hazmi | Nominated by bin Laden as 9/11 hijacker; deceased |
| Riduan Isamuddin, aka Hambali | Indonesian who organized and led Jemaah Islamiyah, Al Qaeda's Southeast Asian affiliate. Longtime ally of Khalid Sheikh Mohammed. |
| Mohammed Mansour Jabarah | Young Kuwaiti Canadian Al Qaeda recruit, sent by KSM to Southeast Asia to distribute money and plot attacks; imprisoned in U.S. |
| Abdul Karim Abdul Karim (Musaad Aruchi) | Abdul Basit's brother; went to university in U.S. with KSM, assisted him in Pakistan after 9/11; arrested in Pakistan in 2004; whereabouts unknown |
| Mohammed Jamal Khalifa | Saudi businessman, brother-in-law of Osama bin Laden; led NGOs and financed radical Islamists in Southeast Asia; associate of Abdul Basit, Wali Khan; deceased |
| Muhammad Naeem Noor Khan (Abu Talha al-Pakistani) | Pakistani computer engineer; KSM associate alleged to have helped plan attacks in London; arrested 2004, released from prison in Pakistan in 2007, no further information |
| Wali Khan Amin Shah | Afghan Manila Air plot coconspirator, bin Laden associate from the anti-Soviet jihad; currently imprisoned in U.S. |

*(cont.)*

| | |
|---|---|
| Konsojaya Trading Company | Shell company in Malaysia with ties to KSM and numerous associates; supported terrorist plots in Southeast Asia, in particular the Manila Air plot |
| Khalid al-Mihdhar | Saudi Al Qaeda operative nominated to 9/11 plot by bin Laden; hijacker; deceased |
| Khalid Sheikh Mohammed (Mukhtar, KSM) | Kuwaiti citizen of Pakistani descent; mastermind of 9/11 and numerous other plots; captured in Pakistan in March of 2003; currently imprisoned at Guantánamo |
| Ibrahim Muneer (Abdul Majid) | Saudi businessman, associate of Abdul Basit in Manila; whereabouts unknown |
| Abdul Hakim Murad | Kuwaiti national of Pakistani descent; childhood friend of Abdul Basit; Manila Air coconspirator; currently imprisoned in U.S. |
| Saifullah Paracha | Pakistani businessman, associate of KSM; accused of holding Al Qaeda funds; currently imprisoned at Guantánamo |
| Uzair Paracha | Saifullah Paracha's son, assisted KSM sleeper agent in U.S.; currently imprisoned in U.S. |
| Adil Qadoos | Brother of the man in whose house KSM was captured; Pakistani army major arrested in Pakistan in 2003 on suspicion of ties to KSM; court-martialed, currently imprisoned in Pakistan |

| | |
|---|---|
| Ahmed Qadoos | Resident of the house where KSM was captured in 2003; arrested with KSM by Pakistani authorities; released within the week |
| Mohammed al-Qahtani | Saudi Al Qaeda member, sent to U.S. by KSM as the twentieth hijacker; never cleared customs, sent back to the Mideast; captured after 9/11; imprisoned in Guantánamo |
| Jack Roche | British-born Al Qaeda recruit from Australia; confessed to plotting attacks in Australia; released from prison in 2007, currently lives in Australia |
| Mohammed Amein al-Sanani | Mohammed Jamal Khalifa associate in Philippines in 1994, member of board of Konsojaya shell company, Wali Khan associate; currently living in Australia |
| Adnan el-Shukrijumah | Saudi-born Florida resident sent to U.S. by KSM as sleeper agent to await further instructions; tasked with casing potential targets, including Wall Street and the Panama Canal; whereabouts unknown |
| Aafia Siddiqui | American-educated Pakistani woman with science degrees from Massachusetts Institute of Technology and Brandeis University; suspected KSM associate; convicted of assault against American interrogators; currently in prison in U.S. |

*(cont.)*

| | |
|---|---|
| Abdullah bin Khalid al-Thani | Qatari minister of the interior, former minister of religious affairs; member of Qatari royal family; aided jihadis, including KSM, who was given an engineering position in the Qatari Ministry of Electricity and Water |
| Abu Bara al-Yemeni (Abu Bara al-Taiz) | Yemeni nominated by Osama bin Laden to take part in 9/11 attacks; unable to participate due to difficulty obtaining visa; currently in Guantánamo |

*A note on names:* Because Arabic contains few vowels, transliteration of names is complex and often variable. We have tried to use the most common spellings. In the case of Khalid Sheikh Mohammed we have used the spelling he uses.

# THE HUNT FOR KSM

# CHAPTER 1
## Mukhtar

*Faisalabad, Pakistan, March 2002*

In the late autumn of 2001, just as the first fresh snows fell, the American military with its NATO and Afghan allies thundered into Al Qaeda's Afghanistan redoubts; the foot soldiers of the terror organization, when still alive and able, largely fled rather than stand and fight. "It wasn't a highly sophisticated effort," said one American intelligence operative.[1] "They were running around like roaches with the lights on, [having] totally miscalculated in terms of how the U.S. would respond." Some had gone into hiding in the southeastern highlands of Afghanistan, but most had fled overland to Pakistan, hiking through the mountain passes that connect the two countries or taking the roundabout route through Iran. Many traveled on beyond Pakistan. Others stayed.

Pakistan was hardly foreign territory to the Al Qaeda fighters. Some had come from there originally; some had been based there during the long war against the Soviet Union; still others had been educated and trained there. Almost all had transited through Pakistan more than once. They knew the place. Something more than familiarity, too, made Pakistan a likely refuge. The country was woven through with a network of jihadi fighters, organizations, and sympathizers. Militant groups had been a feature of Pakistani life almost since the beginning of the nation. The original and persistent reason for their existence had been to oppose India's efforts to control Kashmir, which Pakistan claimed as its own. The Pakistani government, particularly its principal spy organization, the infamous Inter-Services Intelligence directorate, the ISI, had blessed and supported the jihad movements in this role, legitimizing them. In many cases, ISI had created, trained, and equipped them.

Additionally, since the 1980s, there had been a Sunni-Shiite proxy war within Pakistan funded on opposing sides by Arab states in the Gulf, mainly Saudi Arabia, and Iran. An American diplomat in the region at the time described that struggle as "the confrontation to see who was going to be the dominant force in the Muslim world."[2] The intermingling of the original Kashmiri jihadis, the Gulf-Iran sectarian recruits, the later-arriving fighters focused on Afghanistan, and finally Al Qaeda and the Taliban had resulted in an indecipherable—and volatile—mess. Authorities were no longer sure what anyone was fighting for, and sometimes, it seemed, neither were the jihadis. Lack of clear purpose, unfortunately, had done nothing to reduce the fervor or the deadly results. Pakistan for decades had been at war with itself.

This underlayer of violent extremism was particularly strong in the Punjab, Pakistan's rich central province, from which many of the early Kashmiri jihadis had been drawn. Faisalabad, a sprawling industrial and agricultural center of five million in the heart of the province, had been the home office of almost every significant sectarian jihadi group in the country at one time or another. So it wasn't a great shock to intelligence operatives when they received word in mid-March of 2002 that the city might be harboring Al Qaeda fighters.

NSA's computers had collected a string of intercepts that led CIA analysts to believe that a group of jihadis had holed up in Punjab. An intercepted phone call indicated that one of the group might be a man known as Abu Zubaydah, who had long-standing and close ties to the terror group's inner circle of leadership. The estimation of Zubaydah's precise role within Al Qaeda had frequently changed over the previous decade and even then remained fuzzy to the Americans. They nonetheless viewed him as a major figure, one who would know important Al Qaeda secrets. And he would certainly know the most important one—where was the next attack going to be?

The intercepts were inexact about precisely where Zubaydah and his cohorts were. John Kiriakou had arrived in Islamabad a month earlier as a TDYer, or temporary duty assignee, to help lead the CIA's counterterrorism operations in the country. He'd been begging for an Afghanistan posting since September 11, and the Pakistan job came open as he was threatening to resign if not deployed immediately. He was a fluent Arabic speaker and that alone gave him real value, as did his time chasing terrorists in the Gulf and in Greece.

The agency had a clever piece of hardware called "the Magic Box" that could send out an electronic signal keyed to a particular telephone. If it found the phone within range, a ping would be sent back to the device. The agency had Zubaydah's electronic signature from NSA. So for two weeks agents drove around Lahore and Faisalabad pinging for the phone, from two in the morning until dawn, when they thought Zubaydah was most likely to be using it. They made very little progress. The phone they were hunting appeared never to be in the same place two nights running.

One of the agency's top analysts was also TDY'd from Langley to help pinpoint Zubaydah's location. The analyst, Deuce Martinez, was regarded as one of the best "targeters" the agency had. He had arrived for the latest of several stints, just in time for the morning shift after a marathon day of flying. Martinez was told who the target was, and how the intel they had received was so vague as to render it almost useless.

Martinez went to work immediately. He put Zubaydah's name in the center of an analytical report and then added lines radiating outward, representing NSA signals, ground intel, e-mails, and whatever else he could find—phone numbers of people Zubaydah had called or who had called him, and a second layer of calls made by and to the people he had talked to. He used a link-analysis computer program to build images of networks from the raw data. He drew his own crude reconstruction of the analysis on a huge piece of butcher paper pinned to a wall inside the CIA's rooms in the Islamabad embassy. In a few weeks, Martinez had narrowed the range to fourteen distinct addresses that stood out as the most likely sites. Ten of the sites were in Faisalabad, four in Lahore.

Unable to further identify the location and unwilling to wait and risk letting Zubaydah slip away—or, worse, letting him launch an attack—Kiriakou's boss, the CIA Islamabad station chief, Bob Grenier, decided to hit the fourteen sites simultaneously. The mission was so large and expensive he had to get the okay from Langley before launching it. Permission was granted and a planeload of equipment, agents, and weapons was flown in. Three dozen American CIA and FBI agents were rounded up to take part, and one of each was paired with an officer from the ISI. It was an extraordinary number of people for a clandestine operation, but even with that they needed help. They persuaded their Pakistani counterparts to provide the rest of the manpower for their little army. The Pakistanis agreed. It was a huge undertaking with a greater chance of chaos and failure than success.

With the local knowledge the Pakistanis provided, the Americans scouted the sites as well as they could. Two of the Lahore sites turned out to be bad matches—one was a kebab stand, the other an all-girls' school. Many of the remaining sites were mud huts. Two of the Faisalabad prospects, however, were particularly interesting. One large house was curious because the shutters and windows were kept closed at all hours. Even in March, Faisalabad is hot and humid, and keeping everything shut up made no sense. Another property seemed odd because it appeared to be a vacant lot. How could phone calls be made from a vacant lot?[3]

The Pakistanis assisting the Americans explained that in many large cities in their country, each physical property is assigned a telephone number. Whether it is occupied or not, wires are strung so that it can be activated quickly and cheaply when the time comes. One of the Pakistanis climbed the nearest pole and found that the wire assigned to the vacant lot had been spliced and a second line was run to the three-story house next door.

"We got 'em," one of the other agents told Kiriakou.

On the night of the raids, the Pakistanis provided two big buses to take the strike teams from Islamabad to Lahore. At a safe house there, they were divided into site teams of four men each—one CIA agent, one FBI agent, and two Pakistanis. After everyone assembled in one room, Kiriakou climbed on a tabletop, and ordered everyone to synchronize watches—just like in the movies. The two Lahore teams transferred to small trucks and the rest took off for Faisalabad, another two hours down the road. The mission nearly ended right there. The highway to Faisalabad is a toll road and the lead car blew through the first tollbooth without paying. The Pakistani police chased it down and pulled it over. The whole caravan, including two buses full of guys in *shalwar kameez* bristling with weapons and communications gear, had to pull over and sit there and wait until the local cops were persuaded to let the lead car go.

They launched the attacks in the pitch-black two o'clock hour of March 28. The teams stormed the suspected hideouts without warnings of any sort, the Pakistanis going in first. CIA and FBI officials had set up a command post at a safe house in a central location in Faisalabad. They were waiting there in the dark when they began to hear the sounds of a gun battle coming from the direction of the house with the stolen telephone connection. Kiriakou and another CIA officer raced to the house, a pale peach three-story stucco home built behind high walls in the upper-middle-class Shahbaz Town district.

The Pakistan Rangers had rammed through an outer gate and the ground-floor doors, making a racket and igniting a full-scale firefight. By the time Kiriakou arrived, at least one of the residents was already dead. Under attack, three men attempted to flee. They ran to the top floor of the house, then tried to escape by leaping from the house to the one next door. They were spotted from below, pursued, engaged, and shot. One man was dead by the time he hit the ground. Another was screaming in pain, alive but incapacitated. The third man was wounded in the groin, abdomen, and thigh, and was bleeding profusely. Kiriakou wasn't certain, but thought there was an excellent chance the wounded man was Zubaydah. He called Martinez for advice on how to identify the man. Martinez suggested photographing his iris, but the man's eyes were rolled back in his head. Martinez said to photograph his ear, the configuration of which is as unique to each individual as a fingerprint. Kiriakou took a cell-phone photo of the ear and e-mailed it immediately to Islamabad, where it was ID'd as probably belonging to Zubaydah.[4]

One of the Pakistani officers, aggrieved at having one of his men shot, offered to administer justice to Zubaydah on the spot. Kiriakou was firm; he had to deliver the prisoner alive. He stopped the execution.

The men in Zubaydah's house never knew what hit them. At least ten were taken into custody. They had been living in the house for weeks. Beyond just hiding out there, Zubaydah had directed that classes in basic English and electronic bomb construction be conducted inside. He was also trying to arrange for new identity papers to be delivered to them. Among the cache of materials seized in the raid were telephones, stolen and forged passports from a dozen countries—including Somalia and Colombia—bomb-making manuals, military textbooks, diaries, videos, and cassette recordings. The materials were packed off to the embassy in Islamabad, scanned, photographed, and shipped back to Washington, D.C. The CIA team quickly bundled the wounded Zubaydah into the back end of a Toyota pickup, then raced to a local hospital, which was a mess—bugs entered freely from windows left open against the heat, geckos scrambled across the walls, the floor ran with blood and bodily fluids. Needles were cleaned by plunging them into a bar of soap prior to injection. The Americans deposited their dying prisoner on a bed and used a sheet to tie him to the frame, hoping to prevent any attempt at escape.

In the midst of this chaos, a cell phone started ringing. Over and over again. It didn't belong to any of the agents. The Americans soon realized it was Zubaydah's phone, which was in a sealed evidence bag in the room. The FBI, seeking to secure all the evidence from what they regarded as a crime scene, had stowed the phone in the sealed bag to be shipped away with the rest of the materials gathered at the scene. There it remained. Kiriakou and another CIA agent were eager to see who was calling Zubaydah, but they could do nothing but listen as the phone rang unanswered inside its evidence bag.

The incident was a stark illustration of a fundamental difference between the FBI and the CIA—a difference that was becoming ever more apparent as the two agencies jostled with each other on the front lines of the hunt for Al Qaeda in Pakistan. The FBI, given its criminal investigation into the 9/11 attacks, was primarily concerned with the past, with what had happened, with the crime that had been committed. The CIA was interested in the future, what might happen tomorrow, or even today. The FBI wanted evidence; the CIA needed intelligence.

Zubaydah's condition was dire and his captors feared he would die before a definitive identification could be made, and before he could talk. So the Americans raced him by helicopter to a better hospital on a military base near Lahore, where he was stabilized. As soon as they deemed it practical to move him again, Zubaydah was hustled out to the Lahore airport in the dead of night. A CIA Gulfstream jet was waiting in a far corner of the airfield, and the agency wanted to get him out of the country as quickly as possible.

The FBI, as usual, had other ideas. Jennifer Keenan, a senior FBI agent in Islamabad, got a call at three in the morning that Zubaydah was en route to the airport and on his way out of the country. She had previously received instructions that she had to make sure the FBI had a good set of fingerprints from Zubaydah before he was shipped off to wherever the CIA planned to take him. Urgently, she called a couple of other agents and they raced off to the airport. They arrived barely in time. They met the antique 1950s ambulance carrying Zubaydah on the tarmac just as he was about to be transferred to the Gulfstream.

Reading reports on an investigative target, even dozens of them over years, is not the same as actually meeting the target in the flesh. The few photos obtained over the years by the U.S. government had shown Zubaydah as being wiry, even frail, and very bookish. To the agents' astonishment, he was a big, buff man, strong as an ox, with wild hair. His impressive strength was probably the main reason he survived his injuries. Keenan's two agents were big, too, and when they tried to get a set of prints from him on the tarmac, he resisted, consciously or not. As they wrestled with Zubaydah, the pilot of the plane stormed down the stairs, demanding to know what the hell was going on.

Kiriakou, who was trying to help the FBI agents, said they were trying to print the suspect.

"Who the fuck wants him fingerprinted?!" the pilot screamed.

Kiriakou's response was equally forceful: "The director of the FBI!"

After they finally got the prints, the burly FBI agents stepped aside so the CIA could take custody. Two agency officers, both far smaller than the FBI men, eased Zubaydah out of the ambulance and put him on an old-fashioned litter to lift him up the rickety stairway and onto the plane. They dropped the litter, and Zubaydah fell face-first onto the ground. Blood spit everywhere, and he writhed in agony on the asphalt.

The FBI agents grabbed the litter back and hauled Zubaydah onto it and up the steps. As they were about to reach the top, the man on the lower end lost his balance, probably slipping on the blood, and staggered. His end of the stretcher tipped down with him and Zubaydah was about to flip off one side and fall twenty feet straight onto the tarmac below.

That fall almost certainly would have killed him, and with it the government's best chance yet—by far—to ascertain Al Qaeda's plots and plans. The FBI agent at the head of the litter was a well-muscled man named Ty Fairman. He single-handedly held the litter aloft and kept Zubaydah on top of it until his partner regained balance and grabbed his end.

Zubaydah was finally loaded on board. Within a minute or two, he was flying out of Pakistan.

## *Udorn Royal Thai Air Force Base, Thailand, April 2002*

The jet carrying Zubaydah eventually landed at an air base outside the city of Udon Thani in northeastern Thailand. Udorn, as the airfield was commonly known, had a long history with the CIA, having been the jungle-bound home base to the agency's Air America during the Vietnam War. A secure interrogation facility was hastily improvised there. This new facility—one of the first of what would come to be called the black sites—had been arranged by the CIA and its Thai counterparts. It was in most regards perfect—remote, yet with easy access to the world's airways; patrolled by friendly eyes ready to look away when asked.

Caring for and interrogating prisoners were not roles the CIA usually performed, or for which it was especially well equipped. The CIA gathered intelligence, not prisoners. In most cases, the Americans with the most expertise in the histories and handling of radical Islamists were members of the FBI, which had been investigating and preparing prosecutions of Islamist terrorists since the first bombing of the World Trade Center in 1993. But in a secret "Memorandum of Notification," the Bush administration had granted the CIA the lead role in handling Al Qaeda captives.[5]

Winning the job away from the FBI had been an important bureaucratic victory for CIA director George Tenet, a master of Washington infighting. From very early in the War on Terror, Tenet sought to place his agency in control of the flow of information, and won for himself the ability to mold and disburse it as he saw fit. One of the FBI's top counterterrorism officials, Pasquale

D'Amuro, the scrappy former leader of the New York field office's international terrorism operation, fought pitched battles in the Oval Office to protect the FBI's role in the response to 9/11, but lost. His new boss, FBI director Robert S. Mueller III, was in no position to help him. September 11 was Mueller's eighth official day on the job, and he—and the FBI itself—had no saviors in the upper reaches of the Bush White House. Worse, the FBI had been the nation's principal counterterrorism force before September 11, and was seen, in the eyes of many within the relatively new Bush administration, as having failed to protect the United States against Al Qaeda. New circumstances demanded new methods, and the CIA put itself forward.

But when the man thought to be Abu Zubaydah, the first big fish to be netted after September 11, arrived in Thailand in early April, the CIA interrogators were nowhere to be found. Lacking its own expertise, the agency had chosen to use teams of outside contractors to conduct prisoner interrogations of so-called high-value detainees. The Zubaydah interrogation team was still waiting to be dispatched. Some in the CIA had not thus far been persuaded that the wounded man was really their target.

The mystery man nonetheless lay dying. So the initial interrogation—auspiciously, it turns out—fell to two of the FBI agents who happened to know the most about Al Qaeda: Ali Soufan, a brash young agent who was one of its only native Arabic speakers, and a former officer from the army's 82nd Airborne Division who also spoke some Arabic, Stephen Gaudin. Both were veterans of the New York JTTF and highly regarded interrogators, but—even given that—had been uncertain what their jobs would be at Udorn. They had been told in no uncertain terms that their role in Zubaydah's debriefing would be subordinate to the CIA's. They would do what was asked. The orders they were given before being dispatched were firm: "You will help the CIA. If they want you to, you provide questions. If they want you to do guard duty, you're gonna do guard duty, you're just gonna do . . . whatever [they ask you to]."[6] They would be "second chair" to the CIA.

The two were the only agents from the Bureau on the charter flight to Thailand. There were others on board who did not appear to be from the CIA or any other intelligence agency. Gaudin and Soufan had no idea who these people were. The plane landed in Thailand ahead of Zubaydah's flight from Pakistan. When Zubaydah arrived and was wheeled into the crude interrogation facility, the agents realized the other occupants of their plane had been medical personnel. One of the men who ultimately attended to him was a top-notch surgeon from Johns Hopkins who was there as a favor to a top CIA official. Zubaydah was in dire condition. The medical staff went to work.

Although the CIA interrogation team had yet to arrive, the agency personnel who had set up the site were there. Once the prisoner's condition had stabilized enough, the CIA officer in charge turned to Gaudin and Soufan and said, "Aren't you guys going to get in there and start talking to him?" The fear—dread, really—that prevailed then was that the attacks of 9/11 were simply a precursor to whatever would follow. The FBI men asked where the CIA interrogators were and were told it didn't matter—time was short and they needed to find out as quickly as possible if this was Zubaydah and, if so, what he knew. "You two guys are it," the CIA man said. "There's nobody else here to do the interview."

The FBI had perfected and practiced its own style of interrogation over decades. It required agents to accomplish two main tasks—persuade the person being interrogated that the agents genuinely cared for him, and persuade the prisoner that the agents already knew the answers to most questions they asked; lying was futile. As basic as this approach seems, it had held up amazingly well over time. It worked. Soufan and Gaudin were highly regarded practitioners. Gaudin in particular became a star at the FBI for getting one of the 1998 Africa embassy bombers to confess.

Almost all FBI interviews have one overarching purpose. The Bureau is a law enforcement agency whose primary focus is gathering evidence to take to trial. Agents aren't single-minded, however. They say they know the value of information, and have often used the threat of a long prison sentence to get it. Interrogating suspects about a larger universe of coconspirators is a technique that the FBI has used to bring down entire Mafia crime families, for example, despite those organizations' code of silence.

Agents typically start an interview by pulling out their badges, telling the suspect who they are, reading him his Miranda rights, and asking the suspect if he wants to talk. This circumstance was different. All anybody wanted to know from Zubaydah was how to stop the next attack. It sometimes seemed that was all anybody in government wanted to know, period. Because Zubaydah was still in mortal danger from his wounds, the interviews had to be brief and to the point. Then the agents would have to give up the room to the medical team, often for hours, before the prisoner was able to resume. They would alternate in that fashion for days.

Zubaydah was encouragingly cooperative in the first round. Because both agents had studied and investigated Al Qaeda for years, they knew Zubaydah's history, his hometown, his nicknames, his parents' names—even his e-mail addresses. They used this information to test Zubaydah's reliability. In fact, they told him that this was exactly what they were going to do. We'll know when you're lying, they said, so don't waste our time.

"If you'd rather not talk to us, say 'I don't have anything to say,' but don't lie to us," Gaudin told him. Zubaydah lied right off the bat. Asked his name, he replied that he was Abdel Moneim Madbouly, a famous Egyptian film comedian of the black-and-white era. It was like saying he was Bob Hope, such an obvious lie that all three men—Soufan, Gaudin, and then Zubaydah—laughed out loud. When Soufan subsequently addressed him as Hani, his mother's pet name for him, Zubaydah, taken aback, told them they didn't need him to say his name, that they already knew who he was. Gaudin agreed, but told Zubaydah they had to hear it from him. "It's a test. We're testing you," he said.

Many FBI case agents keep what they call to-go bags close at hand for their active investigations. The bags contain all relevant information on a suspect so that all an agent has to do if he's called out of town on a case is grab the bag and go. Gaudin ordinarily used a lawyer's accordion file to hold documents in his to-go bag. But he didn't have one for Zubaydah, and when he got the call to go to Thailand, he only had time to download the wanted posters of suspected terrorists from the FBI website. His Bureau laptop was broken, a common problem, so he loaded the posters onto his PDA, an awkward little handheld computer made by Hewlett-Packard called a Jornada. It was an obscure device, so much so that Gaudin's colleagues teased him about buying the only one ever made. Zubaydah had been around Al Qaeda so long—since the early 1990s—that he was presumed to know everyone of significance in the organization. So one of the tests Gaudin and Soufan would use to assess Zubaydah's reliability was his willingness and ability to identify faces on the wanted posters. Not all the wanted terrorists were Al Qaeda members, but enough of them were so that the test should prove useful.

The world of radical Islam was hardly a unified front. It was fractious, disordered, with different organizations and different agendas that often competed with one another. Even individuals who seemed to have similar goals did not appear to be connected. Before 9/11, the most famous Islamist terrorist in the world was Ramzi Yousef, a nom de guerre for a Kuwaiti-born Pakistani named Abdul Basit Abdul Karim. Yousef had attempted to blow up the World Trade Center in 1993, killing six people, wounding scores of others, and causing hundreds of millions of dollars in damage. He had escaped New York the night of that attack and joined forces with his uncle, Khalid Sheikh Mohammed, in Karachi, Pakistan's commercial capital.

After Yousef's near-glorious success in New York, the two headed to the Philippines, where they hatched plans to assassinate the Roman Catholic pope and the American president, Bill Clinton, and blow up a dozen American-flagged jumbo jets in flight eastward over the Pacific. One Japanese man had been killed during a test run of their homemade explosives. Their plans were scuttled in January of 1995 by Yousef's carelessness, which eventually led to his arrest. Mohammed, however, got away, and had been quietly pursued by a handful of counterterrorism agents ever since.

Mohammed, whom the agents habitually referred to as KSM, traveled the world with aplomb, setting up terror cells in one place, negotiating to sell holy water from Mecca or buy frozen chicken parts in another. So far as the investigators knew, Yousef and KSM were their own bosses, belonging to no organization other than the fictional Liberation Army Yousef had created to take credit for the first World Trade Center attack. KSM had become an obsession to some among his pursuers, especially to the lead agent on the Philippine case, an idiosyncratic former CPA named Francis J. "Frank" Pellegrino. Pellegrino, an FBI agent out of New York, pursued KSM relentlessly to the four corners of the globe; he had come close to catching him more than once, but whenever he got near enough to touch him, his quarry vanished, like smoke on the wind.

The plot to blow up the airliners wasn't regarded as an Al Qaeda operation, and there was no information suggesting Yousef and Mohammed were Al Qaeda affiliates. As bin Laden rose in prominence, the FBI team chasing KSM began to feel as though everyone had forgotten that he, too, wanted to kill Americans—thousands of them at once. KSM was secretly indicted in the U.S. in 1996, thanks in large part to the overseas gumshoe work of Pellegrino and a partner. When the indictment was unsealed at a high-profile news conference following Basit's sentencing two years later, virtually no one noticed, much less publicized it. By then, if your target wasn't Al Qaeda, it didn't matter. Beyond Pellegrino and a handful of other agents, no one spent much time worrying about KSM or even thinking about him. In the year prior to September 11, as hints and clues of a major attack accumulated, the Manila case receded even further into bureaucratic backwaters.

Al Qaeda grew to dwarf all other terrorist targets. Its activities dominated threat reporting within the intelligence community, especially after its bombings of the two U.S. embassies in Africa in 1998 and the American warship USS *Cole* in Yemen in 2000. In the final months before the 9/11 strikes, the intel channels hummed with reports that Al Qaeda was planning something spectacular.

Even the president was briefed on the looming threat. One mysterious name was persistently associated with these Al Qaeda plans—Mukhtar, which in Arabic can mean "the head," "the brain," or "the chosen one." No one knew who, exactly, Mukhtar was, but some of the intel had him trying to send sleeper agents into the United States. The name took on near-mythic proportions after 9/11, when bin Laden himself, in a video, praised Mukhtar as the mastermind of the attacks. Pointing to a position off-camera, bin Laden thanked him profusely. Even after the tape was recovered in the rubble in Afghanistan, the best forensic experts in Washington could find no trace of Mukhtar or his identity on it. When Soufan first saw that video, he thought to himself: "Who the hell is Mukhtar? We need to find him."

Although Al Qaeda had been a high-priority intelligence target for half a dozen years, American knowledge of the organization was surprisingly sketchy. Most of the prior investigative efforts had been focused solely on Osama bin Laden and a few members of his inner circle, including second-in-command Ayman al-Zawahiri and Saif al-Adel, a suspected operations chieftain. These men had been targets of an entire special unit within the CIA. But beyond them, U.S. understanding of Al Qaeda was riddled with holes. Who belonged? How many were they? Dozens, hundreds, thousands? And where the hell were they? What was the organization's command structure? Who did its bidding? What were its ultimate intentions?

In ideal circumstances, Gaudin and Soufan would try to extract exactly this sort of information from Zubaydah; they would build a better understanding through patient, careful questioning. The situation at Udorn was far from ideal. They needed Zubaydah to tell them where and when the next attack was going to occur. The CIA continued to have doubts about Zubaydah's identity. They took his fingerprints and pressed the FBI agents for further corroboration. Gaudin and Soufan were already certain. They recognized him from Bureau photographs. Zubaydah was bigger than they expected. He could have played tackle for a college football team, Gaudin thought. But there was no doubt in their minds it was he.

Zubaydah's physical condition fluctuated a great deal during the first thirty-six hours at Udorn. At times, he seemed about to slip away. The doctors would rush in to resuscitate him, doing whatever they could to keep him alive. During one such effort Soufan and Gaudin stayed in the room while doctors worked to bring him back from the brink. By this point they had begun to establish a connection with Zubaydah. While the medical team worked on him, Soufan held ice cubes to his lips, murmuring to him in Arabic, trying to comfort him. Zubaydah, flat on his back, defecated all over the gurney and himself. Gaudin grabbed clean towels and wiped him clean. Don't worry, they told him, these are good doctors and they are going to take care of you.

Shortly thereafter, Zubaydah was moved to a nearby hospital. Soufan and Gaudin went with him. On Zubaydah's request, Gaudin stayed at his side and held his hand while their prized detainee went through a number of magnetic resonance imaging (MRI) tests, which involve the patient being inserted into a large, claustrophobia-inducing cylinder. Zubaydah was scared. Gaudin reassured him. Once Zubaydah was stabilized again, the agents resumed their interrogation, testing his willingness to cooperate by asking him to identify photographs from Gaudin's PDA. They told him that they would scroll through the photos and wanted Zubaydah to respond only when they showed him a photo of Saif al-Adel or Abdullah Ahmed Abdullah, both of whom were wanted for their suspected roles in the African embassy bombings of 1998. If he was willing to talk about those men, they reasoned, he was probably willing to talk about anything.

Gaudin gave Soufan the PDA with what he thought was a photo of Abdullah, but he had accidentally called up a photo of Khalid Sheikh Mohammed.

Zubaydah suddenly squeezed Gaudin's arm. Gaudin became agitated, thinking Zubaydah was claiming that the photo of KSM was Abdullah. He stopped the session. He told Zubaydah to quit wasting his time. After all we've been through in the last two days, after all we have done for you, he said, don't you dare lie to me.

Zubaydah replied: "No, I'm not lying to you. That's Mukhtar."

Soufan, standing out of line of vision of the photo, was puzzled. Gaudin, still aggravated, said: "I know exactly who this is. This is Ramzi's uncle, the plot against the pope, the plot against the Philippine airline." He rattled off a bunch of information on Mohammed from the Manila Air plot, then said, "I don't want to talk about him. He's not important to me. What's important to me is this test, if you're going to be truthful to me. I'm here to talk about Abdullah. Don't talk to me about this guy anymore."

They resumed the slide show, but Zubaydah interrupted again. "How did you know about Mukhtar?" he asked.

Gaudin finally realized then that Zubaydah must know KSM, which made no sense. Zubaydah was Al Qaeda; KSM was Abdul Basit's uncle, a freelancer. He brought KSM's photo back up on the PDA and told Zubaydah with feigned frustration, okay, say whatever it is you wanted to say about the man in the photograph.

"That's Mukhtar," Zubaydah said. "How did you know that Mukhtar was the mastermind of September eleventh?"

Gaudin was so stunned he nearly fainted. Zubaydah had asked how the Americans had known that KSM was one of the most wanted men on the planet, the mysterious Mukhtar. Of course, they had no idea, but Gaudin gamely told him they knew everything: "We told you we already know the answers. When we ask you questions, we already know the answer."

He congratulated Zubaydah. "See, this is what we're talking about, this is being honest with us. Thank you for being honest." Gaudin was worried he wouldn't be able to maintain his calm in front of Zubaydah any longer and, gathering his resolve, calmly told him he needed to take a bathroom break. He and Soufan went out of the room. Once outside, Gaudin could barely contain himself.

"That's Frank's guy," he told Soufan, referring the Manila case agent, Pellegrino. "Frank's guy is the mastermind of nine eleven."

The pair were stunned. They didn't quite understand how they had done it, but both knew they had uncovered a huge piece of information. They had to tell Pellegrino, their bosses, the world. Gaudin told the lead CIA agent at the site they needed to send cables immediately to their respective headquarters, telling them Zubaydah had produced the single most important piece of the September 11 puzzle to date—that Frank's guy was the mastermind of 9/11.

The CIA man stared blankly at them and said, "Who the hell is Frank?"

The FBI and CIA—so often on parallel tracks that never converged—had been chasing Al Qaeda, the 9/11 plotters, KSM, and Mukhtar without the slightest hint that they were all connected.

When Gaudin finally reached Pellegrino in New York, he told him as best he was able over an unsecured international connection what had transpired. Pellegrino was speechless. The last name he wanted to hear in connection with 9/11 was KSM, Pellegrino said later. "You want to crawl under your desk. I would have preferred any other name in the world."

When Soufan reached Kenny Maxwell, a supervisor on the counterterrorism squad in New York, and told him that "Frank's guy" had planned 9/11, the supervisor's immediate response was that it was another suspect in the Manila Air plot, Mohammed Jamal Khalifa.

No, Soufan said. KSM.

"Shit," Maxwell said. "He's not even Al Qaeda."

It didn't take long for it to dawn on the counterterrorism squad members—and, soon, others in the FBI, the CIA, and the White House—that the identity of the mastermind of the worst terrorist attacks in history had been right there in front of them all along.

The alert went out—aggressively, urgently, quietly. The very public hunt for bin Laden and company continued to dominate the headlines, and preoccupy the U.S. military. But the U.S. arsenal of tracking satellites was spun up and retasked toward a new target. The FBI and the CIA mobilized, and the entire weight of the U.S. war on terrorism was shifted toward an effort to find a man whose last known location was somewhere deep in the underworld of Karachi, Pakistan, enmeshed in a web of jihadis and the intelligence officers who protected them. It would soon become the largest secret manhunt in history, a guns-drawn chase through the streets of some of the world's most dangerous places. But it would be nearly another year—a year full of attacks and plots in the U.S. and everywhere else—before KSM was finally run to ground.

# CHAPTER 2
# Those Without

## *Kuwait, 1960s–1980s*

Badawiya, the neighborhood where Khalid Sheikh Mohammed grew up, sat between the sand and the sea on the southernmost edge of Fahaheel, an oil boom town south of Kuwait City. The neighborhood mosque overlooked a mile-wide field of rubble and weeds, a buffer zone between the neighborhood and the great Shuaiba petrochemical complex and Persian Gulf port. The refinery flare stacks sputtered and glowed around the clock. Al-Ahmadi, headquarters of the Kuwait Oil Company, and the bountiful Burgan oil field—the foundations of modern Kuwait—were just a few miles to the west.

Before oil was discovered at Burgan in 1938, Fahaheel was little more than an obscure date palm oasis on the road to Saudi Arabia. Older Kuwaitis recall driving the route south from the capital through miles of blank sand, the occasional car, camel, or Bedouin tent the only sights along the way. Burgan Field was unusual for its vast volume—Kuwait is fifth in the world in known oil reserves, and fully half its production has come from this one place—and its ease of access. In places, the oil simply bubbled to the surface on its own.

Mohammed's parents arrived from Pakistan on the leading edge of Kuwait's boom years. His father, Sheikh Mohammed Ali Doustin Baluchi; his father's brother, Ali Mohammed; and their young families came together in 1956.[1] Both brothers were religious men and had been recruited to head mosques. Sheikh Mohammed became imam of a drab brown brick mosque in Al-Ahmadi, the administrative center of the Kuwaiti oil industry. The twin minarets of the mosque stood in stark contrast to the Kuwait Oil Company corporate reservation, which surrounded it. The reservation was designed and built by the British and had the look and well-ordered feel of a small military installation. The gridded, tree-lined streets, flower-bedded roundabouts, and white-fenced worker cottages seemed to have been dropped in whole from another, greener world.

Sheikh Mohammed and his wife, Halima, had four children when they arrived in Kuwait. Five more were born after; Khalid second to last. The families traveled on Pakistani passports, but this was as much a matter of convenience as identity. Both Sheikh Mohammed and Halima were ethnic Baluch, from a swath of hard, dry land across the Gulf of Oman from the Arabian peninsula. Baluchistan, as it is known, includes parts of contemporary Iran, Afghanistan, and Pakistan, but existed as an entity in its own right long before the boundaries of any of these modern states were drawn. Sheikh Mohammed and Halima were both born in Karachi, Pakistan's burgeoning commercial capital, but grew up in Sarbaz in Iranian Baluchistan, a couple of hours from the current Pakistan border. Mohammed's Pakistani passport was issued by the consulate in Basra, Iraq.[2]

Baluchistan is one of the oldest inhabited places on earth and its history is one of fierce resistance to whatever would-be ruler was on hand at the moment. Next-door-neighbor Persia, the great power of the ancient world, was held at bay for a thousand years; Alexander the Great suffered his greatest defeat there, and the Arab rulers who swept over the region in the century after Muhammad's death were told by their military strategists to forgo Baluchistan, for "if you send a small Army, it will be defeated, if you send a large Army, they will die of thirst and hunger."[3]

The oil money that drew Mohammed and his family didn't merely enrich Kuwait; it transformed the country utterly. At its first formal census, in 1957, Kuwait had a population of 206,000. In slightly more than two decades, it had grown six times larger and has nearly doubled again since. The growth came almost entirely from abroad. Palestinians and Egyptians arrived by the hundreds of thousands and largely took over the businesses of bureaucracy, civil affairs, and education. Americans and Brits came, in smaller numbers, to run the new oil and banking enterprises. South Asians—Pakistanis and Indians, initially; Filipinos, Sri Lankans, and Bangladeshis later—formed the workforce in the oil fields and refineries and, later, in a vibrant service economy.

The boom made native Kuwaitis among the wealthiest and most cosseted people on earth. Their traditional Bedouin birthright had been a share of their fathers' camels; the post-boom Kuwaiti citizen enjoyed guaranteed state employment, or a stipend if he were jobless or privately employed; marriage bonuses; free mortgages, medical care, and education from childhood through university; and guaranteed income at retirement.

All this and more was available to every Kuwaiti citizen. The majority of residents, however, were not citizens and never would be. Most migrant workers and their offspring were deemed unqualified. This created a caste system dividing those with citizenship, the native-born Kuwaitis, from the guest workers, known locally as *bidoon*—those without. The Baluch, no matter how long they stayed, were among the *bidoon*. This was a fundamental fact of life for the family of Mohammed Ali Doustin. They knew they would never belong. They didn't even know how long they would be allowed to stay. On occasion, the government would notify a family to pack up and leave as soon as possible. It didn't have to be clear why.

Khalid Sheikh Mohammed was born on April 14, 1965. His father was already fifty-seven, and died just four years later.

Khalid's older brothers—Zahed, Aref, and Abed—directed his schooling. Education in the years of Khalid's youth was serious business. Schoolboys wore white shirts and gray slacks, and the headmaster carried a bamboo cane to keep students in line. Khalid was much younger than his oldest siblings and had nieces and nephews his own age. He and his nephews all attended high school together at Fahaheel Secondary School, a three-story brick all-boys school that housed as many as twelve hundred students.

Mohammed, like his brothers, was an excellent student and technically inclined. He was also rebellious. He and one of his nephews, Abdul Basit Abdul Karim, once climbed the flagpole atop their elementary schoolhouse and tore down the Kuwaiti flag.[4] The girls attended separate female-only schools and did not progress beyond secondary school. "Khalid excelled, especially at science," said Sheikh Ahmed Dabbous,[5] a family friend and teacher at the school, which, like Fahaheel, had a diverse student body—Kuwaitis, Palestinians, Egyptians, and the Baluchi contingent. There were strict separations among the students. Each group tended to stay with its own. State-sponsored sports clubs, for example, were formed for the exclusive membership of native Kuwaitis.

Most of the teachers at the public schools Mohammed attended were Palestinians, who flowed into the country following the 1967 war. They made up the largest group of expatriates in the years of Khalid's childhood and adolescence. At one point there were an estimated 450,000 Palestinians in Kuwait, threatening to outnumber the natives. Hawalli, an area of Kuwait City, became known locally as the West Bank. A United Nations program established after the formation of Israel to help resettle Palestinians away from Palestine included an ambitious educational component; by some measures, Palestinians in the 1970s were among the best-educated populations in the world. As they did in other Arab countries, Palestinians in Kuwait predominated in the professional ranks of engineers, physicians, and teachers.

Kuwait became a center of Palestinian political activism. Yasser Arafat worked there as a civil engineer. Khalid Mishal, a founder of Hamas, was graduated from Kuwait University and taught school in Kuwait City. Most of the political energies of the exiled Palestinians were directed toward Palestine and the formation of an armed resistance there (Fatah, the movement for the national liberation of Palestine, was founded in Kuwait in 1959), but just by weight of numbers Palestinians became a significant, although largely veiled, presence in Kuwait's nascent domestic politics.

Two epochal events roiled the Islamic world in 1979: Islamists overthrew the shah of Iran and instituted an Islamic republic; and the Soviet Union invaded Muslim Afghanistan and installed a puppet government. Muslim leaders worldwide, but especially in the Gulf, were eager to ally themselves with the call to jihad that followed the Soviet invasion. It provided an opportunity to show their commitment to Islamic action without much risk. But the Islamic revolt in Iran provoked a more complicated response. In Kuwait, Shiites made up about a third of the population, and they saw Ayatollah Khomeini's rise to power as a model for Islamic reform at home. The government turned to local Sunni Islamists, such as the Muslim Brotherhood, as a show of their own commitment to a more Islamic Kuwait.

The Brotherhood had begun in Egypt in the 1920s, lashing out at the iniquities of the modern world and calling for a return to a more literal interpretation of Islam. The Brotherhood spread throughout the Arab world, where it often formed the core of opposition to autocratic governments; its members frequently were treated as criminals.

The Kuwaiti government tolerated the Brotherhood, which by the 1980s was dominated locally by Palestinians, as a hedge against potential threats from nationalists on the left. The organization was, as in much of the Arab world, illegal, but nonetheless often stood candidates for elections. The ambivalence was common throughout the region; the risk embedded within it was that Islamists would not long be content to be used as a pawn against other government critics and would demand action of their own choosing.

Mohammed's oldest brother, Zahed, became a student leader of the Brotherhood at Kuwait University. Another brother, Abed, attended religious universities in Kuwait, then Qatar. Mohammed followed Zahed's lead and began attending desert camps of the Brotherhood when he was sixteen.[6] The camps were organized as one part recreation and one part proselytization. Speakers came from abroad to spread the word. It was there in the camps that Mohammed first heard the call to jihad. One particularly fiery orator was an Egyptian-educated Pashtun, Abdul Rasul Sayyaf, who called the young men in the camp to come to Afghanistan to join the holy war against the occupying Soviets.[7]

While much of the ruling elite worried about the persistence of rural, desert values in a modernizing, urbanizing culture, the Islamists were worried about the opposite—the secularization of the new Kuwait. Fewer and fewer families attended mosque regularly. The Brotherhood saw itself as a bulwark against this steady decline. It recruited members quietly, often approaching them covertly in times of personal turmoil or trouble. Its members kept close eyes on local mosques to see who might be newly susceptible to the renewal of a religious lifestyle.

Another key element of the Brotherhood's ideology was a virulent anti-Semitism, which historically had not been a hallmark of Islamist thought. Sayyid Qutb, the Brotherhood's founding theoretician, had preached a rigid, relentless campaign to blame the Jews for almost everything. That message was tailor-made for the crestfallen years that followed Israel's repeated displays of military dominance over the Arabs. An earlier generation's attempt to shape a secular, pan-Arab identity was swept away in the Jewish victories, and pious young men like Mohammed were particularly willing to embrace a vision of a religious future.

When Mohammed graduated high school, Zahed was teaching at a local technical school. Zahed had planned on graduate school in the United States, but the family decided only one boy could afford to go abroad—as *bidoon,* they did not qualify for the generous government scholarships provided to native Kuwaitis. The older brothers chose to send Khalid to the west for further schooling. Mohammed's old high school teacher Dabbous said Mohammed had made clear for years his desire to go abroad: "From the beginning of his studies it's science. He wanted to go to America for this reason. He wanted to become a doctor [PhD] there." The brothers chose Khalid. They traded their future for his.

## *North Carolina, 1984*

Traveling on a Pakistani passport, Mohammed arrived in the winter of 1984 in tiny, remote Murfreesboro, North Carolina, to attend Chowan College, a two-year school virtually unknown in the United States but advertised abroad by the Baptist missionaries it graduated. For Mohammed, it must have been like landing on Mars. There were dusky rivers meandering through dense pine forests, cotton fields, and tobacco patches. Not a sand dune in sight.

Mohammed told school administrators he had heard of the college from a friend in Kuwait. He applied to the school shortly after graduating from Fahaheel Secondary School in 1983. He listed his brother Zahed as his father on the enrollment forms. His bill—$2,245 for the spring semester—was paid in full on the day of his matriculation, January 10.[8] Chowan had been founded in 1848 as a sort of finishing school for young Southern women. Later, under financial duress, it reduced its curriculum and became a two-year junior college. Its leafy setting in isolated Murfreesboro—population about two thousand, with no bars and a single pizza shop—ensured that everyone remained on the straight and narrow.

Chowan did not require the standard English proficiency exam then widely mandated for international students. Foreign enrollees often spent only a semester or two there, improved their English just enough, and transferred to four-year universities. Dominating the international contingent by the 1980s were Middle Eastern men, about fifty of whom were enrolled each year. Mohammed, although Pakistani by birth, spoke Arabic fluently and was integrated into the Arab contingent.

The Arab students were the butt of jokes and harassment in the anti-Muslim era that followed the 1979 Iranian takeover of the U.S. embassy in Tehran. The local boys razzed them, calling them Abbie Dahbies, a play on Abu Dhabi.

Some American students found the foreigners impenetrable. "They seemed to be praying all the time," said John Franklin Timberlake, a 1984 Chowan graduate who became a police officer in Murfreesboro. "Just chanting, like. We never understood a word of it. Sometimes we'd come home late on a weekend night, maybe after we'd had a few beers, and they'd still be praying."[9] The foreign students, regardless of religious affiliation or inclination, were required along with everyone else to attend a weekly Christian chapel service.

A group of the Middle Easterners lived in Parker Hall, a brick tower overlooking Lake Vann, a small pond on campus. They often cooked, ate, and prayed together. As was their custom, they left their shoes in the corridor, an apparently irresistible target for locals, who sometimes moved the shoes from the hallway to the lake. Other students occasionally propped big garbage pails filled with water against the doors of the "Abbie Dahbies," then knocked and ran away. When the young men answered the door, water flooded the room.

Mohammed did well in the pre-engineering curriculum he took for the sole semester he was there. He left in the spring for North Carolina Agricultural and Technical State University in Greensboro, a historically black college on the Piedmont plain in the central part of the state. Unlike gentrified Chowan, A&T was located in a large, growing, fractious city and had an activist past. Jesse Jackson was a graduate, and on February 1, 1960, students at A&T staged the first Civil Rights–era lunch-counter sit-in at a downtown Woolworth. By the time Mohammed arrived, African Americans still made up the majority of students, but there were good-size blocs of white Southerners and Middle Easterners.

For most of the Middle Easterners, this was their initial exposure to Western life. They were excited to see the movies, hear the music they had dreamed of at home. Once they arrived, some were appalled at what they witnessed. Others were thrilled. Like college students almost everywhere, they loved the party life. The better-off among them drove their new Porsche roadsters and Mercedes coupes to and from campus. Like many other religious Muslims, Mohammed developed a dislike for the U.S. in his time here and a disdain for many of his fellow Muslims.

One of Mohammed's nephews, Abdul Karim Abdul Karim (Abdul Basit's brother), had left Kuwait the year before Mohammed and spent two semesters in Oklahoma. He transferred to A&T with Mohammed and majored in industrial engineering. Mohammed was in the mechanical engineering program. The men lived a couple of miles off campus in bland apartment complexes with names like the Yorktown and the Colonial. They shared cars and accumulated parking tickets in large numbers, one friend said. They seldom mingled outside their groups and tended to skip organized events. In the fall, when football dominated the Aggie social calendar, the foreign students arranged soccer matches in the park.

Some of the American students were resentful of the Middle Easterners, feeling they knew English well enough to do the work in lab classes but didn't carry their fair share.

"It was the college life: we used to get together three, four times a week, watch the games, chat, drink, you know," said Sami Zitawi, a Kuwaiti native who recalled large get-togethers on Friday, the Muslim holy day. "We used to go to the farmers, buy a lamb or a goat. Butcher it with a knife. . . . Every Friday night someone would have a big dinner: fifteen, twenty, twenty-five students." The butchering, he said, was often comically inept. The men sometimes organized variety shows—skits and small plays in which Mohammed was an active participant.[10]

While the Middle Eastern students seemed monolithic to the Americans, there were deep divisions within their ranks. "Basically, what you saw was a microsociety of our home," said

Mahmood Zubaid, a Kuwaiti architectural engineer. "Everybody fit in where they felt most comfortable.... There were Kuwaitis, Palestinians, Jordanians. About two hundred to three hundred people in total, but they tended to associate with just their own group.... We hung around only with Kuwaitis. The community we were in, out of the two hundred or three hundred, was actually only about twenty people."

Even within the Kuwaiti group there were deep divisions in politics, culture, status (the native Kuwaitis were on full government scholarships, while the Palestinians and Baluch paid their own way), and especially religion. At the other extreme was a strong core of religious conservatives who tried to act as moral police.

The fun-loving Arabs called them the mullahs. Mohammed was a mullah. There was plenty at A&T for Mohammed and other true believers to be distressed about. Some of the Arab students, like many Americans, treated college life as one long, barely interrupted party. Some had fancy cars and pretty American girlfriends. They went to the clubs; they drank and smoked whatever was available. One Kuwaiti student so resented the efforts at moral policing he would place a bottle of Johnnie Walker scotch on his table whenever the mullahs came by. The party boys tried not to call attention to themselves, but the mullahs noticed. They monitored airports for the arrival of new students and tried to bring them to their side of the battle.

Arab governments monitored relations among their overseas students and would disperse students if they determined any kind of fundamentalist cell was forming. "We had a lot of our students coming back from the U.S. radicalized," said one high-ranking Arab official. "I'm not talking about religious guys going to the U.S. and coming back as fundamentalists. I'm talking about cool guys," he said.[11]

Mohammed was religious, studious, and private, but friendly and capable of a laugh. He had little contact with Americans, and when he did found them to be debauched and racist.[12] He also had a hard time following their traffic laws. He crashed his nephew's

Oldsmobile into a car driven by locals, was found guilty of causing the wreck, and later ordered to pay damages. He lost his right to drive, ignored the order, and ended up spending a few hours in the county jail, a hulking concrete structure that takes up most of a block a mile west of campus in downtown Greensboro.

At the end of 1986, after just three years, Mohammed and his nephew Abdul Karim were graduated from A&T. Almost a third of the mechanical engineering graduates were Middle Easterners. As at Chowan, there was no photo of him in the yearbook. Unlike some of his classmates, who saw their time in Carolina as a high point in their lives, Mohammed was embittered and eager to leave America.

His old high school teacher, Sheikh Ahmed Dabbous, sought him out shortly after he returned home to Kuwait. He found a changed, dour, disenchanted young man.

"When he goes there, he sees most Americans don't like Arabs and Islam," said Dabbous.

" 'Because of Israel,' he says. 'Most Americans hate Arabs because of this.' He's a very normal boy before. Kind, generous, always the smiling kind. After he came back, he's a different man. He's very sad. He doesn't speak. He just sits there.

"I talked to him, to change his mind, to tell him this is just a few Americans. He refused to speak to me about it again. He was set. . . . When Khalid said this, I told him we must meet again.

"He said, 'No, my ideas are very strong. Don't talk with me again about this.' "

## *Peshawar, Pakistan, 1989*

Peshawar sits on a delta of tableland that narrows as it backs up against the Hindu Kush mountain range in northwest Pakistan. The landscape is harsh, with little arable land. The possibilities for a hard life are great; those for livelihood, meek, now that the Silk Road on which it sits has long since ceased to be a commercial thoroughfare.

The local Pashtun population has for generations dodged invaders, traders, and missionaries. The Pashtuns are a tough, wily bunch who have survived—even thrived—for centuries by being able to bend with whatever winds blow through, but they are always careful to take care of their own. Guns are regarded as a man's jewelry and, along with gold and women, are said to be one of the three things for which a Pashtun man will fight. Given the region's history and the prevalence of weaponry within it, that list seems abbreviated. Over time, there have been few periods of calm.

In the 1980s, Peshawar became the rear-echelon headquarters for the Afghan resistance against the Soviet Union's occupying army. While Mohammed was away in America, at college, his brothers—Zahed, Aref, and Abed—moved to Peshawar to support the jihad against the Soviets. By the time of Mohammed's graduation, the pattern of the war had been set. The smaller, nimbler Afghan guerrilla groups had mastered the main act of any resistance—frustrating the enemy—and the war had devolved into a holding action. It had also become a clarion call across the Muslim world. Abdullah Azzam, a Jordanian scholar, had moved to Peshawar years before and almost single-handedly created the modern notion of jihad. Only from the barrel of a rifle, he said, should jihad proceed.

Would-be fighters were drawn from around the globe. Among those who answered Azzam's call was Osama bin Laden, scion of a wealthy Saudi Arabian family. Almost immediately upon returning from America to Kuwait, unable to find work, Mohammed set out to join his brothers.

Armies have always had camp followers. They've changed over time from improbable parades of jugglers and peddlers to the contemporary brigades of missionaries and refugee-resettlement workers. In Peshawar, the headquarters of the resistance, more than 150 relief organizations set up offices during the war. There were so many charities wanting to work in the region that three separate coordinating councils were required to sort out their good deeds.

Before he left Kuwait, Zahed Sheikh Mohammed had gone to

work for a Kuwaiti charity called Lajnat Al-Da'wa al Islamia, or the Committee for Islamic Appeal. LDI was one of the largest charitable organizations in the Middle East. In 1985, two years after he joined the organization, LDI's leaders asked Zahed to move to Pakistan to run their war-relief operations. He was already well established and respected by the time Khalid arrived.

LDI was one of the largest agencies in the region. It had more than twelve hundred employees in Pakistan and Afghanistan and a $4 million annual budget. It operated hospitals, clinics, and twenty-two Qur'anic study centers.[13] As head of a large, well-endowed, and influential charity, Zahed became a figure of importance. He worked out of an office on Arbat Road in Peshawar's University Town, the newest and most Westernized neighborhood in the city, and knew virtually everyone of importance there—Afghan resistance leaders, Arab donors, Pakistani spies, even journalists.

Some charities were suspected of being little more than fronts for laundering jihadi money, but LDI was never accused of wrongdoing. Zahed was strict about not mixing relief work with the resistance. Zahed, the eldest of the brothers, was the most moderate among them. Abed was the most zealously militant, and Khalid followed his lead. LDI spent millions of dollars on schools and clinics and the promotion of the Kuwaiti brand of Islam. Other Arab charities did the same, and their religious schools flourished not just in Peshawar but throughout Pakistan and in areas of Afghanistan controlled by the resistance.

When Mohammed arrived in Peshawar, in 1987, it was a place full of spies, intrigue, and high adventure. The Americans, Russians, Saudis, even the Chinese had scores of agents on the ground. The buccaneering Texas congressman Charlie Wilson periodically rolled through carrying American gifts, the latest of which—Stinger missiles—had just arrived. The fight against the Soviets had been going on for eight years, and the resistance was beginning to sense the prospect of victory. "The Afghans were ecstatic," a Western diplomat who was stationed in Peshawar at the time said. "They thought they were really doing some stuff over there."[14]

Mohammed trained at the Sada camp organized by Azzam. Like most of the Arab camps, Sada spent as much time on ideological rhetoric as battlefield technique. Azzam was a mesmerizing speaker and Mohammed was taken with his message on the necessity of jihad. He would quote passages from Azzam's teachings even decades later.

After he finished the camp training, Mohammed went to work at *al-Bunyan al-Marsus,* the newspaper published by Abdul Rasul Sayyaf's Ittihad-i-Islami, the Islamic Union, one of the Afghan-refugee political parties headquartered in Peshawar. Mohammed's brother Abed was already working at the newspaper when Mohammed began. If Zahed and Aref were older and calmer and Zahed, in particular, was a stabilizing influence, Abed was the most fiery Baluch brother. He had undergone formal religious training in the Gulf emirate Qatar, and was widely respected for his knowledge.

Among dozens of competing potential beneficiaries, seven political parties had been designated by the United States and Saudi Arabia as worthy recipients of the hundreds of millions of dollars they poured into the war against the Soviets. Sayyaf's Islamic Union was at the head of the pack. Sayyaf had been jailed in Kabul and arrived in Peshawar later than most of the other insurgent leaders. This turned out to be an advantage, as the other parties had become bogged down in their own competitions for funds and recruits. Sayyaf was untainted by these rivalries and became a favorite of the CIA.

Sayyaf was a rarity among Afghans, who tended to view Arabs as odd and their interpretation of Islam as impractical. Sayyaf had been educated at Al-Azhar University in Cairo, had spent considerable time in Saudi Arabia, and spoke fluent Arabic. Like Zahed and Khalid Sheikh Mohammed, he was a member of the Muslim Brotherhood and had, in fact, spoken at one of the desert camps Khalid attended as a boy. He was not much of a military man—he'd been a university lecturer before the Soviet invasion—but he was a phenomenal fund-raiser. "Sayyaf had fully internalized the Saudi conservative Islamic message," said Alan Eastham, principal officer in the U.S. consulate in Peshawar in the mid-1980s. "He could give a stem-winder, too. A good fund-raiser, a guy who could go to Saudi Arabia and come back with a pot full of money."[15]

In addition to his work at the party newspaper, Mohammed taught engineering at Sayyaf's university, Dawa'a al-Jihad, which means "convert and struggle." Dawa'a al-Jihad was a rough but functioning college; as many as two thousand students came to learn engineering, medical technology, and literature, and also to train at the neighboring jihadi camps that Sayyaf ran.

The campus had student dormitories, athletic fields, a library, and laboratories, all connected by eucalyptus-lined walkways. It was located about thirty miles southeast of Peshawar, just down the road from the mosque and madrassa where many Taliban leaders were schooled. Twenty-foot-high mud walls separated it from the sprawling Jalozai refugee camp, home to more than two hundred thousand Afghans who had fled a decade of war at home. With Sayyaf's financial support, Mohammed established a curriculum to educate the refugees and prepare them for war against the Russians.

Sayyaf attracted men from all over the Muslim world. Mohammed made lasting acquaintance with several Southeast Asians at Sayyaf's camps, including an Indonesian known by the nom de guerre Hambali, who would remain an associate for the next fifteen years.

While he was in Peshawar, Mohammed married one of his cousins—the daughter of a maternal aunt. The Baluchi brothers were a part of the small, semipermanent community of foreigners around Peshawar; these included Azzam, Egyptian Islamic Jihad founder Ayman al-Zawahiri, and bin Laden. Many of the more well-off Arabs bought houses in Hayatabad or University Town, the most modern and expensive neighborhoods in Peshawar. Bin Laden and his large family of wives and children lived in a big new house in Hayatabad. Mohammed lived at the refugee camp.

Most of the Peshawar Arabs prayed at the small Saba-e-Leil mosque, behind a stucco arch inlaid with pink marble on a dead-end alley off Arbat Road, not far from both Sayyaf's and Zahed's offices. Parts of Peshawar came to look like an Arab town, and this was a bustling little neighborhood, with bakeries, water-buffalo butchers, tailors, and travel agents for booking passages home. There were Arabic newspapers and magazines published locally. Men wore kaffiyehs and their wives were fully covered in Wahhabi black. Tailor shops were kept busy sewing the latest Eid fashions. They lived in many ways a normal life. Khalid even took graduate-level classes by correspondence, earning a master's degree in Islamic culture.[16] The brothers blended in with their Arab colleagues. They wore red-and-white checked head scarves and looked more Arab than Pakistani. Zahed and Khalid, both short, stout, and heavy-bearded, looked enough alike that, despite Zahed being eight years older, some people could not tell them apart.

Many of those who came to fight the holy war never got far beyond the city. "Saudi, Gulf families would send their kids to Afghanistan in the summer for some school project," Eastham said. "They'd send them through a training camp, give them a weapon, and send them into Afghanistan. They worried to death about it, didn't want them to get killed. These were the donors' kids. You had to accept them. It drove the Afghans crazy because the Arabs had an air of superiority about them, an arrogance." They were largely regarded by the various Afghan armies as a nuisance, to be tolerated in exchange for the petrodollars that followed them.

Bin Laden's family owned one of the largest construction firms in the world, and under his direction, the Arab jihadis spent enormous energy constructing camps and hideouts in the mountainous terrain across the border in Afghanistan. For a time, Mohammed worked as a hydraulic engineer for a Japanese company named Maruzen. The company sent him to Japan to learn its management system. When Mohammed returned to Afghanistan, he maintained and repaired hydraulic drills used in the construction of defensive positions—trenches and caves—in the mountains.[17]

By this time, Soviet leader Mikhail Gorbachev had already decided to end the Soviet occupation of Afghanistan, which was a failure in almost every regard. The Soviet army did not control the country in any genuine way and could not suppress the insurgency.

The war was draining the Soviet treasury and was extremely unpopular among the citizenry. It had become the Soviet Vietnam.

Gorbachev began removing troops in 1988. By February of 1989, the last Soviet soldier marched in retreat across the Friendship Bridge over the Amu Darya. The Afghans had once again repelled an empire. But the war didn't stop, or even slow much. The Afghans, victorious against the foreign invader, did as they had so often done in the past—they turned on one another.

The Soviets left behind a government led by a former head of the secret police, Mohammed Najibullah. Sayyaf, among others, argued that the government could be upended with a quick and convincing military victory. The resistance, including Sayyaf's Islamic Union and eight other Peshawar-based Afghan political armies, chose to attack Jalalabad, a government garrison town not far from the resistance's own headquarters across the border in Pakistan.

One long-standing debate among the Afghan Arabs had been what role they should play vis-à-vis the Afghan resistance armies. Some of the Arabs wanted to form separate combat brigades, to make their own fight. Azzam argued that the Arabs were there to serve the Afghans and should fight at their behest. The debate resurfaced during preparations for the Jalalabad attack. A small group of Arabs, including Mohammed's brother Abed, wanted to lead its own attack. They were dissuaded and instead fell in behind the Afghan ranks. It didn't matter. The attack was ill-conceived and poorly executed—a real goat fuck, as one Western analyst described it.

Casualties were heavy in what turned out to be a two-month siege. Even fighting from the rear, the Arabs fell victim to the Jalalabad defenses. A group of them wandered into a minefield. One misstep triggered a lethal series of explosions. Among the dead was Abed Sheikh Mohammed.

In a normal life lived in a normal time, a man like Abed—a religious scholar by training; a pious, devout man by every description; a man who was idolized in Qatar for work he had done educating wayward young men—would never have been near a battlefield. His death was felt with a special sense of loss. Zahed and Khalid were crushed. "With the Eternal Ones," Azzam wrote in a eulogy, "did this emigrant rider pass on, accompanied by the hearts of all who knew him." Khalid and one of his wife's brothers did what they could to establish a legacy for Abed, getting financial support from Sayyaf for a school Abed had been trying to get off the ground—a coup, since when the Soviets left Afghanistan, the rivers of cash the U.S. and the Saudis had poured into the resistance trickled to an end as well. Many among the jihadis blamed these erstwhile sponsors for the ignominious loss at Jalalabad and the wasted lives, including Abed's, that went with it.

Full-scale internecine war broke out after the failed attack. The various elements of the Afghan resistance attacked not just the forces of the government, but one another. It was a period of deep disconsolation among the foreign fighters in Peshawar. They argued among themselves.

Azzam, the creator of jihad, and bin Laden, its moneyman, had a serious falling out over strategy. The two had cooperated to open the Office of Services to coordinate recruitment and planning. Bin Laden, however, had taken sides with Egyptian jihadis, who wanted to use money that had been raised for the Afghan fight to fund activities at home in Egypt. Azzam gave a lecture in which he declared that the use of the money for anything beyond Afghanistan would be unlawful. Bin Laden left the organization soon after. Then, a mere month later, Azzam, the heart of the Arab jihadi resistance, and two of his sons were killed by a roadside bomb on Arbat Road en route to Friday prayers at the mosque. Some blamed Afghan leaders or, later, bin Laden. Others blamed the American intelligence services. The murder was never solved.

The Americans were also accused of actively opposing the establishment of an Islamic government in Kabul. Some among the mujahideen felt they had been duped into serving America's interests and then tossed aside. Ahmed Shah Ahmedzai, a Sayyaf deputy, said that when the Americans left, they didn't even say, "Bye-bye, Afghans."[18]

The repercussions of the Iraqi invasion of Kuwait in August of 1990 were experienced by some in the resistance as a further insult. The counterattack, led by American forces, infuriated bin Laden, who felt that the Saudis, by allowing the U.S. to base its soldiers in the kingdom, violated a sacred dictate to keep infidels out of the holy land. He confronted the royals, offering to use his own holy army to protect the kingdom. One man who attended the meeting at which bin Laden made his offer said bin Laden produced a sixty-page document outlining his plans.[19] He said he had twenty thousand men ready to fight and another forty thousand in reserve. He told a prince in attendance that he would do this to serve Allah, not the king. The family, flabbergasted at his naiveté and insulted by his disdain, declined the offer.

Bin Laden began attacking the U.S. and Saudi governments in speeches, saying there was no difference between the Soviets and the Americans—they were all infidels and would all be swept away in the coming Islamic tide.

While bin Laden turned his attention elsewhere, Afghanistan deteriorated into full-on civil war, and men kept coming to fight in it. Among them was Abdul Basit Abdul Karim, Khalid Sheikh Mohammed's younger nephew and comrade in the removal of the Kuwaiti flag from their elementary school back in Kuwait. Basit had gone abroad to Wales to study electrical engineering, and in 1988 came to Peshawar on break from school. He returned in 1991 and developed a reputation as a clever designer of explosive devices. Across the border from Peshawar, he trained at Khalden, the first and biggest of the guerrilla warfare camps, and taught courses in bomb making.

Many of the original Afghan Arabs had already left the region, more or less for good. Khalid and Zahed were still in Peshawar, but the glory had gone out of the fight. Everything seemed changed for the worse. Azzam and Abed were dead. Disillusionment and resentment at the American and Saudi abandonment of the rebel cause were prevalent. One friend of the Baluch brothers said: "In 1991–92, their whereabouts, their meetings, their thoughts, it became more secret. The hatred for Americans—it was among every Arab who came to Afghanistan.... They all thought America had imposed its rule by vetoing Islamic rule in Afghanistan through its agents in Pakistan."[20]

## *Doha, Qatar, 1992*

In 1992, Zahed Sheikh Mohammed left for a business opportunity in the United Arab Emirates. With both brothers gone—Abed for good—and the anti-Russian jihad complete, Khalid went through a restless period. He tried to move on to the next holy war, this one in Bosnia, moving there for a brief period and contributing to the cause, mainly by organizing donations—but he didn't stay long. He returned to Peshawar briefly before he was invited to move to Doha, Qatar.

Abdullah bin Khalid al-Thani, a member of the ruling family and a minister in the government, arranged a job for Mohammed as a project engineer in the Ministry of Electricity and Water. As an expression of his faith, Abdullah bin Khalid provided what amounted to a retreat for former jihadis. "A lot of these guys had what were basically gentlemen's truck farms. It was a hobby," a Western official who was stationed in Doha at the time said. "Grow cabbages, raise ducks. An expensive hobby, since the government would give you water for residential use, but not for agriculture; you had to pay for your own.... The house was always overstaffed, a lot of unemployed Afghan Arabs. These guys would stay for a while; some of them they tended to get a little plumper. There were always these guys hanging around, and maybe a couple of Kalashnikovs in the corner."[21]

Perhaps influenced by the large circle of acquaintances his late brother, Abed, had built there, Mohammed accepted the position and moved his family to Doha in 1993. How much he worked at the job is uncertain. What is clear is that he hadn't quit the fight. Mohammed established a small fund-raising operation there, recruiting men throughout the Gulf to hunt for individual donors, often finding them among the older, wealthier men at local mosques. Mohammed's recruits would wait for them to emerge from the mosques after prayers before cornering them for small donations. This was a common practice throughout the region, officially frowned upon but allowed. The system worked because the corner men were able to use the Muslim custom of tithing as leverage against their marks. Mohammed would periodically make the rounds, collecting the money from his growing network of operators.

Mohammed was an adept and relentless networker with a gift for small talk and instant familiarity. A friend recalls running into him once on a street outside a mosque in Doha. While they talked, a constant stream of people kept coming up to Mohammed to say hello, shake his hand, exchange warm good wishes. Mohammed seemed to know them all and had a kind word, or maybe a joke, for each. He couldn't have been more charming.[22]

It is hard to hide in a place like Doha, one of the world's smallest capitals. Security officials there were aware of Mohammed's activities and allowed him to continue. "We knew he was sort of in possession of money and sending it somewhere," a U.S. official said. It was never clear whether Mohammed was part of any larger organization; whether there were lines of authority through which he reported or if he was a sole proprietor. His sort of small-time, informal fund-raising, usually involving donations in the hundreds, not thousands, of dollars, was ubiquitous for religious causes throughout the Gulf. Mohammed simply adapted it to a new cause—jihad, in its many guises. Mohammed flew in and out of Doha, popping up in the UAE, Bahrain, Pakistan, and occasionally Kuwait. His name was almost never mentioned in broader counterterrorism discussions, and it wasn't evident that he was anything more than a bit player.

# CHAPTER 3
# Jihad

*New York City, 1992*

In early September of 1992, a pair of men traveling with fake passports arrived from Peshawar, Pakistan, at New York's John F. Kennedy International Airport and presented themselves at immigration control. One of the men, Ahmad Mohammed Ajaj, carried a crudely forged Swedish passport with his picture pasted in it. The document was instantly recognized as fraudulent. A subsequent search of Ajaj's checked baggage revealed diagrams and chemical recipes for making bombs. He was arrested on the spot. The other man was Abdul Basit Abdul Karim, Khalid Sheikh Mohammed's nephew. He had a valid Iraqi passport in the name of Ramzi Ahmed Yousef, but the passport did not contain a visa for the United States. He had no checked luggage, just a carry-on bag. He had stowed most of his materials, including the bomb recipes, in Ajaj's bag. Questioned about the lack of a visa, he immediately admitted the passport was not his, gave his real name, and requested political asylum. The immigration holding facility was full, so he was assigned a court date and released on his own recognizance. He took a taxi to New Jersey, went to a mosque, and soon recruited a makeshift crew to assist him in blowing up the World Trade Center.[1]

Basit and Mohammed had separated when, after high school, Mohammed went to Chowan, in North Carolina, and Basit to the technical college in Wales a few years later. They reunited briefly in Peshawar, when Basit, on a break from school, visited in 1988, and again when he returned in 1991. By then the Soviet war had ended but the mujahideen training camps remained, churning out fresh batches of would-be warriors. Basit became so adept at making bombs at Khalden that trainees called him the Chemist.

Basit didn't waste time on debates about the future of jihad and where it should be waged; he began making plans and finding men to carry them out. His first recruit was the hapless Ajaj, a Palestinian who had immigrated to the United States in 1991 and worked at menial restaurant jobs before leaving to take jihad training in Afghanistan—without thinking to renew his visa. After his training, he was stranded in Pakistan. When Basit offered him a first-class return ticket to the U.S. in exchange for carrying his bags, he accepted. Basit also gave Ajaj the bad passport that led to his arrest, while he kept the valid Iraqi passport, purchased at a Peshawar bazaar for a mere $100, for himself.

Basit was equally persuasive with others, including Pakistani cousins who credited him with guiding them on a path to jihad. Months prior to his arrival in the United States, Basit had renewed acquaintances with a childhood friend from Kuwait, Abdul Hakim Murad. Murad at the time was in the United States, struggling to get licensed as a commercial pilot. He went to five different flight schools before eventually earning his license.[2]

When Basit contacted Murad, he told him he had taken up the cause of jihad and wanted to attack Israel. This would come as no surprise to anyone who knew him. Basit used to profess his devotion to the Palestinian cause by declaring himself Pakistani by birth, Palestinian by choice. Israel was a tough target, however; it was alert to danger and its defenses were formidable. Basit said he would attack Jews in the United States instead. He knew from

Mohammed's college experience and Murad's travels around the country for flight training that access to the United States was generally simple and that, once there, the freedom of movement was nearly absolute. He asked Murad if he could suggest any Jewish targets. Murad shared Basit's low opinion of Israel. "If you ask anybody, even if you ask children, they will tell you that the U.S. is supporting Israel, and Israel is killing our Muslim brothers in Palestine," he said.

Murad agreed to think about potential targets and, while Basit scouted Brooklyn for Jews, gave it some thought. Eventually, Murad told Basit that the World Trade Center would make an inviting target. New York had a lot of Jews, he knew, and the Twin Towers were bound to be a workplace for many of them.

Throughout his time in New York that fall and winter, Basit stayed in touch with his uncle Mohammed. They talked often by telephone. Some of their conversation was social, some of it related to Basit's project, for which he was strapped for cash. The bomb he wanted to build didn't need to be hugely expensive, but it nonetheless took money to buy the materials and to live in the meantime. Mohammed was impressed with how easily Basit seemed able to operate in the United States. He pitched in, wiring $660 to the bank account of one of Basit's accomplices.

Basit finally settled on Murad's suggestion. He had several different ideas on what sort of bomb he could build. He toyed with the idea of building a device that contained cyanide, the idea being that the release of the deadly gas into the Trade Center's ventilation system would neatly kill all its occupants. This design proved too daunting and expensive, so he settled on the cheapest sort of bomb he knew how to build—an ordinary fertilizer bomb made with urea nitrate. He built several small prototypes and drove out to the New Jersey countryside to blow them up. "Making chocolate" was how he described the process to Murad.

The eventual attack was a ramshackle, almost cartoonish affair. Basit designed and built a bomb that in the end cost only $3,000. The first time they tried to put the bomb in place in the parking garage, his crew crashed their vehicle en route and had to delay the attack. On February 26, the day of the actual attack, Basit overslept by several hours and his accomplices let him slumber on. Though hours late, the bomb was successfully stowed, although inefficiently arranged, behind shipping crates in a rental van and parked in the basement of the North Tower. After setting the timer, Basit had only seven minutes to get himself and his helpers out of the building. He jumped from the van to a getaway car, which then got trapped behind a cargo truck for several agonizing minutes in the basement. They made it out with mere moments to spare.

Basit intended the bomb to topple the North Tower into the South Tower, somehow bringing them both to the ground. When the bomb exploded, the damage was much less significant. Still, it fractured several structural columns and shook the giant tower.

Basit fled the country that same night on a first-class flight to Pakistan from JFK, leaving his ragtag crew to suffer the consequences. On his way out of town he mailed letters to news organizations claiming responsibility for the attack:

> We are, the fifth battalion in the LIBERATION ARMY, declare our responsibility for the explosion on the mentioned building. This action was done in response for the American political, economical, and military support to Israel the state of terrorism and to the rest of the dictator countries in the region.

Basit went on to detail a litany of complaints about the evils America had done in the Middle East and elsewhere, and signed the letter in the names of Al-Farrek Al-Rokn and Abu Bakr Al-Makee. There was no Al-Farrek or Abu Bakr. There was no Liberation Army, either—just Basit and Mohammed and their fervid imaginations. The World Trade Center was just the beginning. With the Trade Center bomb, Basit and Mohammed had come upon a new, off-center notion of jihad: not just a war against states, but a nonstop, all-out war on all enemies, anywhere they could be reached.

## *Federal Plaza, New York City, 1993*

Basit's truck bomb provided the first glimmerings of a new realization for the few Americans who thought about such things—international terrorism was a nearly unknowable threat. It could spring from the ground almost anywhere and, contrary to most expectations, it did not have to be sponsored by pariah states.

This should not have come as a great surprise. The United States had significant experience with terrorism over the prior two decades. Almost all of it came from domestic sources—the Weathermen, Black Panthers, and scores of other, less-well-known groups. There had been hundreds of bombings across the nation, very few of them sponsored by opposing states. Nothing that had occurred approached the ambition of the Trade Center attack, but several of the explosions had caused significant injury, death, and expense.

At first, investigators were not even certain that the Trade Center had been bombed. Initial reports suggested some organic cause, perhaps an electrical transformer explosion. Federal officials did not immediately respond, leaving the first investigations to local authorities. An FBI agent who happened to be in the neighborhood having lunch when the bomb went off ambled over to the site, took one look, and ambled back to the office.[3] Within the first hours, however, clear evidence of a bomb was uncovered and federal agents descended on the basement.

The New York City field office of the FBI had long been the largest and most headstrong of the bureaus spread across the country. It had to be. Virtually every kind of crime the Bureau dealt with occurred within its jurisdiction. Its leaders had always felt that no one understood what they faced as well as they did. As a result, the office had every peculiarity of every other office plus some of its own invention.

Organizationally, it was within the federal judicial district known as the Southern District of New York. This was sometimes referred to—mockingly, but enviously, too—as the Sovereign District of New York. It was in many ways a separate fiefdom from the rest of the Bureau, creating its own rules and procedures. The agent in charge of the office, unlike all but one other agent in charge, held the rank of an assistant director of the entire FBI.

If the New York office's relationship with the rest of the Bureau was rocky, its relationship with its New York neighbor—the New York City police department—was worse. The Bureau had been an insular organization from its start under J. Edgar Hoover, famed for doing things its own way and its own way only. The NYPD equaled or surpassed it in hubris, dwarfed it in size, and was equally blind to its own flaws. The two agencies argued about almost everything—who would get what cases, where they would be tried, who would interview which witnesses. At times, unable to reach any compromise whatsoever, they interviewed witnesses twice, neither side willing to either give up the right to do so or to trust the work of the other.

In an attempt to bridge some of these gaps, the two organizations had in the 1970s teamed together and built a task force to investigate bank robberies, which were often federal crimes. This prepared the ground for the formation in 1980 of a Joint Terrorism Task Force (JTTF) staffed with a dozen FBI agents, most of who came from its M-9 special bomb squad, and a dozen NYPD detectives. It would later grow to include hundreds of people drawn from the FBI, NYPD, DEA, the Port Authority, fire departments, and scores of other agencies—especially after 9/11.

Before the 1993 Trade Center attack, there was no template—nor, it seemed, was there any need—for fighting international terrorism, and the JTTF worked mainly on domestic terrorism. What little foreign intelligence work was being done focused on Sudanese and Egyptian diplomats at the United Nations, not international terrorists. (The Bureau's first investigative work on Osama bin Laden would occur because bin Laden was then living in Sudan and the Bureau had previously done the investigative work that led to the deportation of a Sudanese diplomat.) This was not glamorous work, nor was it particularly well rewarded.

The FBI historically was an organization driven by data. Its meticulously maintained archives of fingerprints and case files were among the largest and most useful criminal databases in the world. Internally, statistics drove the FBI's bureaucracy. You got promoted by accruing numbers—interviews, arrests, convictions. By its own metrics, this was a strict meritocracy. But to view it that way would be to ignore those superior agents who, for whatever reason, seldom made arrests.

Counterterrorism was in a uniquely bad position within this system. Until something horrible happened, no one paid it much attention. Agents could get stuck there. If you were lucky, you'd rack up an arrest every couple of years and a conviction every decade. It wasn't the place you wanted to be in the Bureau unless you really cared about what you were doing. The real action was in chasing mobsters and white-collar criminals, slapping the cuffs on them and perp-walking them into the courthouse.

CT agents were pitied—or, worse, scorned—within the Bureau. Some thought you got stuck doing terrorism cases only if you were lazy or incompetent. The degree to which terrorism was a bureaucratic backwater was made obvious in a meeting not long after the World Trade Center bomb exploded. Federal prosecutors, New York police, U.S. Treasury agents, the FBI, and the CIA gathered to share information. After preliminary discussions were completed, one of the CIA men in attendance (none of whom would reveal their names) addressed the lead prosecutors and in all sincerity asked: How do we stop international terrorism?

The FBI guys were dumbfounded. Isn't that your job? they asked.

As it turned out, no. The CIA was in the international intrigue, information, and great power struggle businesses. Its knowledge of and methods for counteracting Islamist terror were virtually nonexistent. The FBI did not have much more institutional knowledge.

What it did have in the Trade Center bombing, however, was a crime—a federal crime—and it was the Bureau's responsibility to investigate it.

The big break in the Trade Center investigation occurred within hours of the attack. Investigators, laboriously sifting through the debris in the North Tower basement, found a piece of the wreckage of the Ford Econoline van that Basit had used to transport the bomb. An alert cop examined it for a VIN number and found one. From there it was a simple matter of running the number through motor vehicle databases, which revealed that the van was a Ryder rental vehicle. Investigators then found the agency that had rented the van, and the name of the person to whom it had been rented. They caught another break when the renter, a man named Mohammed Salameh, called the rental agency to report the van stolen and ask for his $400 security deposit back. Because Basit was the financier and had fled the country, leaving his accomplices on their own, Salameh was broke and desperately needed the cash from the deposit. When he showed up to collect his money, he was greeted by an undercover FBI agent pretending to be a Ryder manager. Refund in hand, Salameh was arrested on his way out. Once investigators had him in custody, the others involved in the conspiracy were quickly identified. The lone exception was Basit, whom the others knew only as Rashid.

Seven men were implicated in the attack. Each was assigned his own team of investigators. Frank Pellegrino's team got Rashid.

Pellegrino was a young FBI agent from Long Island. He'd been a certified public accountant at Coopers & Lybrand before deciding to give up the security—and boredom—of that career in 1987. "If I had to add up another book of numbers I was gonna shoot myself," he told friends. He had gotten his start in accounting because his junior varsity baseball coach taught the subject at Elmont Memorial High School in Nassau County and he thought he'd get an easy ride. His Irish mother had been a detective from a long line of Irish cops and so he applied at the Bureau. He waited more than a year for a response, and was thinking he'd stay in accounting, when the call finally came.

Pellegrino was ambitious. Once he joined the FBI he almost immediately began taking night classes back at St. John's University in Queens, where he'd gotten his accounting degree. In a remarkably quick four years, he had earned a law degree while working long days at the FBI. The Bureau was full of accountants and had a fair sprinkling of lawyers. Few, if any, agents were both, though anyone in the field office would tell you that Pellegrino didn't look or act at all like an accountant or a lawyer—or an FBI agent, for that matter.

Pellegrino's early experience at the Bureau was typical for the time. Like others in the Southern District, he spent the first years of his career on drug cases. He was then moved to the counterterrorism squad, which largely entailed surveilling people going in and out of mosques. When Neil Herman, head of the JTTF, gave Pellegrino his Trade Center assignment, it was at best inauspicious; "Rashid" seemed like a sideshow to the main event. Nonetheless, Pellegrino and two other men from the JTTF, Treasury agent Tom Kelly and Brian Parr from the Secret Service, tracked leads all over Brooklyn and Queens. Others among the WTC attack team seemed more important. Several had connections to a radical preacher, Omar Abdel-Rahman, known as the Blind Sheikh. It was to one of the Blind Sheikh's mosques that Basit had gone when he first arrived in the United States. But as the other suspects were gradually rounded up, they all talked about the mysterious Rashid, who flew in and out of their lives in a virtual heartbeat, apparently bearing the World Trade Center plan with him. He had more wherewithal and savvy than the others. He seemed to have connections overseas. When investigators learned that Rashid had flown out of the country the night of the attack, he took on even more importance.

Investigating the bombing remained a slow process. Information was scant. Pellegrino's team eventually tracked back through the immigration system and found Basit's real name and where he was from. Bit by bit, they began to assemble a profile, and all signs pointed east—to Pakistan.

## *Islamabad, Pakistan, 1993*

An international manhunt was launched for Basit, with a reward of $2 million for his capture. Tens of thousands of matchbooks were printed up with his photo emblazoned on them. The matchbooks were air-dropped over half of Pakistan. Basit—or, in reality, his alter ego, Ramzi Yousef—became a kind of celebrity in the jihadi world. Every time a bomb went off anywhere, his name came up. And when his name came up, one or more of the team of Pellegrino, Parr, and Kelly hit the road.

It got to be kind of a joke. Because Basit had officially become public enemy number one, he was spotted everywhere. He was driving a gasoline-filled truck in Bangkok. He was bombing American embassies in Asia. Nothing came of the early leads and rumors, so the agents were left to scour every bit of evidence they had on Basit's crew. They tried to trace the money behind the attack, but it had required so little that even that task proved daunting. They did find a record of a bank transfer into the local account of one of Basit's comrades—Salameh—that they couldn't figure out. It was for $660 from someone identified on the wire transfer record as Khalid Shaykh from Doha.

It was such a paltry sum that the investigators almost certainly would have ignored it if they had anything better to go on. They didn't, so they recorded it and hoped someday it would make sense. Efforts to get information in Doha were fruitless. As they began constructing Basit's personal history, they learned he had been raised in Kuwait, part of a large Baluchi extended family there. They eventually determined that "Khalid Shaykh in Doha" was Basit's uncle on his mother's side, Khalid Sheikh Mohammed.

The investigators assumed Basit was in hiding somewhere,

probably among friends and family in Pakistan, especially since he had called there often from the U.S. Pellegrino had a theory honed from his days chasing fugitives in Manhattan and Queens: "Everyone goes home. I don't care if you're a fugitive from Washington Heights, New York, or wherever, you want to go home and talk to Mom at some point," he'd say. Pellegrino thought Basit would make his way back home, and eventually that's where he went.

He disappeared for a time into Baluchistan, the unruly desert region that straddles Iran and Pakistan, but he didn't stay quiet for long. He was treated within the growing jihadi community as a kind of folk hero, a man-about-town in Quetta, the provincial capital of Baluchistan, as well as Peshawar and Karachi.

Pellegrino and Parr flew to Islamabad, the Pakistani capital. The FBI abroad was in a uniquely helpless position. They had authority to pursue criminal cases wherever the cases took them, but they had no infrastructure to assist them. A few of the larger embassies had an FBI representative (known as the legal attaché, or legat) stationed there full-time. Most did not. Agents were reliant upon the goodwill of the resident CIA station chief, the ambassador, and local officials. Cooperation from all these sources varied greatly. Typically, the CIA chiefs and their case officers were agreeable to setting up meetings. The Pakistanis were another story.

Pellegrino and Parr met with local security officials in an attempt to enlist their help tracking down Basit. They brought with them a series of phone numbers Basit had called from the United States. They wanted to know who the numbers belonged to. They assumed they were family and friends, but had no way to be sure. The security official in charge of the meeting took an uncommonly long time looking through their request. The whole while he was reading through it, he kept wagging his head no. He didn't say anything, just shook his head over and over again. Pellegrino and Parr knew they were wasting time. Then the official finished examining the papers, looked up, and said, "We'll help you."

He never did, of course, setting the tone for years of passive-aggressive behavior. The Pakistanis always said yes and then never helped, even when they were asked to procure the most mundane items, such as bank and phone records. U.S. investigators managed to get Pakistan to raid the home of Mohammed's brother Zahed in an effort to find information on Basit and other coconspirators. But Pellegrino and Parr spent a month in Pakistan and left with not much more than they brought with them. They returned to New York with little on Basit and nothing on his mysterious uncle.

## *Karachi, Pakistan, Summer 1993*

Basit's boyhood friend Abdul Hakim Murad had recently returned from the U.S., where he had finally earned his commercial pilot's license and was living in Karachi. He was having difficulty finding a job. He and Basit met up. Basit was in a talkative mood and went on at length about the need for good Muslims to give their lives, if needed, to the struggle.

They talked about the enemies of Islam and potential targets: Benazir Bhutto, then the prime minister of Pakistan; nuclear power stations; a government official in Iran; the U.S. consulate there in Karachi; and a variety of other U.S. government buildings. There was an idea to assassinate President Clinton.

Basit also took Murad around Karachi, introducing him to a small network of friends. They met with a man who said his name was Abdul Majid. He was a Saudi import-export businessman, he said. His real name was Ibrahim Muneer.

That first meeting with Majid was at Majid's Karachi apartment, near the roundabout in Sharifabad, a pleasant leafy area near one of the largest public parks in the sprawling city. Majid was very interested in learning everything he could about Murad's pilot training: how long it took, how expensive it was, and who could qualify for it. Basit took Murad to meet Majid a second time. They had dinner at one of the barbecue places out in the Clifton district, by the sea. Again, Majid grilled Murad about the technical difficulties, or lack thereof, associated with flying.

Basit and Murad returned to Majid's apartment in August, but Majid was out of town—in Saudi, tending to business, Basit said. Another man was there instead. Basit introduced Murad to Wali Khan Amin Shah, an Afghan veteran of the anti-Soviet jihad.

By now, Basit had persuaded Murad to join the cause. Murad even came up with an idea of his own. He proposed packing an airplane full of explosives and dive-bombing it into the Pentagon or CIA headquarters. He, Abdul Hakim Murad, would pilot the aircraft to glory. Basit said it was certainly an idea worth considering. The two of them then moved to an open-air compound in a warehouse district in Lahore for several weeks. There, Basit taught Murad to build bombs. Making chocolate. In one practice session, a detonator exploded in Basit's face. He lost partial sight in one eye and had to be taken back to Karachi and hospitalized. As Murad sat with Basit during his recuperation, Majid showed up and paid all the bills.

## *Peshawar, Pakistan, Autumn 1993*

Not surprisingly, given Basit's growing acclaim, Pellegrino and Parr eventually got a tip on his whereabouts. A source had a copy of a request for a set of forged identity papers. They were to be delivered to a shop in Peshawar. Pellegrino saw the documents and immediately recognized Basit from the accompanying photo. He rushed back to Pakistan.

The FBI had no permanent presence in Pakistan at the time, and the legat, or legal attaché, responsible for Pakistan and the region worked out of Bangkok. The Bureau had to rely on others for everything. Pellegrino didn't even have an office to work from while there. The legat flew in to help arrange surveillance of the Basit document exchange, but while Pellegrino was optimistic, the legat told him not to get his hopes too high.

The surveillance was to be conducted by the Pakistanis, and the legat doubted it would go as planned. Pellegrino waited a week.

Basit never showed up. He had been tipped off. He knew it was a trap.

Pellegrino was disappointed, but accepted the missed opportunity as part of his learning curve. He met with the CIA station chief and the State Department security team in Islamabad, and they hammered out a plan to be carried out if Basit popped up again. Next time, nobody would know about an operation to get him except those whom Pellegrino wanted to know. What the FBI agent didn't know was that Basit—and his uncle Khalid—were just getting started. He also didn't know the full extent to which American authorities would find it impossible to actually do what they wanted to do in terms of getting to people like Basit in a place such as Pakistan.

# CHAPTER 4
## Bojinka

*Manila, the Philippines, 1994*

Mohammed and Basit were physical opposites. Basit was more than six feet tall, lean and lanky, usually clean-shaven. With a beak-like nose and half-blind right eye, he nonetheless achieved a sort of rakish handsomeness. Mohammed was half a foot shorter, stout, bearded, and usually bespectacled—a stolid Friar Tuck to Basit's dashing Robin Hood. Their personalities were similar, however. What they shared most—in addition to their outsize ambitions—was a rough, happy-go-lucky charm that they used to persuade others to go along with what must often have seemed outlandish schemes. They were raconteurs, and had an affability about them that suggested they would make excellent dinner companions. They flirted with women and charmed men. They brought this same casual air to their plots, a kind of off-the-cuff, what-the-hell approach, as if blowing up buildings full of people were a perfectly normal thing to do.

For men who were still very young—Mohammed not quite thirty and Basit three years younger than that—they were already men of the world. Both had left their small Kuwaiti hometown and gone off to strange new worlds for school. They were multilingual, fluent in Arabic, Urdu, Baluch, and English, and moved easily through a globalizing world. They put on different identities as though they were changes of shoes.

Basit had invaded the world's greatest metropolis, New York City, nearly knocked down two of its tallest buildings, and walked away without batting an eye. From his base in Doha, Mohammed traveled the world, ostensibly on business, but building a loose web of ad hoc terror associates. Unlike many terrorists who preceded them, they lacked a focused ideology. They had one foot in the world of the Middle East from their boyhood in Kuwait and the other in Asia from their ethnic roots in Iran and Pakistan. They picked targets to suit the moment. Manila was next.

Mohammed and Basit arrived in the Philippines in the summer of 1994, Basit in July and Mohammed in early August.[1] They lived in neighboring hotels in Quezon City, the largest single city in Metropolitan Manila, as the capital region is called. Basit used numerous aliases, the most common being Adam Ali. Mohammed called himself Salem Ali, although he registered as Khalid Mohammad Mohammad at Sir William's Hotel and stated his residence as Doha, Qatar. Basit started a relationship with Aminda Custodio, a dancer he met at the hotel bar, and the two of them moved to the nearby Tiffany condominiums in the Greenhills neighborhood. Mohammed was a frequent visitor.

They were joined in Manila by a third man, Basit's friend Wali Khan Amin Shah, the Afghan mujahideen whom Mohammed had known since the Soviet war. Khan, too, befriended a local bar girl and they moved in together.

The three men met at the corner 7-Eleven, at shopping malls and hotel bars, and at karaoke clubs in the Ermita district and the EDSA entertainment complex. Basit dated a girl who sold perfume at a big mall. Mohammed chatted up her sister. The men discovered a dental clinic staffed almost entirely by attractive female dentists and suddenly discovered the joys of getting their teeth cleaned. They paid princely sums to local women to open cell phone and bank accounts, telling them that they were recuperating veterans of the Soviet war in Afghanistan. It was an easy enough sale—Khan was missing three fingers on one hand and Basit was half blinded and scarred from his bombing accidents. Mohammed sold himself as a Gulf businessman, variously from Saudi Arabia or Qatar. He exported plywood, he said.

Mohammed and Basit used the Tiffany condo as their lab, experimenting with chemical mixtures for the miniature bombs Basit was designing. When Basit moved out and left the country in mid-September, Mohammed moved in. Mohammed drove a rented Toyota sedan and wore khakis and polo shirts. He tipped well and ordered in hamburgers for dinner.

The two men had developed a workable idea for an airplane bomb before Basit left, and Mohammed ran a test to see if they could get all the ingredients of the bomb onto an aircraft. He planned to fly from Manila to Seoul, South Korea. The key ingredient in the prospective airplane bomb was nitromethane, which was inexpensive and readily available in the Philippines. Mohammed emptied the contents of fourteen contact lens solution bottles, taking care not to break the plastic seals on the bottles. He then refilled them with the nitro. He carried thirteen of the bottles in his carry-on bag on his flight to Seoul. Basit had previously carried a single bottle on a flight from Hong Kong to Taipei.

To test his ability to clear airport security while carrying a metal detonator, Mohammed carried a small metal bolt. He taped the bolt beneath the arch of his foot, then covered his foot with a sock. He wore clothing with metal buttons and jewelry to confuse the scanners, then placed condoms conspicuously in his bag to support the cover story that his main purpose in traveling to the Philippines had been to meet women. He did not have a visa for Korea, but planned to claim that the Korean embassy in Manila had told him that a visa was unnecessary. He set off alarms at the security scanner and was asked to undress. This included his shoes, but not his socks, and he was passed through. He realized later that he had left a detailed plan for the attacks in his carry-on bag; it contained all twelve of the targeted flights as well as the time the bombs were intended to explode. Security officials didn't notice the plan, but did ask why he was carrying so much contact lens solution.[2]

I found a great sale in Manila, he said.

He raised other suspicions, too, by having purchased his ticket only one day beforehand. He explained that his visa was about to expire and that he had to leave the Philippines and travel to another country to renew it. The customs officers accepted the explanation and allowed Mohammed to fly to Seoul.

When he landed at Kimpo, Seoul's international airport, he was prevented from entering the country because he had no visa. He was held at the airport for ten hours, but again, no one searched him, and he was put on a plane back to Manila. As soon as he reached Manila he flushed his fake identity papers down the toilet in an airport restroom, then caught the next flight to Karachi, where he reconnoitered with Basit. Satisfied that all the preparations were proceeding according to plan, Basit returned to Manila while Mohammed hopped a flight to Doha to visit his family.

Later in the year, Khan and his girlfriend took a room in the Doña Josefa Apartments, a transient hotel not far from Ermita. The Josefa was a part of a world that is largely invisible to most people. Its plain, gray, water-stained stucco was perched at the end of a large squatters' encampment full of makeshift barbershops and two-stool cafes. The impermanence of its population made it the ideal environment for men who came and went and explained little.

The Josefa's other recommendation was its location facing President Quirino Avenue, a main artery connecting the old government and financial center of Manila and the neighborhood where the Vatican ambassador to the Philippines lived. This provided a tactical advantage for Mohammed and Basit's latest plan: to assassinate Pope John Paul II.

The pope had scheduled a visit to the Philippines for the second week in January of 1995. While in the city, the pope intended to stay at the papal nuncio's residence, less than a half mile from the

Josefa. Conveniently, his motorcade would have to pass the Josefa along President Quirino Avenue numerous times during his visit.

The papal visit would be a huge event for the island nation. A former Spanish colony, it was the most Catholic country in Asia and hadn't hosted a pope for fifteen years. The Filipino practice of Catholicism was often deeply romantic, even sentimental. At Easter, for example, many villages sponsored elaborate passion plays, re-creations of Christ's suffering and death. In one town, the dramas had become so extensive that by the 1990s young men had themselves nailed to crosses as part of the festivities. Catholicism was serious business in the country, and a papal visit was to be cherished.

Only in the south of the nation did Catholicism not hold sway. The populace was Muslim in the southernmost dozen or so of the country's seven thousand islands, which marked the eastern edge of the great Islamic expansion during the twelfth and thirteenth centuries. The unique religious practice of the southern provinces was recognized by the national government, which bestowed autonomous region status there. But special status wasn't enough for everyone. Some in the south had gone to Afghanistan during the Soviet jihad and brought the revolution, and expertise in warfare, home with them. Some wanted their own country and were willing to kill to get it. Islamist insurgents had been battling the Philippines government for a decade.

The largest of many bands of rebels were the Moro Islamic Liberation Front and the Abu Sayyaf Group. Both groups had formed connections to the wider web of jihadis exported across the globe by the Afghan camps. The camps were like a factory's conveyor belt, a Clinton administration official once said; would-be terrorists kept tumbling out of it. Abu Sayyaf alone, fed by a rabid anti-Catholicism, had grown from its founding ten members to more than five hundred in five years. Authorities counted more than one hundred terror attacks in the same period.[3]

Mohammed and Basit chose the Philippines as a base of operations for practical reasons. Labor, rent, and food were all cheap. The radical Islamists of Abu Sayyaf and Moro (the Tagalog word for "Moor") were close at hand. Members of both groups had trained in mujahideen camps during the Afghan jihad, and Basit and Mohammed had acquaintances among them. Basit and Khan had even been asked to help train some of them and had spent time in the southern islands. In some ways, they could not have chosen a better city to set up shop. Manila was especially cheap, and its built-in networks could be relied upon to help with logistics.

In other ways, they could not have chosen worse. The carnage from the previous Islamist attacks—hundreds of deaths, bombings of drive-in restaurants and railroad cars, kidnappings by the score—had focused official attention on Islamic extremism in a way that was unlike almost anywhere else on earth. Radical Islam wasn't theoretical here. Thousands of police and intelligence agents throughout the country were hard at work trying to penetrate and stop the groups. They were ever alert to potential threats. Key suspects throughout the country were under constant surveillance. Philippine police wiretapped every phone that was feasible to wiretap, within the law or not. In the months before the pope's visit, precautions were increased still more.

Basit and Mohammed did not appear to have any particular animus toward the Catholic Church. Members of Abu Sayyaf had suggested the pope as a target to Basit. Basit agreed, but decided to leave Abu Sayyaf out of the actual operation; he said he'd be happy to give the locals all the credit afterward.

Basit had found the southern insurgents unsophisticated. He didn't think they would benefit from his bomb-making expertise. Mainly, he said, they liked to shoot their guns,[4] and he and Mohammed had bigger plans than their small-arms expertise could underwrite. But the local jihadi networks offered other advantages. Khan had been a close associate of Osama bin Laden during the Afghan war, and had visited him after bin Laden moved to Sudan. Khan had also been friends with the man who ran the International Islamic Relief Organization in Peshawar. Either bin Laden, the IIRO man, or both could have provided introductions to Mohammed Jamal Khalifa, a Saudi brother-in-law of bin Laden's who ran the East Asian branch of IIRO. Khalifa had fought in the Afghan campaign, too, but had left early, in 1985. He moved to Manila, took a Filipina wife, and established a wide range of businesses—timber sales, rattan furniture manufacture, agricultural seed distribution—and charitable organizations to fund Islamic education and, authorities said later, insurgencies. He was a substantial donor to both Moro and Abu Sayyaf. He helped fund their training camps in the southern jungles. Khan became an intermediary between Mohammed and Basit on the one hand and Khalifa's local network on the other.

Khan was also the go-between with one of Mohammed's friends from the Afghan camps, an Indonesian named Hambali. Khan, Hambali, and Mohammed Amein al-Sanani, an associate of Khalifa's, were among the founding directors of Konsojaya, a shell company the group set up in Malaysia to transfer money to Manila. One of Khan's school friends from Saudi Arabia, Ibrahim Muneer, joined him in the Philippines and Malaysia and probably guided the creation of Konsojaya. Muneer was an actual businessman, though, and a fairly successful one. He operated an import-export company out of Karachi. Among other enterprises, he was said to have had the royal concession for the export of holy water from Saudi Arabia to Pakistan. Konsojaya, according to its incorporation papers, was intended to be just such a trading company, exporting palm oil from Malaysia to the Arab world. Pellegrino would later find that the company actually did make one deal, buying a load of vegetable ghee and shipping it from Singapore to Karachi. But the shipment got caught up in customs at the port in Karachi. The Pakistanis held it up for taxation and the Konsojaya executives didn't have the money to pay people off. So they let it sit there and the ghee spoiled.

Beyond that, it's not clear what other deals, if any, the company ever did, although it gave the plotters credentials that allowed them to pass themselves off as businessmen. They had cell phones registered to the Konsojaya account, and the company served as a point of contact.

In late 1994, Basit returned to Manila and soon moved into the Josefa. Khan and his girlfriend, Carol Santiago, moved out to an apartment on Singalong Street. Using various aliases, Basit collected the materials—nitromethane, citric and nitric acid, wire, cotton balls, Casio watches—needed to make the bombs he and Mohammed had experimented with during the summer. By telephone, he and Mohammed discussed different ways to kill John Paul, including suicide bombers disguised as priests, remote-control bombs, and an aerial attack. Basit ordered custom-made clerical cassocks. When they learned that President Clinton was to visit during the same period, they discussed ways to kill him, too.

With both the pope and the American president about to make appearances, it was a nervous season in the capital. A typhoon had blown through earlier in the month, cutting power and uprooting trees that still lay strewn along the streets. Philippine authorities were hyper alert to threats against the pope. Given both Abu Sayyaf's and Moro's history of attacking Catholic clergy, they added security throughout the capital. Basit and Mohammed, worried that they couldn't penetrate the heightened defenses, turned instead to another, more innovative attack.

Mohammed and Basit had been talking for months about ways in which they could use commercial airliners as terror targets, dating back at least to the first time Murad mentioned using airplanes as missiles in Pakistan. Basit thought he could devise small, electronically controlled explosive devices that could be disassembled and smuggled aboard airliners. Once aboard, the device's parts could be reassembled, connected to a modified digital watch that would serve as a timer, then set to explode after the man who assembled the device had deplaned.

Basit researched flight schedules and identified a dozen American-flagged jumbo jets that would all be in the air, most eastward-bound for America, at the same time. They called the plan Bojinka, Serbo-Croatian for "big noise." Mohammed, Basit, Murad, Khan, and another man would all place bombs on different planes. If they could make it work, it would be an astonishing catastrophe, an amazing victory. Who would then doubt the power of the Liberation Army?

Late in the evening on December 1, Wali Khan rode his motorcycle to a mostly deserted movie theater in a Makati district shopping center, placed a small version of the Basit-designed explosive device under a seat, and left. The bomb worked on schedule, blowing up an empty seat and injuring a handful of late-night moviegoers

The next step was to make sure the bombs could be assembled on board an aircraft. Basit built a slightly larger version of the bomb Khan had placed in the movie theater, then booked passage on a flight from Manila to Tokyo that included an intermediate stop in Cebu. Basit boarded the flight in Manila, set the timer, and planted the device beneath the seat in front of him. A flight attendant noticed that he then kept switching seats, moving all over the cabin. She didn't know he was trying to get further and further out of range of the bomb. He got off the plane in Cebu. The bomb went off exactly as scheduled on the next leg of the flight, killing a Japanese businessman and nearly dooming the entire aircraft, which the pilots heroically managed to land with a gaping hole in its fuselage. A slightly larger bomb would have brought the entire plane and its passengers down.

With the test run successful, Basit and Mohammed began final preparations. Mohammed planned a return to Manila for early January.[5] Basit called Murad in the Gulf and asked him to come to Manila. Murad had been expecting the call. Basit gave him instructions to buy a variety of hair dye products and to check in to a low-rent hotel upon arrival. When Basit met him at the hotel and took him over to the Josefa, Murad wasn't surprised to see Basit's apartment full of bomb-making materials—"chocolate"—but was very surprised to see Ibrahim Muneer, whom he knew as the Saudi businessman Majid. Muneer wore gloves every time he visited.

Just after Christmas, Muneer and Basit left Manila for a weekend. They told Murad they were going scuba diving and gave him instructions to begin constructing the bombs. When they returned, Basit and Murad set about making more bombs in earnest. Muneer disappeared. Murad had the impression Muneer was living with Basit at the Josefa before Murad arrived, but had moved elsewhere in town. Muneer left the apartment that night. Murad would never see him again.

The plot ended there. A chemical fire ignited by the ever-careless Basit flushed the two from the apartment. The smoke caused the fire department to respond, then the police. The cops made a bit of a mess of it, going into the room without a warrant and discovering the trove of bomb-making materials. Alarmed, they went shopping for a judge who would sign a search warrant with no evidence of the need to search other than a small fire. Twelve judges denied them. The thirteenth authorized the search, which uncovered an astonishing litany of chemicals and bomb-making gear—gallon jugs of nitrobenzoyl; grape juice bottles full of acid; switches, watches, alarms. They also found a chemical dictionary, two Bibles, two crucifixes, and a manual on how to hear Roman Catholic confessions. It took two full-size police vans to haul the stuff away. Murad was arrested later that same night, after Basit sent him back to get his Toshiba laptop from the apartment. Khan was arrested outside his apartment a few days later. Basit had simply disappeared.

Mohammed didn't have to disappear. No one yet knew he had ever been there.

# CHAPTER 5
## Making a Case

*Manila, the Philippines, January 1994*

Just as Pellegrino surmised he would, Basit flew back to Pakistan via Singapore the night of the Josefa calamity. He got away, but hardly clean. He had left behind so many clues that he might as well have waved a red flag on the way out of the country.

He had sent Murad back for the laptop for two good reasons. One, it was dangerous to go back himself; better somebody other than he. Indeed, Murad walked right into the police handcuffs. Or, rather, he ran. When he was spotted returning to the hotel, a policeman yelled at him, and he turned and ran. The cop fired and missed, but Murad tripped over an uprooted tree trunk and was arrested. Two, the laptop was worth going back to get. It contained enough information to identify Basit, Mohammed, everything they had planned, and almost everyone they knew. Among the names and phone numbers: Khalid Sheikh, similar to the name on the wire transfer before the World Trade Center bombing. There was also a copy of a letter apparently asking for money and signed by "Khalid Shaikh + Bojinka":

To: Brother Mohammad Alsiddiqi:

> We are facing a lot of problems because of you. Fear Allah, Mr. Siddiqi, there is a day of judgment. You will be asked, if you are very busy with something more important, don't give promises to other people. See you on the day of judgment. Still waiting.

When the police first took Murad into custody, they didn't really know who they had or what crime, if any, might have been committed. What they had was a mountain of evidence, and, soon enough, as Murad began talking about the World Trade Center bombing, they began to suspect they might actually have Basit—the infamous Ramzi Yousef—in their custody. They put the word out to the United States.

When the call came into the JTTF at 26 Federal Plaza in lower Manhattan, Pellegrino, unusually, was in the office. He had spent much of the previous two years chasing faint leads around the five boroughs, then the five continents, without great success. He and his colleagues knew who Basit was, but not much else.

Sensing a big break in the case, he rushed to get to the Philippines. The Filipinos, however, were in a near panic about the pope's imminent arrival and had virtually shut down the country. Nobody could get in or out until the pope was safely packed off to wherever his world tour took him next—not even the FBI and its team of forensic experts, who could help determine who the Filipinos had in their custody.

By the time Pellegrino arrived on January 16, the local investigation was well under way. Filipino police and intelligence agents had determined that the man in their custody was not Basit but Murad. For a few days they also had Khan locked up, but he escaped jail—almost certainly with the help of a bribed jailer—and left the country two days before Pellegrino arrived. He didn't resurface for months. Still, the computer and documents gathered at the Josefa and at Khan's apartment on Singalong Street provided dozens of leads. They showed that Khan, in particular, had traveled extensively and had contact information for, among others, Osama bin Laden and his brother-in-law Khalifa, the IIRO executive. In the short time he was in custody, Khan admitted that he had received money from Khalifa. The police had been watching, and wiretapping, Khalifa for two years, so they knew his connections to Abu Sayyaf and Moro. And he was connected to these transients, too?

Coincidentally, Khalifa had been arrested in the United States just two weeks before. He was at that moment in a Northern California jail, being held formally on suspicion of visa violations. Khalifa was wanted in Jordan after being convicted in absentia for involvement in a bombing campaign there. The Jordanians wanted him extradited. The U.S. inclination at the time was to accede to such extradition requests. In fact, it wasn't a formalized policy, but in practice the U.S. preferred to ship suspected terrorists out of the country rather than go through the headache and expense of investigating and trying them. Mary Jo White, the U.S. attorney in Manhattan, thought this was crazy. Extradition didn't solve problems, she said, it merely delayed them. What was to keep a suspected terrorist who had been extradited from returning to the United States and attacking again at a time of his choosing?

As was usual for the New York field office, when agents left town for an investigation they often took federal prosecutors with them. This helped focus the avenues of inquiry. The prosecutors knew what they needed to take a case to court, relieving the agents of the need to reinvestigate everything later, when the prosecutors would want to see the evidence and hear the witnesses. Michael Garcia and Dieter Snell, two of White's young assistant U.S. attorneys from the Southern District, were partners in the Manila Air investigation. Garcia and Pellegrino butted heads, in part because Garcia, the prosecutor, wasn't the only lawyer of the two. But by their second or third extended tour of Southeast Asia, the two had become close, a model of how agent and prosecutor could work together.

They were also accompanied wherever they went by a CIA "minder," whom they grew to tolerate and even, at times, appreciate. He could be helpful in gaining the clearance needed to set foot on foreign soil, and to make their visits less threatening to the in-country CIA station chiefs, who didn't like FBI agents and prosecutors straying into their airspace. Anything that could possibly be used in a criminal prosecution—and thus be brought out into the open—was anathema to the CIA, to the point that its on-the-ground people usually stayed far away from the visiting law enforcement investigators. In return, the federal agents usually welcomed the lack of attention even if it meant less help. "There was not a close working relationship between the FBI and the agency in Manila," one participant recalls.

When Pellegrino learned from the Filipinos that there was information suggesting that Khalifa was funding Basit, he and the attorneys pleaded with their superiors to keep Khalifa in custody in California until they could build a real case against him. They had no problem persuading White. Richard Clarke, the White House counterterrorism adviser, also was desperate to keep Khalifa in custody, believing he was financing not only the Philippine Airlines plot but Al Qaeda operations in Southeast Asia as well.[1] But the State Department—in fact, secretary of state Warren Christopher himself—was angling to send Khalifa away as a favor to the Jordanians.

The Basit investigation had become a point of political contention even before the events in Manila. There were three competing interests: the Southern District of New York, which was running the criminal investigation; elements within the headquarters of the Department of Justice who wanted to bring control of the case to Washington; and the CIA, which wanted the criminal investigation shut down entirely so its agents could have an open field in which to explore the intelligence implications of the case.

Enough connections had been drawn between Basit and the wider jihadi world that the CIA wanted access to the information, if not to the case itself. Pellegrino and others at the FBI and Justice wanted to criminally prosecute Basit.

As a matter of policy, information derived from a criminal investigation was not routinely shared with intelligence agencies, and information derived from intelligence operations was not shared with criminal prosecutors. The division resulted from a desire to protect the rights of those accused of criminal activities; much intelligence information would never be allowed in an American courtroom, and the point of the nonsharing policy was to avoid contaminating criminal cases.

The wall, as it was called, was often misunderstood and frequently interpreted too broadly. The agents assigned to collecting intelligence sometimes couldn't, or wouldn't, talk to their colleagues who were working the criminal side of the same cases. Big things—like leads and plots and potential sources—fell through the cracks.

"People were sitting next to each other, literally, and not sharing information," said Neil Herman, then head of the New York JTTF. "Sometimes because they couldn't, other times because they just didn't want to or didn't think to. One would be from the criminal division, another [from the] FCI [Foreign Counterintelligence] division. And they wouldn't talk to each other. It got to be comical at points. It was crazy."

The larger issue was whether the Basit/Khalifa case should be treated as a criminal matter at all. Shouldn't it be handled as an intel-gathering effort? White's answer was not so simple: yes, but the criminal case should also proceed, with both sides working together to the degree that they were able to. Some top DOJ officials in Washington disagreed, and told her to shut down the criminal investigation, citing "the wall." She refused. Things got heated, and White had to send two of her top deputies to a series of meetings in Washington and New York just to preserve a law enforcement element of the case, and, especially, a supervisory role for her office and the New York FBI. She won the battle, but it was only the first salvo in a much longer war over the wall, and over what kind of information, if any, could be handed over to prosecutors and FBI agents from those on the intelligence side. White was in no mood to lose Khalifa, a crucial part of the case, just because yet another government agency wanted to do a favor for someone. But the negotiated settlement didn't mean her office and the New York FBI got anywhere near the kind of intelligence that they believed the CIA was gathering in Manila and elsewhere.

Meanwhile, Pellegrino was growing concerned that the Filipinos would let Murad go for lack of evidence before the FBI could build a case against him. He ended up spending almost three months in Manila investigating, but did not participate in the extensive interrogations of Murad by the Filipinos. He found lots of evidence anyway—enough for a federal grand jury to indict Murad in New York—but very little insight. Who was in charge? Who was the planner? Who had the ideas?

Mohammed's role was blurry; Pellegrino unearthed information showing he was more actively involved in Manila than he had been in Basit's New York operation, but he remained in the background. He had come early to the Philippines and left early. The investigation later turned up a lone fingerprint of his on the chemical dictionary found in room 603 and enough information from witnesses to persuade Pellegrino that Mohammed was a figure worth pursuing. Still, he was one of many suspects, a second-tier figure, as one intelligence analyst described him; he was still regarded more or less as Basit's uncle.

Khalifa seemed the likeliest suspect to have played a major role. He had the organization and the money—and the bin Laden connection. Holding him until they could find more evidence was essential. But after four months in American custody, Khalifa suddenly dropped his opposition to deportation to Jordan. Did he fear talking about Manila? Had he cut a deal with Jordan? No one knew, but once he said he was willing to go back to Jordan to stand trial for murder, there was little argument to keep holding him for visa violations. White dispatched Pellegrino and Garcia to Jordan to see if they could work out some kind of deal, but even the Jordanians said it was a mistake to send Khalifa back to them. Pellegrino later lamented that Khalifa and the U.S. marshals acting as his escorts were transiting through JFK International at about the same time he and Garcia were landing on their way back. Khalifa was soon sent to Amman and, almost immediately, a key witness against him in the bombing case recanted. He was released and went home to Saudi Arabia, beyond the reach of American investigators. Although Pellegrino wondered about the larger issues, he was an FBI agent and the FBI's method of approaching investigations was to let the evidence lead you. You go find information. Then you work with what you have and go get more. Time-consuming and exacting, certainly, but not brain surgery. Only when there is no more information to be found should you worry, and for now there was plenty of information still to be gotten, and plenty of places to go look for it. Much of what he had pointed toward Malaysia.

## *Islamabad, Pakistan, February 1995*

Mohammed and Basit vanished off the screen again. No one knew exactly where either had gone.

Basit had fled through Asia, flying to Singapore the night of the fire, then on to Pakistan. Once again, however, he did not go to ground. He immediately started arranging another plot in Thailand. He recruited a young South African named Istaique Parker to help him smuggle bombs onto the cargo holds of airliners leaving Bangkok. Parker, wary, abandoned his assignment, telling Basit that security was too tight. They returned to Pakistan in early February. As ever, Basit was full of new ideas for targets and ways to get at them—embassy bombings, kidnappings, airplane attacks. Parker was scared to death. Basit had told Parker that Parker's name was on the laptop left behind in Manila, and that he had no choice but to go all-in. The knowledge that he might be a suspect himself led Parker to turn on Basit. When he read in a magazine that the

United States was offering $2 million for information leading to Basit's arrest, the choice between going to jail or getting rich became clear. The next day, he called the U.S. embassy in Islamabad and told officers there he knew Basit and where he might be.

Parker made at least one visit to an embassy official who turned him away. It took some additional effort to persuade other officers at the embassy that he knew what he was talking about, but members of the State Department's Diplomatic Security Service eventually listened and believed him. Cables flew around the globe.

Parker had called the embassy on February 3, a Friday. By Saturday, Ralph Horton, the lead FBI agent for much of Asia, had flown in from Bangkok to run the operation. FBI supervisors in New York and Washington, assuming Basit was about to be caught and knowing that the Pakistanis said they could have him, put together a plan to get Basit out of Pakistan that was so detailed it resembled a military operation. Permission was worked out on the ground in Islamabad, where there was a sense of urgency. The government, then headed by Benazir Bhutto, who believed she herself had once been a target of Basit and KSM, readily agreed to assist in the raid and hand him over.

The Americans planned to fly Basit out of Pakistan as quickly as possible. They readied a plane and lined up agents from the Bureau, the Diplomatic Security Service, the Port Authority, and other agencies to handle the rendition. The plane left New York on Sunday. Detective Matthew Besheer of the Port Authority's intelligence unit was assigned to the contingent that would pick up Basit once the overseas flight landed at an air base north of New York City. Pellegrino, who was still leading the investigation in Manila, was told to get to Pakistan as soon as possible to accompany Basit on the flight home. He immediately went to the Pakistani embassy to get a visa. It was a Saturday. They said they could do nothing until Monday. He couldn't believe the guy he was chasing in the Philippines was exactly where he had predicted he would be—at home in Pakistan—and that Pakistani officials were once again getting in the way.

Parker had told the embassy officials he knew Basit was in Islamabad but didn't know precisely where. He said Basit didn't intend to stay there long, that he was preparing to go to Peshawar. For two days they looked but couldn't find him. On Monday, Parker called again. Basit was still in town, he said, but intended to leave soon. If the Americans were going to get him, they couldn't wait for all their people to be in their assigned spots. This was the time.

Pellegrino was still en route. He had finally gotten his visa on Monday, flown straight to Karachi, then run to catch a 7:00 p.m. flight to Islamabad. Karachi, a city of more than ten million people, had a small airport with the look and feel of a facility in a midsize American city—Des Moines, maybe. Walking through it, Pellegrino heard someone call his name. It was an FBI explosives expert named Wally Higgins in his trademark cowboy hat. With him was fingerprint man Jackie Bell. They were all part of the team that would formally identify Basit and bring him back. They thought they were in good shape timewise. The move on Basit wasn't supposed to occur until the next day. But the Islamabad flight was delayed for two hours, then four, then more. The group ended up spending the whole night in the terminal. Pellegrino was dying.

Parker received information that Basit was going to spend the night at the Su-Casa guesthouse, then leave for Peshawar—the gateway to the autonomous tribal areas—in the morning, where they would be unlikely to capture him. Surveillance was put in place at the Su-Casa. They tracked Basit when he left the hostelry in the evening with a companion. The two spent an hour in a nearby market, and Basit returned to his room. The snatch team moved into position early Tuesday morning.

Parker, as previously agreed, visited Basit in his room in the morning. He left the Su-Casa immediately after, running his hands through his hair as he exited the building. This was the sign. The team moved in. They marched through the lobby and stormed the second-floor room, where Basit was taken by surprise. They identified him, then quickly bundled him out of the room, out of the house, and into a waiting car. He was taken immediately to the airport and was on his way out of Pakistan within the hour.[2]

At about the same time, Pellegrino and company finally took off on the short hop from Karachi. Bill Miller, a State Department Diplomatic Security Service agent stationed in Islamabad, was waiting for them on the ground when they landed. He's already gone, he said. Pellegrino was crushed. He was the guy chasing Basit for two years. Basit was his guy and now others would get to interrogate him on the long flight home. There was nothing he could do. "I'm sorry, Frank," Miller told him. "Do you want to have dinner instead with me and my wife?"

Except for his personal disappointment, it probably mattered little that Pellegrino missed the Basit flight back to the U.S. Secret Service agent Brian Parr, who had worked with Pellegrino at the beginning of the WTC investigation, and FBI special agent Chuck Stern, another veteran of the JTTF, approached Basit on the plane. After being read his Miranda rights, Basit readily waived them and consented to be interviewed. His only condition was that no notes be taken. He said he thought that if there was no record of the interview, he could safely deny it ever occurred.

"He was friendly. He seemed very relaxed and he seemed actually eager to talk to us," Parr testified later.[3]

Parr and Stern agreed to the condition, although they fudged the rules by making extensive notes during breaks in the interrogation. Basit was surprisingly willing, even enthusiastic, to talk about his exploits. He confessed to both the airline bombing plot and the WTC attack, and provided a surprising amount of detail. At one point he sketched a diagram of where in the World Trade Center basement he wanted to park the van holding the bomb. Parr took the diagram, but Basit asked for it back. He then tore off the portion of the paper on which the diagram was drawn, popped it in his mouth, and ate it.

The interview with Basit lasted six hours, on and off, as the plane flew back over Europe and the Atlantic. It landed at an airfield in Orange County, New York, just north of New York City. Basit was cuffed, shackled, and blindfolded, then loaded into one of the Port Authority's choppers, a Sikorsky copiloted by a one-legged Vietnam vet, for the last portion of the trip into Manhattan, where he was to be jailed. Besheer, the Port Authority cop assigned to the JTTF, hopped aboard and they flew down the east side of Manhattan to avoid the fog coming off the Hudson River on the west side, then circled the tip of the island, coming up past the twin towers of the Trade Center. It was a cold, brilliantly clear winter's night. The towers shimmered in the frigid air.

Bill Gavin, an old FBI hand, unmasked Basit just as they came upon the towers.

They're still standing, he said.

Basit replied: They wouldn't be if I had had more money.

Hearing this, Besheer could barely contain himself. He'd been one of the first responders at the '93 Trade Center attacks and had been injured in them. Isn't this his stop? he muttered. Let's open the doors and let him out.

## *Cape Town, South Africa, April 1995*

Istaique Parker, the young South African who turned Basit in, was eager to accept the $2 million reward for his assistance, but he declined an offer to go into the federal witness protection program. Give me the money, he said, and I'll take care of myself. The U.S. policy for paying out rewards required that the money be delivered in person, receipt acknowledged. The JTTF asked Besheer to hand-carry the money.

Parker, who had been secretly spirited into South Africa under heavy guard, wanted the money in small U.S. bills. The cash constituted a considerable pile. Besheer packed it in two large duffel bags, skated past security at Newark, and hauled the bags to Cape Town, where Parker was living.

Besheer and a representative from the State Department agreed to meet Parker downtown. Besheer opened the duffels and asked Parker to count the cash.

That's okay, Mr. Matthew, Parker said. I trust you.

Besheer told him it wasn't a matter of trust. These are the rules I have to follow. You have to count it all.

You learn something new every day, it's said. Before he had gone to South Africa, Besheer had no idea how long it might take to count $2 million. He and the other Americans didn't want Parker to lose count, so they watched in silence. It took four hours.

# CHAPTER 6
# Sorting It Out

*Manila, the Philippines, April 1995*

Two months after Basit was brought back to New York, the Filipino police transferred Murad to American custody. The Filipinos had held Murad since the night of his arrest, January 6, but hadn't allowed the Americans access to him. The isolation of Murad and the escape of Wali Khan Amin Shah from Filipino custody had raised questions about the local investigation.

Under harsh interrogation, Murad had told the Filipino investigators almost everything he knew. Pellegrino was in the country much of that time, but he wasn't convinced he would ever get to talk to Murad. He thought the Filipinos might release him. By the time Pellegrino loaded him onto an aircraft bound for New York in April, Murad must have thought he had already given away every secret he ever had. So he told them all again to Pellegrino and another FBI agent, Tom Donlon, on their flight across the Pacific.[1]

He admitted the plan to bomb airliners. He described his own recruitment. He said Basit had attacked the World Trade Center. He said Basit's Liberation Army was just him and Basit. He told the agents about future ideas for attacks against nuclear plants and the CIA headquarters. He identified possible sources of funds for the operation. In short, he described plans for the most ambitious attacks against the United States since Pearl Harbor. During the course of this, Murad also validated the FBI's basic plan for interrogations: have agents who know what they are talking about asking informed questions of subjects they have treated respectfully. But he said little about Khalid Sheikh Mohammed. Pellegrino believed that was because Murad had at best only a vague notion of who he was.

With Basit and Murad in custody, the FBI was still trying to build a picture of the overall plot. Investigators had identified and captured what looked like half of the main group. Khalid Sheikh Mohammed, Wali Khan, and Ibrahim Muneer were still at large. There was evidence of a larger group centered around Mohammed Jamal Khalifa, his aides, and acquaintances. The Filipinos were even more convinced that was where the real story lay, and so, to a degree, was Pellegrino. While tapping Khalifa's phones in recent years, the Filipinos saw a network of contacts spreading across the Philippines through Southeast Asia and into Saudi Arabia and other Gulf locations where deep-pocket donors lived. Khalifa used his businesses and the local office of the Saudi-based IIRO to disguise funds he donated to local Islamists. The FBI agents were looking at leads heading off in a thousand different directions, but Malaysia in particular continued to look like a center of activity.

Konsojaya, the trading company Khan had been instrumental in establishing in Kuala Lumpur in 1994, had interesting connections—enough to raise significant and immediate suspicion. Khalifa had called its offices repeatedly. One of the other founding directors, Mohammed Amein al-Sanani, was an officer in other charities connected to Khalifa. Al-Sanani and Khan had multiple connections, as did Khan and Khalifa's number two, Ahmad al-Hamwi. Even with Yousef in custody, it seemed to Pellegrino he had missed as much as he understood. Who were these people, and how could they afford to do what they were doing? Pellegrino wasn't convinced Konsojaya was anything but what it seemed—a trading company. Basit and Mohammed weren't rich; they didn't seem to have huge sources of funds. Money was tight enough to make them worry about cash transfers into their bank account of as little as $2,000. You gotta eat even when you're blowing things up, Pellegrino thought.

Basit's concerns over money gave the FBI one hot lead. Soon after arriving at the federal lockup in Manhattan, he called "Khalid" at the water ministry in Qatar, and when there was no answer, he left a voice mail saying he needed $2,000 for his commissary account.[2]

The records seized in the investigation revealed a constant stream of air travel and hotel rentals. Where did the money come from? Pellegrino's team's principal task in the next year was to ensure they had gathered the evidence and witnesses needed to prosecute Basit and Murad. But they also wanted to track these plots down to their ultimate beginnings, and figure out who else involved in them really mattered, and what they were up to.

## *Langley, Virginia, 1995*

Pellegrino wasn't alone in his lack of understanding. Radical Islam was beginning to be recognized more broadly as an emerging problem that had to be investigated, understood, and countered. The CIA had only grudgingly ceded to the FBI its lead role in terror investigations abroad as well as at home, a status that had been formalized by a presidential order signed in June of 1995, essentially defining terrorism as a crime.[3] Presidential Decision Directive 39 made the FBI the chief counterterrorism organization, and because the FBI was the FBI, that meant perpetrators were to be hunted down and evidence was to be assiduously collected and presented to grand juries. Indictments and trials would follow. The CIA was chagrined, but lent its assistance to tracking down suspects and smoothing the way with the authorities in host countries. The agency's contacts with foreign security services were much more extensive than the FBI's, and the agency had used those contacts to bring two of Basit's accomplices in the World Trade Center attack back for trial. In fact, the CIA routinely complained that information sharing was a one-way street, the same criticism the FBI would level in the opposite direction a decade later.

The CIA's central problem with the FBI's approach was that it was reactive. Events would occur—a bomb, a shooting, a kidnapping—and crimes would be alleged and suspects sought. This was fine as far as it went, but it did nothing to actually stop terrorism from happening. The agency had established groups to study and track the problem, notably the Counterterrorist Center, established in 1986 (the name was changed to the Counterterrorism Center in 2002). But the CTC had evolved into more of an analytical unit with a variety of branches studying different potential terrorist threats. In 1996, the agency made another attempt at creating a more proactive organization. It was formally called the Bin Laden Issue Station and was modeled on the agency's overseas stations in that it would combine intelligence gathering with operations. It was the first and only CIA station ever created to dedicate its efforts to one man. The station, located in a northern Virginia office park as a way of creating physical separation between it and CIA headquarters, would treat bin Laden as if he were a country.

Osama bin Laden was hardly a complete mystery. The youngest of many sons of a wealthy Saudi industrialist, he'd been known as a leader of the Afghan Arabs in Afghanistan in the 1980s. Since then he had been viewed primarily as a kind of terrorist tourist, someone who dabbled in terror financing. Concern began to increase when he was kicked out of Saudi Arabia and moved to Sudan in 1991. There, he had built an economic base, controlling much of the nation's agricultural sector, and installed the underpinnings of a terror organization. He established military training camps in the desert and was believed to have formed an alliance with Egyptian jihad groups bent on overthrowing Hosni Mubarak.

CIA director George Tenet years later described the agency's view of bin Laden: "We saw him as a prominent financial backer of Islamic terrorist movements who was funding the paramilitary training of Arab religious militants operating in, or supporting fellow Muslims in, Bosnia, Egypt, Kashmir, Jordan, Tunisia, Algeria, and Yemen."[4]

He was widely regarded as a venture capitalist of terror, someone who listened to pitches and decided which to fund, largely from his share of the family fortune. The new bin Laden unit would be dedicated to the proposition that he was more than a financier.

The station was to be led by Michael Scheuer, a career analyst who had become frustrated with the fact that all the reams and reams of analysis produced by his agency seldom seemed to lead to action. Every report simply generated another, and they were all neatly stacked on shelves, never to be looked at. Scheuer wasn't a field agent. He had rarely been out of the country. But he was smart, imaginative, and scared to death. He had worked on the radical fundamentalist desk for years, and was convinced some very bad things were coming America's way, especially from bin Laden.

Scheuer was also uncompromisingly combative, a real son of a bitch by almost everyone's account, even his own. If it weren't for his obvious intelligence, his main skill might have seemed to be pissing people off. Years later, the CIA's number three official, Jim Pavitt, had even encased a letter from Scheuer in Lucite and displayed it prominently on his desk. "Dear Jim," the letter read. "I think you suck." Pavitt liked to tell people that Scheuer was "the only person at this place who ever had the balls to talk to me like that. Seeing it every day keeps me grounded."[5]

Scheuer liked to say that he needed to talk that way for anyone in upper management to actually pay attention to him.

For his part, Scheuer thought the agency—and Pavitt, for that matter—was mainly hampered by its stupidity. There were only a handful of people in the United States government outside of the New York JTTF's counterterrorism squads who thought radical Islam represented a genuine threat to the country—Richard Clarke, the White House's top counterterrorism adviser, and Scheuer chief among them. Both men had a difficult time getting anyone else to take them or their concerns seriously. In fact, as many thought the two were unhinged as treated them seriously. Terrorism was out of fashion.

The CIA in many ways was crippled by its failures, just as the FBI was crippled by its successes. The FBI may have been moribund, caught up in its own history, unable to see beyond its walls to the larger world in which it was working. Local cops would often deride the Bureau, saying the only thing it was really any good at was catching bank robbers, although it wasn't hard to find cops who questioned even that. The Bureau's activities were aimed at handcuffing ordinary criminals, people who broke the law for profit or for personal pride. They had little experience with radical Islamic fundamentalists, who broke the law because they believed God wanted them to. As such, the Bureau's habit of paying people to inform against their criminal colleagues just didn't work.

Whereas the FBI wanted to just keep repeating the things at which it had succeeded, the CIA was scared to death to do so. Its appetite for victory had been curbed by revelations of its past participation in coups and assassinations, and the agency's resources had been cut back substantially. Stations were closed around the globe, agents dismissed, and the double agents they had recruited left out in the cold. "Risk" had become a dirty word. Field agents complained that bureaucratic kudzu had crawled through the place and strangled it from the top down.

The bin Laden station was intended as a pilot project to break the stranglehold. It would be an actual CIA "station," with case officers who actually did things, working just next door to the agency's sprawling campus in Langley, Virginia. Nothing like that had even been contemplated before, and it created a lot of jealousy and sniping.

Scheuer would start with a tiny staff—fewer than a dozen agents—but he wanted to bite off huge portions of the terrorist portfolio. He was to have responsibility, of course, for bin Laden, but he was also intrigued by Basit and what had happened in New York City and Manila. He wanted Mohammed and Khalifa under his purview as well. He was already looking hard at them in his current position at the CIA's Islamic Extremist Branch. He warned his superiors that the analysts with the most experience covering KSM were going with him to the new organization; there would be no one left behind familiar with the case.

Before transferring to the new organization, he formally proposed taking responsibility for both Mohammed and Khalifa, but was not given initial approval to do so. Afraid of what could happen—that is, afraid that KSM would somehow get lost in the bureaucratic clutter—he continued tracking Mohammed, even delaying the move to his new job for months.

When Mohammed went to ground in the latter months of 1995, "once his trail went cold," Scheuer moved to the new operation. And in the meantime, the man who would be replacing him complained that Scheuer was trying to take too much of the best work. Scheur appealed but lost.

"So, typically, they chose the worst solution. They cut the baby in half," Scheuer said. "I got Khalifa, he got KSM. And I don't remember reading a single intel report from the field about where he was [after that], what he was up to, or who he was with."[6]

## *Federal Plaza, New York City, Autumn 1995*

Pellegrino's hunt for information about KSM, which had been going on for almost two full years, was wearing other people out, especially since they didn't think there'd be any huge payoff if they ever actually found the guy. International terrorism had fallen back off the radar of those who mattered in the Bureau and, more important, off the radar of those above them in Washington. The World Trade Center attack seemed aberrant, an isolated event without meaning beyond its immediate victims and circumstances. In an era of tightening budgets, and as vivid memories of the experience faded, it was not something to which a lot of resources would be devoted.

The lack of fanfare—and any obvious career payoff—was also making it difficult to keep other investigators interested in the case. Pellegrino had already worn out another potential partner who was tired of all the travel. Lots of agents felt the same way, and a few passed on partnering up on such a grueling assignment. The FBI was a *domestic* agency, after all.

Still, Pellegrino needed help. He wondered about this veteran Port Authority cop, Besheer, who had accompanied Yousef on the helicopter ride. Besheer had more or less assigned himself to the JTTF. He had come over to the Trade Center the day the North Tower had been bombed and never returned to his office. While terrorism seemed a backwater to many, to Besheer it was the most important work he could do. He was raised Catholic but he was also Arab American—half Lebanese, half Syrian—and felt he somehow owed his country this service. He even learned a few words of Arabic from his father, a tailor, and from his mother, a seamstress in the family's tiny shop just a few dozen blocks from the Twin Towers.

After years as a beat cop, he had been promoted to detective and in 1992 had been assigned to do a study on security at the World Trade Center. His report stated, presciently—but fruitlessly, it turned out—that the Trade Center garage was vulnerable to truck bombs. The report was largely ignored until the day of the attack. Besheer was sent over to the crime scene, and for the next year he did whatever was asked of him. Even with high security clearance, he ended up digging through stacks of parking tickets, any record that somebody wanted chased. It was pure grunt work. He did it all tirelessly and without complaint.

Pellegrino appreciated Besheer's attitude. He appreciated something else as well. Pellegrino had a mischievous sense of humor and a high-pitched cackle that erupted easily and often, so he took note when Besheer assumed the role of office cutup. Besheer played practical jokes on colleagues, in one case wiring a flashbulb so that it would go off when another agent opened his desk. He and Pellegrino put a piece of fish underneath another agent's car's backseat. The guy would show up at the office smelling like rotten fish and have no idea why. Given the stress and grimness of the job, Besheer's antics were a welcome relief. They also bonded over being 5 foot 8, shorter than most agents.

Pellegrino and Besheer had worked together the prior fall on an unrelated case—a shopping mall bomb plot in suburban New York—and had gotten on well. Pellegrino was impressed by Besheer's experience as a beat cop and also by his fearlessness; by then the detective had been stabbed and assaulted and had suffered other indignities while working some of the toughest beats within Port Authority, like the squalid bus terminals. He was also drawn to "Matty" Besheer's standing as a sort of outsider, not one of those out to win a popularity contest. He had taken to calling him Bash, in recognition of the fact that the tough Port Authority cop from Brooklyn always had a much more aggressive way of getting things done than FBI agents like Pellegrino were allowed to have. One morning, after participating in the prominent arrest of one of the first World Trade Center bombers, Besheer came to work to find a copy of the front page of a New York newspaper on his desk. The paper featured a photo of Besheer leading a handcuffed suspect on a perp walk to the detention facility. Besheer appears serious in the photo. A colleague who occasionally joshed with him about his allegedly divided loyalties, given his Arab American heritage, had attached a Post-it note saying, "Matt, why the long face? Was he a relation?"

Not long after getting the first news out of Manila, Pellegrino asked Besheer to step out of the office for a minute. The task force quarters were wide open, a bullpen, and it was hard to have any privacy there. Out in the narrow hallway, Pellegrino leaned against one wall. Besheer leaned against the other. If you cared to look, there was a gorgeous view of the city out the window at the end of the narrow corridor.

Pellegrino told Besheer they had an international target they needed to chase. Did Besheer want to go along? It would require huge amounts of time on the road, maybe in uncomfortable circumstances.

Absolutely, Besheer immediately said. Count me in.

Shouldn't you check with your bosses at Port Authority? Pellegrino asked.

Count me in, Besheer said.

It was a leap of faith, as Besheer actually did need permission. But he had watched Pellegrino at work over the previous two years, and in a squad room mostly full of good, but not necessarily the most ambitious, guys he stood out. Besheer thought the JTTF generally had a robust collection of talent, not all of it being put to the best use. Pellegrino was the real deal, he thought. Everybody by and large wore what might as well have been FBI-issued dark suits. Their desks were perpetually clean. Pellegrino's desk was a mess. By outward appearances, so was he. He looked rumpled. His hair was long, at least by FBI standards. He wore T-shirts and jeans and comfortable shoes made for walking the streets for hours. He was always busy, always late, always in a hurry. Sometimes he'd forget things, as if there were too much in his head to find it all on command.

Besheer, ten years Pellegrino's senior, saw a younger version of himself, a striver, a dirt dog, a relentless son of a bitch. "You could see that look in his eyes, that nothing would stop him," Besheer said.

Besheer eagerly signed up for the hunt. If this guy is going, he thought, I'll be happy to go with him. Maybe even protect him; free him up to do his free-association analytical work.

They first had to pitch Herman, the supervisor. And when

some within the FBI and DOJ balked at promoting Besheer because of his "lowly" Port Authority background, Pellegrino appealed to Mary Jo White, who, as the U.S. attorney for the Southern District, was the JTTF's de facto overseer. White could be intimidating when she chose to be, despite her diminutive size. It helped that she was personal friends with FBI director Louis Freeh and attorney general Janet Reno.

Pellegrino pitched her on the importance of continuing the investigation. First, they needed to find Wali Khan, he said. We can make a case against him for the movie theater bomb, if nothing else. White "got" terrorism, and said sure—bring Besheer aboard and go for it. But she reminded Pellegrino they hadn't yet gotten enough evidence from Manila to indict Khan. "Make time, make grand jury time, and indict him," she said. "And then get your ass to the Philippines and find some goddamn evidence."

## *Kuala Lumpur, Malaysia, 1995*

Mohammed, meanwhile, was apparently not concerned about being tracked by anyone. He kept up what had become a peripatetic lifestyle, traveling the globe. He sometimes used fake papers in his travels—they were widely available for a pittance. In Pakistan in particular, a cottage industry in identity papers had developed during the anti-Soviet war to serve mujahideen who preferred to have the paper record of their participation in the jihad obscured. Like much else that was initiated during the war—the training camps, the calls to jihad, the intermingling of the Pakistani intelligence establishment with various jihadi groups, the ISI's involvement in the opium trade—the document industry continued unabated long after the war had ended. Mohammed took advantage of this when needed. He used more than two dozen aliases.

In the summer, Mohammed traveled to Malaysia from Qatar, via Sudan and Yemen, to meet with Khan, who had settled in Malaysia after escaping from the Philippines. On the same trip he met with Hambali and Hambali's colleagues in their regional militant organization, Jemaah Islamiyah.

Building JI was a remarkable achievement accomplished in very little time. Hambali and his Chinese wife, Noralwizah Lee Abdullah, had moved in 1991 from his native Indonesia into a tiny wooden shack in a migrant quarter of a small village, Sungai Manggis, south of Kuala Lumpur. Sungai Manggis was just minutes from the western Malaysian coast, and from there an hour by boat across the Strait of Malacca to Indonesia. It was a well-traveled path for poor Indonesians who came to Malaysia for work.

When they arrived, Hambali and his wife carried a single bag each. They cooked, ate, and slept on the floor. Five years later, Hambali commanded a network. He did it by sheer hard work. He started out doing odd jobs in the village. Soon, he began showing up outside the gold-domed mosque on the southern edge of the nearby market town of Banting, selling kebabs out of a trishaw.

Hambali switched from kebabs to patent medicines and began traveling—on business, he said—disappearing for weeks at a time. At home, he received what became a steady stream of visitors. They spoke English and Arabic and sometimes carried shopping bags from duty-free shops.

Hambali prospered. Soon he was driving a red Proton hatchback and juggling calls on a pair of cell phones. Many of those calls, investigators later determined, were made to Mohammed Jamal Khalifa in Manila.

Hambali had eluded detection altogether when the Manila Air plot unraveled. He had remained in his little hut along Manggis River Village Road, an unlikely place from which to command anything, about as far off the beaten path of world affairs as one could get. Yet Hambali sat in his tiny Malaysian village and meticulously planned, then patiently built, Jemaah Islamiyah into an extraordinarily disciplined network. It had more structure than anything bin Laden ever attempted, with strict geographic sectors that covered all of Southeast Asia, an organizational chart in each of the sectors, and command tables delineating clear lines of authority and responsibility up and down. Unlike Arab terror organizations, which tended to be haphazard and ad hoc, Jemaah Islamiyah was strictly regimented. Its regional commanders held regular meetings and assessed monthly taxes on members.

Hambali gathered money and men. He recruited a diverse group—small-time traders, artisans, and factory workers, but also engineers, businessmen, middle managers, and university lecturers. They found Hambali a man of tremendous, if quiet, charisma. "He was such an unassuming person," said Mohamad Sobri, a former soldier in the Malaysian army who became one of Hambali's followers.[7]

Hambali made a regular circuit of small prayer groups to promote a goal—uniting Southeast Asia's Muslims into a single, powerful Islamic force. With nearly three hundred million Muslims throughout the region, it would be by far the biggest Islamic nation on earth. At the end of every session, followers passed a hat around the room and put in whatever small amounts of money they could spare. Hambali's network had also helped Basit, who was at the time among the most wanted men on earth, enter the Philippines surreptitiously by the well-worn smuggling route through the southern islands. The back door, they called it.

As was often the case, Mohammed met with Hambali not to serve some specific purpose but rather to build and maintain his own evolving network. Why he thought he needed connections to a terror network in Southeast Asia was known only to him.

As often as he traveled under an alias, Mohammed traveled freely under his own name. In the fall he moved back to Bosnia to work for an NGO, the Egyptian Humanitarian Relief Agency, in support of Bosnian Muslims in their war against the Serbs. Not only did Mohammed travel under his own name, he registered with the government as Khalid Sheikh Mohammed, an engineer. The Sarajevo police department and state security service had his address, 11 Bjelave Street, in downtown Sarajevo. It was even mentioned in the report of a state security agency that worked closely with U.S. authorities.[8] If KSM was hiding, he was strangely conspicuous about it.

The CIA was crawling all over these NGOs because so many

of them were used as fronts to shovel millions of dollars to mujahideen organizations. Some of those funds even came from the U.S. government, which was anxious to stop the war and the campaign of "ethnic cleansing" against Muslims. A contemporaneous CIA report named the organization that Mohammed worked for as one affiliated with international terror.[9] The report alleged that high-ranking government officials in Saudi Arabia, Kuwait, and Pakistan were bankrolling the terror fronts. The Pakistani ISI was said to be training some of them. Once again, the Americans were looking right at Mohammed, but it was as if he wore a cloak of invisibility. He was there, they were examining the very organization he was working with, but they did not see him or ignored him if they did. Investigators later came to suspect that Mohammed helped build a bomb that was used to blow up a police station in neighboring Croatia. At the time, KSM wasn't thinking much about charitable giving. "Most, if not all, of this travel appears to have been related to his abiding interest in carrying out terrorist operations," the 9/11 Commission would later say about KSM's travels and activities during this time, some of it funded by Abdullah bin Khalid al-Thani, the member of the Qatari ruling family who invited him to stay in Qatar and arranged for his government job.[10] In retrospect, it seems clear that Mohammed was assembling bits and pieces of a new kind of international organization—one that was ad hoc almost by definition but one in which the individual pieces would be available to him upon request.

On Christmas Eve in 1995, Pellegrino was about to get on a plane and go to Bosnia in search of KSM. Local law enforcement there had indicated that they knew who KSM was and where he was living. But before Pellegrino could leave, he was told that Mohammed had already gone away, slipping again through his and the FBI's hands.

Mohammed wasn't long gone from Malaysia when Pellegrino and Besheer rolled into Kuala Lumpur, seeking to enlist the help of the

Malaysian security services in their hunt for Wali Khan. Too much of the evidence they had found in Manila pointed to Malaysia as Khan's logical hiding place. We don't know where he is or who's hiding him, they thought, but we think he's here.

The initial meetings with the Malaysians were formal, and the locals weren't very forthcoming. Besheer and Pellegrino spent weeks in town, however, investigating Konsojaya and other Kuala Lumpur connections to the plot. Besheer put his formidable relationship and networking skills to work, developing teasing alliances with, among others, Dato Yousef, a top official in the Royal Malaysian Police Special Branch. Soon enough they found themselves making toasts in a Chinese restaurant called the Cheers Palace. Besheer had grown a short ponytail and Yousef started calling him Yanni after the Greek American singer. Anything for you, Yanni, Yousef said. Let me know where he is and Khan will be dead in half an hour.

"No! We need him alive!" Besheer told him. "We need to take him with us!"

Pellegrino and Besheer left the problem to the Malaysians and went first to Okinawa, where the Japanese had stored the remains of the Philippine Airlines flight Basit had bombed in his trial run. Parts of the plane had to be disassembled, examined, tagged as evidence, and shipped to New York to be used as exhibits in a trial. Besheer took control of the operation. His attention to detail was perfectly suited to the task. Pellegrino went on to Manila.

Within weeks, the Malaysians came through. They had located Khan in the northwestern part of the country, on a small island called Langkawi, thanks in large part to some business cards found back at the Josefa. They transmitted the information to the regional FBI office in Thailand. Horton, the FBI legal attaché in Bangkok, then passed the word to Pellegrino and Besheer.

Pellegrino was alarmed because Khan hadn't yet been indicted in the United States, and there was a real possibility of him being caught and released—and disappearing forever. He asked Horton to get the Malaysians to hold off on any action for a couple of weeks. He raced back to the U.S., testified to the grand jury, and the indictment soon followed. Then he got on a plane and flew back to Malaysia.

Everybody in the New York office knew what had happened when Pellegrino went to take Basit into custody in Pakistan—how his flights kept getting delayed and he had ended up missing the rendition plane by perhaps thirty minutes. So on his way out the door in New York, he got a hearty send-off in the form of a chorus of friendly catcalls. Don't miss the flight, Frank! Don't miss the flight!

The Malaysians were happy to turn Khan over to the Americans, but, as was often the case, they didn't want it known they were cooperating. So a Boeing 707 with all its markings obscured was flown into Kuala Lumpur for the pickup, with the top FBI counterterrorism official in New York, Thomas Pickard, aboard. Pellegrino and Besheer met in Kuala Lumpur, then flew to Langkawi. Once there, they had to sit on the tarmac in the getaway plane for six hours, sweating in the Malaysian heat, waiting for Khan to be delivered.

Finally, a van rolled up with Khan aboard. He was brought onto the 707 and they were preparing to taxi out and take off. But Besheer, ever the relationship builder, had brought a load of swag—FBI and JTTF baseball caps, vests, shirts—for the local cops, and word somehow got out that he had them on board. Before they departed, Besheer cracked open his stash and began handing it out. The local police descended on the plane, looking for their share of the booty. Within minutes, every Malaysian cop in sight was careening around the airport with an FBI cap on. Stealthy, indeed.

On the flight home, the plane had to refuel in order to make it all the way to New York. The protocol was that an accused person being brought back to the United States would be tried in the jurisdiction in which he first landed. So the normal refueling options—Guam, Hawaii, and Alaska—were ruled out because the New Yorkers did not want to lose jurisdiction. It was known within the JTTF as the Mary Jo White rule: our jurisdiction or bust. Not even

JFK would do, as that was in the Eastern District. This necessitated in-air refueling, a ridiculously expensive option but one that was on occasion employed.

The KC-135 Stratotankers used to do the refueling always came up in pairs, in case something happened to the first plane. Besheer wholeheartedly loved everything about flying. Pellegrino hated it just as much. So Besheer would go up front to the cockpit to watch the refueling while Pellegrino buried his head somewhere in the rear.

On the flight from Kuala Lumpur, the first planned refueling was over Guam. It was a brilliant blue-sky day, and Besheer was in the cockpit watching. As the tanker came in for the hookup, a massive black thunderhead appeared out of nowhere, completely obscuring all visual contact with the tanker. The pilot of the 707 had to break off. They were flying blind in the cloud and didn't know exactly where the tanker was, so the pilot put the 707 into a steep dive to get out of the vicinity of the other plane as quickly as possible. There was never any real danger to the passengers, but the dive caused all sorts of commotion on board.

Besheer hadn't known it, but Pellegrino was in the lavatory when the breakaway occurred. The dive was so steep it caused a momentary weightlessness on the plane. Pellegrino suddenly was floating through the lavatory, his pants around his ankles. When the plane stabilized and he came out, he was a horrible color of green. He looked at Besheer and glared. I fucking hate flying, he said. Besheer burst out laughing. Later, they found out their boss's boss, Pickard, had thrown up all over the back of the plane.

## *Manila, the Philippines, Winter 1995*

On the flight and in subsequent interrogations, Khan had been less forthcoming than Basit and Murad had been. He lied diligently throughout the interview on board the flight. Pellegrino, ever the well-trained FBI man, thought that the lies could be useful in and of themselves, and took careful note of them; maybe he could use the lies against him in court. It was this sort of thought process that differentiated FBI agents from perhaps anyone else who has ever investigated international terrorism—they were driven almost to the exclusion of all other motives by the need to make cases.

After they delivered Khan in New York, Pellegrino returned to Manila and Besheer went back to Okinawa, where he meticulously identified, tagged, and stowed in a shipping container every relevant piece of the Philippine Airlines plane that they might use as evidence in a trial. He had it all sent off to the U.S., making sure to have a fellow agent at JFK personally deliver it to the evidence vault, so the chain of custody couldn't be questioned by even the most persistent defense attorney.

Pellegrino and Besheer then tracked down every witness and piece of evidence they could identify. Besheer had never spent much time abroad and was sometimes dumbfounded by the way life was lived outside the United States. Manila was a palace of wonders for him, and he demanded that, in their few hours of downtime on such trips, they race around so he could take tourist photos of local Catholic churches and other attractions. The pictures would later come in handy at trial, to show juries what it was like "over there." One night, they were at the house of one of the bar girls Basit had befriended. They were in a sitting room right off the kitchen interviewing her mother when Besheer's eye was caught by movement on the drain board next to the kitchen sink. He saw rats scampering across the counter. He turned back to look at Pellegrino, who was sitting next to the mother on the couch. Just then, two huge cockroaches appeared atop the back of the couch, just behind Pellegrino's head. Besheer jumped up instinctively. Pellegrino did, too, without even knowing why. They finished the interview standing up.

They interviewed hotel clerks, chemists, movie theater ticket takers, and naked go-go dancers. Pellegrino visited the dental clinic with the pretty dentists and traded an FBI pin for the X-rays and dental records of one of the suspects. They spent hours in photo-processing shops, going through boxes of negatives, looking for photos of KSM and the others. The dancers were generally more impressive than the clerks. And often more helpful. They ended up making many trips to see the girls, who often lived out on the squalid periphery of the metropolis, usually with their families. Besheer, always the detail man of the two, found that by bringing a large tub or two of ice cream—a luxury the girls couldn't afford—they would get their questions answered more easily, and at greater length. They usually brought mango, because it was their own favorite flavor—and they would end up stumbling out at the end of the interviews with a stomachful of sugar and cream.

While Besheer brought the treats, Pellegrino brought a kind of guileless charm. He could get anyone to talk in part because he seemed such an unthreatening, fundamentally decent guy. He fought with his bosses, but he was every source's best buddy. People liked him and they told him things.

One afternoon, a family member mentioned that one of the girls had received letters from Khalid Sheikh Mohammed—not love letters, exactly, but more of the flirty "how-you-doing?" variety. In one of them, he told the woman he was a Catholic priest. Later, she got a Christmas card from him. Whatever the content of the letters, their real value lay in the envelopes, one of which Mohammed apparently had filched from his ministry office in Doha. It had a return address printed on it. Mohammed had taken care to obscure the address with Wite-Out, but removing it was a simple matter for the FBI lab techs once Pellegrino and Besheer bagged and tagged the envelope and sent it to Quantico.

Persistence is often undervalued. It isn't usually the brilliance of insight, or great courage or persuasiveness, that ends up making or breaking a case. It's the value of keeping at it. It hadn't been easy or heroic. It had taken months of pounding the pavement in some of Manila's seedier slums, often without a real reason to do so. But with the finding of a single envelope with an obscured return address, Pellegrino and Besheer finally had a fix on Mohammed.

# CHAPTER 7
## A Near Miss

*Doha, Qatar, December 1995*

One thing Basit, Murad, and Khan had in common was how little they had to say about Khalid Sheikh Mohammed. His name, aliases, and fingerprints were scattered through the evidence being accumulated, but he remained at best a blurry figure. By the middle of 1995, Pellegrino and Besheer knew who he was, but they generally didn't know where he was until he wasn't there anymore. They also suspected he was a significant player, given all the evidence found in searches in Manila, but they didn't know how culpable he was, or for what. Their first thought was to track him down and interview him.

Then Mohammed's name started appearing in strange places. The Italians arrested some people and his phone number was in one of their phone books. Someone was picked up in Canada and his number was in that phone book, too. "This guy knows too many people," Pellegrino thought. "Too many bad people." Mary Jo White agreed. So Pellegrino and Mike Garcia, one of two lead assistant U.S. attorneys on the Manila Air plot, decided not to pursue an interview for fear of alerting him to their interest. They thought instead about ways to arrest him.

The phone number everyone had was the same—his Qatar phone. Coupled with the return address from the Manila letters, there was little doubt that Mohammed was spending some amount of time in Qatar. Qatar is a small place, just a thumb of land slightly larger than Connecticut jutting off the eastern edge of Saudi Arabia into the Persian Gulf. Its capital, Doha, was not the type of sprawling metropolis where you would go to hide out. Everybody knew everybody there, unless you were someone who performed contract labor—one of the tens of thousands of Bengalis, Filipinos, and Nepalese who dominated the market for physical work. So knowing that Mohammed, or KSM, as his American pursuers had begun calling him, was in Doha made finding him fairly simple. He was, in fact, found.

The FBI didn't have a legat in Doha, or anywhere in the Gulf, for that matter, and ran its entire Middle East operation out of Rome. It alerted intel officials and later that year, 1995, the CIA moved an agency asset—an informant—to Doha. The man was chosen because he wouldn't raise suspicions, having traveled widely as a Middle Eastern businessman. The asset struck up a relationship with Mohammed. He "would have tea with him and coffee . . . they would have dinner. We knew the apartment he lived in, we knew his job and schedule, who he worked for," said a CIA official with direct knowledge of the investigation.[1] Mohammed lived openly, working as an engineer in the Ministry of Electricity and Water. That is, when he was in town and showed up at the ministry. He continued to travel the world, raising money and constructing his international terrorist network, and was often gone for weeks at a time.

Once they identified where he was, and that he appeared to be continuing to plot against the U.S., Pellegrino and Besheer scrambled to put together a case to bring before a grand jury in hopes of getting an indictment. The CIA obtained a fingerprint from a glass in Doha that matched the one on the dictionary from the Manila apartment. If there was one moment when they knew they had enough, besides the print match, it was when they finally obtained photos of KSM and got the Filipino girls to identify him as the man mixing chemicals with Basit in Manila. They needed to move fast before KSM vanished again.

Pellegrino's boss, Neil Herman, testified before a grand jury while Pellegrino and Besheer were still overseas. KSM was indicted in January of 1996. It was sealed so that Mohammed would not know he was being pursued. A dossier on who KSM was and why it might be a good idea to take him out of circulation was prepared for President Clinton. It included the FBI's belief that KSM and the others had worked on a plot to assassinate Clinton himself, figuring that wouldn't hurt efforts to get his attention and support—which would be needed to execute the kind of extraordinary judicial rendition of KSM they had in mind. The question then became how to do it.

It was a rule of thumb in foreign affairs for American officials to do what they could to avoid embarrassing other governments. In many places, the most embarrassing thing a government could do was to be seen cooperating with America. This was the case in Qatar, which, like almost every country in the region, had a considerable conservative Islamist element within the population. In Qatar, that element was more than well represented within the government, too.

The Qatari government did not want to give its internal opponents any leverage. A Clinton National Security Council official described it as "a distinct reluctance to actually get involved in doing something that would...expose them to having violated their own rules and laws."

The head of state, Sheikh Hamad bin Khalifa al-Thani, had earlier in the year overthrown his father's government and begun an ambitious modernization campaign. This included liberalizing the political structure and—most shocking of all—the media. Al Jazeera, the pan-Arab television network Qatar launched in 1996, was the prime example of this, but there were many others. To some members of the emir's own family as well as neighboring governments, it felt like too much—way too much—modernization. The Saudis, the overwhelming power of the region, were particularly agitated.

The National Security Council staff in the Clinton White House wanted to do a "snatch and grab" and trundle Mohammed back to New York to face trial, as it had with Basit. The administration had had several other successes with such renditions, still a relatively new process, and wanted to send a team to get KSM. The NSC asked for recommendations, and a deputies' meeting was called in late 1995 at the White House to discuss the feasibility of such an operation. There are basically two sorts of meetings called at the White House that involve the entire national security apparatus: principals' meetings, involving the president, cabinet officers, and agency heads; and so-called deputies' meetings, at which the same agencies and departments are represented by the second or third in command—the deputies—who tend to be far better informed about details than their bosses. These meetings are usually where the real work gets done.

The deputies' meetings also tend to be more freewheeling, and in this one, Sandy Berger, the deputy national security advisor to President Clinton, asked for proposals on how they could get KSM. The CIA said it didn't really have the assets in place. The Department of Defense, trying to avoid another *Black Hawk Down* type of debacle, presented plans for what almost amounted to an invasion. Both were ways of saying no without saying no. Those who favored the rendition had imagined going in covertly with a team of perhaps twenty-five people. That was nowhere near the Pentagon's estimation of its needs. "We were off by orders of magnitude," said Jamie Gorelick, the Department of Justice's representative at the meeting.[2]

The State Department said it didn't want to do anything to upset the delicate politics of Qatar, another way of saying no without having to say the word. This argument seemed shallow to those pushing for a snatch.

"The Qatar government had no interest in screwing up its

fragile relationship with us," said one U.S. advocate of a raid. "If we had gone in and nabbed this guy, or just cut his head off, the Qatari government would not have complained a bit.... The Qataris had no choice but to eat whatever shit we chose to feed them.... There was no U.S. agency advocating KSM's rendition. There was an NSC proposal that was shot down by every agency that had a jurisdiction and role. Why? Everyone thought terrorism was a joke and that the NSC staff dealing with this were a bunch of idiots."[3]

But the internal politics of Qatar were probably more of an impediment than the raid's advocates imagined. In fact, in the midst of discussions about what to do, a countercoup was mounted against al-Thani. It was foiled, but it demonstrated anew the fragile state of the Qatari government, which was slow in responding to the American inquiries on the matter.

It would have been difficult to proceed without Qatar's assent, said a U.S. diplomat in the region at the time. "We could not have snatched him. That would not have been either politic or possible," the official said. "There's always the guy who's seen too many movies, who wants to send a commando team into a lower-middle-class neighborhood in Doha to try to snatch him." But, he said, "I don't think anybody ever seriously considered that a possibility."[4]

Absent the backing of the Pentagon and the cooperation of Qatar, there was little that could persuade the White House to go in after Mohammed. It wasn't a question of desire. It was the purely pragmatic question of what could be done, especially without Qatari support. On the ground in Doha, CIA case officer Melissa Mahle concocted a plan that would make the Washington debate irrelevant. It was motivated by her fear that to involve the Qatari government in any way would result in Mohammed being tipped off. A veteran Middle East hand, she believed that any Qatari involvement would amount to giving Mohammed a free pass out of the country. It was Mohammed's frequent travel that gave impetus to the idea. The idea was to lure KSM abroad by having a friendly Qatari official whom KSM knew ask him to fly somewhere to do a favor for him. They had a man who was willing to make the request. The plan was for the FBI to put an agent, Pellegrino, on the same flight and arrest Mohammed as soon as the plane landed on foreign soil.[5]

With no snatch and grab approved at the deputies' meeting, the CIA plan was set aside and the administration was left to try persuading the Qataris to hand KSM over to the FBI, exactly what Mahle had warned against in letters and protests to officials in Doha and Washington. The Qatari foreign minister flew to Washington for meetings with FBI director Louis Freeh and others, and he seemed reasonable, even eager to help. But once he returned to Qatar, no action was forthcoming. Freeh sent the foreign minister a letter reminding him of the dangers KSM presented. "A failure to apprehend KSM would allow him and other associates to continue to conduct terrorist operations," Freeh wrote.[6] He mentioned that Mohammed was suspected of terrorist involvement by several countries and that the Qataris themselves agreed. They had reported that KSM was involved in some unspecified plot to construct a bomb. Freeh's letter seemed to have no effect whatsoever.

While the diplomats debated with the Qataris on how they could or could not help one another, a rendition aircraft and FBI were moved into nearby Oman. Pellegrino was there, waiting; he was called to Doha to help explain again to the Qataris why the American government wanted Mohammed. The idea was that Pellegrino, the man with the nitty-gritty details on how bad an actor KSM was, would be able to persuade the Qataris to help.

Pellegrino flew to Doha. He never met a single Qatari official.

For two weeks, he cooled his heels at the embassy and the local Sheraton while the American ambassador, Patrick Theros, negotiated with the Qataris, at times with a CIA official also in attendance. Pellegrino got so exasperated that one afternoon he called Garcia, even though it was 3:30 a.m. New York time, and said, "Clear your head," and then asked the assistant U.S. attorney to please impress upon Theros how much the Justice Department wanted Mohammed, and to tell him why a U.S. plane and a team of agents was waiting to go wheels up next door in Oman. Garcia could be a very forceful person, and even half asleep he made his case. Nothing seemed to matter. There was even an attempt by former president George Bush to persuade the Qataris, with whom Bush had had good relations, but there was no progress in the meetings, which went on for days.

Melissa Mahle would later blame the FBI for the stalemate, saying it never should have risked involving the Qataris. The FBI blamed Theros and the Qataris. It is not difficult to imagine the Qatari government's reluctance to assist the Americans. Radical Islam as a global force didn't appear to threaten America. At the time, even bin Laden was mostly regarded as more of a nuisance than a danger. Outside the FBI, there were very few people anywhere in the world who thought Khalid Sheikh Mohammed was a significant player in anything. Pakistani intelligence, for example, did not seem to be concerned about him. The Qataris apparently didn't care, and seemed to be supportive of KSM's jihad.

Then one day Theros came back to the embassy from yet another meeting with the Qataris. Pellegrino had been waiting anxiously for an update. Theros had one: the Qataris, who were supposed to be watching KSM, had "lost" him.

How, an American official asked, do you lose somebody in Qatar? Theros said that by "lost," he meant that KSM had slipped out of the country. Pellegrino was less tactful. Looking at the ambassador, he said: "You motherfucker..." Almost as an afterthought, he threw in, "Sir."

Theories abounded as to who could have tipped Mohammed, some more plausible than others, but the mystery was never solved. Those involved said they had come within an hour, maybe two, of taking KSM into custody. After he was gone, the Qataris denied the Americans access to his apartment or office. At the White House, an angry Richard Clarke demanded a postmortem from the CIA about how it could have happened, whether intelligence indicating that sympathetic Qatari officials had undermined the U.S. effort and aided his escape with travel documents were true, and where KSM might have gone. "How many flights *are* there out of Qatar?!" he wanted to know. Clarke said he never got anything from the agency. White, the U.S. attorney, called Freeh and Reno in Washington to say, "Let's keep this pedal to the metal because we are really concerned about him." But Doha was the last easy chance to catch KSM. It really would not have been a great deal more complicated than any of a thousand arrests that are made every day around the world. From that point on, Mohammed was aware he was being sought, and behaved like it. But he didn't curtail his far-flung activities. In fact, having lost his home base in Doha, he might have traveled more. His itinerary—if it's Tuesday, it must be Brazil—read like some mad tourist jaunt. He juggled identities and appearances to suit his objective of the moment.

## *Foley Square, New York City, Summer 1996*

Basit had been indicted for two separate sets of crimes—the 1993 World Trade Center bombing and the 1995 "Manila Air" plot, which was what prosecutors called the attempt to destroy a dozen airliners. He had different accomplices in each case, so two trials would be needed. Mary Jo White, the U.S. attorney, decided to bring the Manila case to court first, mainly because most of its witnesses were in the Philippines. Given the logistics of getting them to New York, delaying that trial until after the Trade Center trial would only increase the difficulty of persuading the witnesses to testify. Trial preparation had the unavoidable consequence of taking Pellegrino and Besheer away from the hunt for the remaining plot members, including KSM.

Besheer was given the thankless task of securing and wrangling the witnesses, a logistically demanding endeavor even for a domestic prosecution in the United States. Civic culture in the Philippines is not similar to that in the United States. Going to a courthouse in Manila to testify in a criminal proceeding simply because you've been asked to do so would seem an odd choice to many Filipinos. Going to New York to testify because some

Americans asked you to would not be a question of choice, but perhaps of sanity. Why would you?

The answer, as it happened, was as varied as the potential witness. Some wanted nothing. Others wanted a plane ticket. Some asked for money, for relocation, for citizenship, a job.

It became a full-time occupation for Besheer for many months in the run-up to the trial. He had a hard time even locating many of the potential witnesses. He was heavily reliant on the Filipino police and intelligence agencies, both as witnesses and as sources of contacts and introductions. Getting them was never a sure thing.

Many of the police officers who were potential witnesses worked under General Hermogenes Ebdane of the Philippine National Police. Besheer called and made an appointment to see him. Besheer and Pellegrino arrived at the general's office as requested at eight o'clock sharp the next morning. The police-office compound also contained housing for officers, many of whom lived on the premises. There were chickens scratching through the dirt outside the building. Besheer and Pellegrino waited in an outer office, drinking the ritual Nescafé instant coffee, which seemed to be the universal drink served to government visitors throughout Southeast Asia. Finally, the door to a back office opened and the general strode through, dressed in a camouflage-pattern wifebeater and boxer shorts. He welcomed the Americans into his office.

They explained what they needed, and it was as if Ebdane had suddenly realized the importance of the meeting. Please wait a moment, he said. He left the room for a minute or two, leaving the two JTTF reps to stare at an elaborate oil painting of the general sitting at the same desk, in full military regalia. When he returned, he had put on his uniform shirt, full of medals and epaulets. The boxer shorts remained. Besheer and Pellegrino could barely contain themselves, especially when they looked at the portrait on the wall above Ebdane. Besheer kept his gaze directed at the general, Pellegrino at the floor, while Ebdane issued the order agreeing to the request.

Many of the witnesses had to obtain passports, and there was always the fear that some of them would skip out when they arrived at the Hawaii refueling stop or once they got to New York. Besheer pinned a number on the lapel of each witness, and assigned Bureau officials to keep track of them and make sure they were all accounted for while in transit. He also had officials watch them in New York, and arranged tours and trips to baseball games at Yankee Stadium.

The prosecution's case against Basit, Murad, and Khan had some holes in it—not because of the physical evidence, which was voluminous, but mostly due to the way the evidence had been obtained. Exactly when the Filipinos had entered room 603 at the Josefa was unclear. Had the defendants been tortured during interrogation? How capable were the accused of acknowledging their rights when so informed on their rendition flights to the United States? Could they understand English well enough to give informed consent? The language question pertained mainly to Murad and Khan. Basit's English was excellent—so good, in fact, that the judge, Kevin Duffy, allowed him to represent himself. Basit was a lively figure in the courtroom, often referring to himself as his client or the accused.

The trial was extraordinary in other ways. Media coverage was extensive. Retaliation for Basit's arrest had been threatened in both Pakistan and the Philippines, and some of the local authorities who had been helping the Americans were targeted. Police snipers were posted on rooftops around Foley Square in lower Manhattan, where the trial was held.

For reasons never explained, Basit was charged and prosecuted under his alias, Ramzi Yousef, and even he referred to himself by that name. Duffy sent out five thousand summonses for potential jurors, thinking that press coverage of the bombing had been so extensive that it would be difficult to find jurors not affected by it. The selected jurors were promised anonymity.

During the trial, Duffy ordered the warden of the jail where Basit was housed to appear in court, where the judge lacerated him for the conditions in his facility. It was also revealed during the trial that Duffy's life had been threatened by the defendants and that he was under guard twenty-four hours a day, which gave Basit cause to ask for Duffy's recusal from the case. Duffy did not recuse himself, nor did he suspend proceedings when on July 17, 1996, in the midst of the trial, TWA flight 800, a Boeing 747 en route from JFK to Rome, exploded just off the coast of Long Island.

One thing not revealed at the trial was a top-secret effort by the FBI to monitor Basit's jailhouse conversations with an informant, convicted mobster Gregory Scarpa. Basit took a shine to Scarpa, especially to his claim that he could provide him with the ability to make telephone calls from inside the jail. Unbeknownst to Basit, and with Scarpa's help, the calls were monitored by the FBI. Some of the calls were made to a man Basit referred to as Bojenga, who seemed to be a coconspirator in Basit's plots. Some authorities believed Bojenga was KSM. In one internal memo that the New York squad sent to FBI headquarters, investigators detailed how Basit told Scarpa of an unidentified person who had provided information on coconspirator Wali Khan, leading to his arrest.[7]

"In sum, it appears that there is a threat to or by some unknown subject in or formerly in Qatar, possibly Khalid Shaik Mohammad," the memo said. "The person to be kidnapped, tortured, and killed is believed by Yousef [Basit] to be an informer. Yousef is passing a 'coded' message [to] Bojenga to torture the informer first to find out his 'recruiters' and kill them as well. . . ."

In addition, Yousef suggested that Bojenga attack the U.S. embassy in Qatar, or a less secure embassy elsewhere, as retaliation for participation in the arrest of Wali Khan.

Through the monitored calls, the FBI also knew Basit was communicating with KSM through their relatives. They also knew Bojenga was involved in more terrorist plotting. The clues that came out of the relationship between Basit and the government informant, and from Basit's phone calls to the outside, were not pursued aggressively, if at all. Many of the telephone conversations were in Baluch and Urdu and weren't translated for weeks or months. Pakistan, where many of the calls were directed, wasn't much help. And the Bureau couldn't contact officials in Iran, where other calls were made to Basit's relatives, because the U.S. government had declared it a state sponsor of terrorism.

During the course of the trial, Basit flirted with court reporters, asking one out to dinner; he told outrageous lies, suggesting, for example, that he wasn't even in the Philippines when the alleged crime occurred; and kidded back and forth with Pellegrino and Besheer, who were in court every day to back up the prosecution team. Pellegrino and Besheer both also testified, Pellegrino at length. He was prickly on the stand, often giving monosyllabic answers to complicated questions from defense lawyers. Given that Basit was acting as his own attorney, the trial also featured the cross-examination of a law enforcement officer, Pellegrino, by the man he had been chasing for two years, Basit.

KSM's name wasn't mentioned once during the trial—on purpose, because prosecutors believed that if he didn't know they were looking for him, he might not hide, despite the fact that he was well aware of the effort to catch him in Qatar.

The three defendants were found guilty on all counts. At the close of the trial, Basit made a remarkable statement:

> You keep talking also about collective punishment and killing innocent people to force governments to change their policies; you call this terrorism when someone would kill innocent people or civilians in order to force the government to change its policies. Well, when you were the first one who invented this terrorism.
>
> You were the first one who killed innocent people, and you are the first one who introduced this type of terrorism to the history of mankind when you dropped an atomic bomb which killed tens of thousands of women and children in Japan and when you killed over a hundred thousand people, most of them civilians, in Tokyo with fire bombings. You killed them by burning them to death. And you killed civilians in Vietnam with chemicals as with the so-called Orange agent. You killed civilians and innocent people, not soldiers,

innocent people every single war you went. You went to wars more than any other country in this century, and then you have the nerve to talk about killing innocent people.

And now you have invented new ways to kill innocent people. You have so-called economic embargo which kills nobody other than children and elderly people, and which other than Iraq you have been placing the economic embargo on Cuba and other countries for over 35 years....

The Government in its summations and opening statement said that I was a terrorist. Yes, I am a terrorist and I am proud of it. And I support terrorism so long as it was against the United States Government and against Israel, because you are more than terrorists; you are the one who invented terrorism and using it every day. You are butchers, liars, and hypocrites.

Duffy responded with eloquence:

Ramzi Yousef, you claim to be an Islamic militant. Of all the persons killed or harmed in some way by the World Trade Center bomb, you cannot name one who was against you or your cause. You did not care, just so long as you left dead bodies and people hurt.

Ramzi Yousef, you are not fit to uphold Islam. Your God is death. Your God is not Allah.... You weren't seeking conversions. The only thing you wanted to do was to cause death. Your God is not Allah. You worship death and destruction. What you do, you do not for Allah; you do it only to satisfy your own twisted sense of ego.

You would have others believe that you are a soldier, but the attacks on civilization for which you stand convicted here were sneak attacks which sought to kill and maim totally innocent people....

You, [Abdul Basit], came to this country pretending to be an Islamic fundamentalist, but you cared little or

> nothing for Islam or the faith of the Muslims. Rather, you adored not Allah, but the evil that you yourself have become. And I must say that as an apostle of evil, you have been most effective.

Duffy sentenced the three men to prison for 240 years each.

Afterward, the prosecution team gathered in Mary Jo White's office and celebrated what was at the time the Justice Department's most momentous victory in an international terrorism case. It was made even more significant because at the outset, Main Justice, as headquarters is called, passed on the case after Murad's arrest, given the difficulties and perceived lack of evidence. "They didn't have the balls to do it; they weren't prepared to go out as far on a limb as we were," one central participant would later say.[8] White and her New York prosecutors had wrested the case away from Eric Holder, who was then the U.S. attorney for the District of Columbia, even though his office was in charge of prosecuting all international cases at the time. She did so by promising the Justice Department that her team would be successful. "You better win," she told the New York team of Pellegrino and Besheer, Garcia and Snell at the time.

Now a smiling Besheer went to White to get her reaction. He was ecstatic, and relieved, given how much of their lives he and Pellegrino had put into the investigation and preparation for trial. "It's a damn good thing you won," she said, straight-faced, before breaking into a wide smile.

That feeling of euphoric victory, however, was short-lived. With Murad, Basit, and Khan locked away, the momentum of the Manila investigation all but evaporated, and so did official FBI support for it. In part this was prompted by the horrific crash of TWA 800. Many, if not most, investigators initially suspected terrorism as the cause of the accident in which 230 people lost their lives. But it quickly became apparent to many of those on the JTTF and elsewhere that it was more likely a straightforward accident. The cause proved elusive, however, so the pressure to fully investigate it persisted. John O'Neill, head of counterterrorism at FBI headquarters, did not share the local investigative skepticism about a terrorist cause. He and others made the TWA probe a high priority and tried to siphon agents off other jobs to help.

Neil Herman, head of the JTTF, fought to keep his team together and on track in their other investigations, including the unfinished business from Manila. His chief investigator on the crash concluded fairly quickly that there didn't seem to be any criminal cause. The crash, nonetheless, remained a diversion and a drain on resources. Herman himself was redeployed to the TWA flight 800 probe against his wishes.[9]

After the trial, Pellegrino and Besheer returned to their investigation, especially to the Philippines and Malaysia, once again sifting through all the evidence, looking for anything they might have missed. They ran down every phone number and every contact again, and found new leads on the ground. The Justice Department and FBI continued to cloak the investigation in secrecy, even though the publicity surrounding the hunt for KSM's nephew—and the reward money—was what led to Basit's arrest. They tracked Mohammed's travels as well as they were able, then approached the governments of the countries to which he had gone to see what they might have on him. They did the same with Mohammed Jamal Khalifa, Mohammed Amein al-Sanani, and Ibrahim Muneer. They still didn't have a solid idea how the conspirators all fit together, especially KSM. Prosecutor Mike Garcia later described the investigators' plight: "We really thought we had him [in Qatar]. And after that we never had an idea of where he was."[10]

## *Tora Bora, Afghanistan, 1996*

Mohammed fled immediately after the escape in Doha to Pakistan. In many ways, Karachi, Pakistan's sprawling commercial capital, had always been more his base of operations than had Doha. It amazed Pellegrino how many other places Mohammed was reported to have gone in the mid-1990s. Some seemed downright bizarre.

He had flown to Brazil, for example, using one of his identified aliases, and headed for the lawless tri-border area adjacent to Argentina and Paraguay, which had become a sort of Star Wars bar for terrorists and organized crime syndicates. Why Brazil? In applying for his visa in Malaysia, Mohammed said he was investigating business opportunities. What business? As near as anyone could determine, he tried to negotiate a deal to buy frozen chicken parts. Chicken? What did that have to do with anything? Pellegrino just shrugged. It was like the palm oil in Malaysia—even terrorists have to eat.

More important, the man Mohammed listed as his local contact in Brazil was the local leader of the al-Gama'a al-Islamiyya, a militant group based in Egypt. The man was later arrested as a suspect in a plot to bomb the American embassy in Brasilia.[11] Pellegrino thought about going to Brazil and never went. Later, looking back on it, especially when it became clear that Al Qaeda was using such import-export businesses as a way of moving operatives internationally and laundering money, he concluded it was near the top of his list of regrets in terms of what he didn't do to find KSM and bring him to justice.

Pellegrino and Besheer tracked Mohammed, belatedly, to Singapore, Malaysia, China, and back to the Philippines. KSM went to Chechnya, hoping to introduce himself to Ibn al-Khattab, the leader of Muslim rebels there, but was unable to arrange a meeting. The point of his ceaseless traveling was twofold: he raised money through his private business, mainly arranging import-export deals, whether for chicken parts or circuit boards; he also recruited men to his cause and established a network of allies. He often posed as a wealthy sheikh. He was something of a hustler, a charming, easygoing guy who met associates in fancy hotels and bars.

One trip no one knew about until much later was Mohammed's visit to Afghanistan sometime late in 1996. Osama bin Laden had just returned there to live, having been effectively driven from Sudan by the constant pressure the U.S. government was exerting on the Sudanese.

When he'd been in Malaysia he'd met again with Hambali. He was ever more impressed with the orderly, steady way Hambali and his partners were building their regional terrorist organization. What they lacked, Mohammed thought, was a solid jihad program. They were doing everything right, but they weren't at war. He invited Hambali to join him in a trip to Afghanistan to meet bin Laden.

Bin Laden's reputation among jihadis had grown since the end of the campaign in Afghanistan. He had spoken out publicly against the corrupt "apostate" regimes that held power throughout the Arab world. In Sudan, he had begun building an infrastructure through which Islamist resistance could be organized and focused. More and more, he seemed the vehicle through which so many grievances could be addressed. Maybe it was possible to rebuild a Muslim caliphate after all.

Mohammed persuaded Hambali to come meet bin Laden. Bin Laden was impressed, and Hambali stayed on in Afghanistan for a time, doing some work for Al Qaeda's media apparatus. Mohammed and Hambali were worldly men who had traveled and seen much. They could lend their experience to bin Laden's efforts.

Mohammed had another reason for coming to Afghanistan: the idea he and Yousef had about attacking America from above was viable, he thought; all he lacked to carry it out were the significant resources necessary to fund it. Bin Laden had resources, Mohammed had ideas. Mohammed wanted to marry them.[12]

Mohammed had tried to see bin Laden in Sudan the year before. He had met with bin Laden's military commander, Mohammed Atef, but hadn't seen the exiled Saudi financier. After they both arrived in the Afghanistan-Pakistan region at approximately the same time—Mohammed fleeing the Americans in Qatar, bin Laden fleeing them in Sudan—a meeting was set up at bin Laden's compound in Tora Bora.

The two knew each other from their days in Peshawar during the Soviet war. Mohammed regarded the meeting as one of equals. He had the cachet of being the uncle of Basit, who was regarded as a hero within radical Islam. Investigators thought less highly of Mohammed, regarding him as subordinate to Basit, possibly limited to raising money. This new plan would resolve any doubts about his importance. He told bin Laden he didn't want to join Al Qaeda—in fact, he refused to do so—and merely sought resources to fund a spectacular attack against the United States. Mohammed explained to bin Laden the plan he and Yousef had concocted, then told him how it might be modified. Basit, the bomb maker extraordinaire, was behind bars, probably forever, and Mohammed needed to either replace him or find some way around the need for the bombs. Murad had provided the answer with his idea to crash-land an aircraft full of explosives into CIA headquarters or some other high-value target—a nuclear reactor, maybe. If you did this, you needn't go through the precise and exacting process of building Basit's bombs. You didn't need bombs at all. Murad's idea essentially converted the airplanes into missiles. Bin Laden dismissed this as inconsequential.

We could do it on a broader scale, Mohammed said. Flying airplanes is not that difficult. Even Murad had gotten a license. We could train pilots in the United States, then when they were ready, simultaneously hijack as many as ten planes from the East and West Coasts of the United States and fire them all into buildings on the ground. Then, Mohammed said, I would land a final airplane in the middle of the United States and walk out onto the tarmac and explain to the Americans why this terrible thing had happened and what they ought to do to prevent it from happening in the future. Bin Laden was noncommittal. He told KSM he appreciated the ideas and would give the matter due consideration.

# CHAPTER 8
## Thin Air

*Langley, Virginia, 1997*

It is almost axiomatic in the affairs of democratic governments that there is always too much or too little of everything. There is seldom just the right amount. The pendulum of public opinion can be wildly destabilizing, and the Central Intelligence Agency was not immune from this. In the heyday of the Cold War, when the continued existence of the nation seemed threatened, the CIA was the country's first line of defense. And offense, too. Instigating coups and assassinations of heads of state became almost routine. Almost nothing was too wild to try. You want a lethal exploding cigar, we'll whip one up in the shop. But, as ever, after the agency's excesses were revealed under the bright lights of congressional hearings, the pendulum swung sharply in the other direction. Throughout the 1980s and 1990s, round after round of budget cuts were felt most sharply in the agency's operations abroad. Spying is a very expensive business. Training can take years. Missions can take decades. Without the money to cover it, the CIA retreated from the world. More than its swagger went missing.

Assets—spies, in ordinary language—were dropped wholesale.

Embassy staffs were slashed. Field stations were closed entirely. Recruiting of a new generation of case officers virtually halted. Lest it be found to violate someone's sensibilities, the agency developed a deep aversion to risk and to assignments without clear expectations of success. If something seemed hard to do, it was often not done; or, more than likely, not even attempted.

This was the situation as the world was becoming dimly aware of a rising new problem—international Islamist terrorism.

Even if the agency had wanted to, it would not have been able to use many of the tools it had used so successfully in the past. They were suddenly outmoded, or ill-suited to the task, because success was no longer a matter of who had the best technology. Paying Soviets to spy against the Soviet Union and a system that the potential asset probably hated to begin with was one matter. Paying Muslims to spy against coreligionists who shared the belief that they were fighting a holy war on behalf of God and their people was another. Every once in a while, as in the case with Istaique Parker, the man who turned in Basit, money could still be part of the motive. But Parker's real inducement was fear. He thought Basit was going to kill him.

Then there was the plain fact that these new enemies lived in very harsh and uncomfortable places where nobody spoke a familiar language. Within the agency, they called it the diarrhea syndrome: few wanted to be assigned to a portfolio that was not only dangerous but unhealthy. As a result, the CIA's collection capability withered, and the agency came to rely much too heavily on what's called liaison intelligence—that is, not intelligence you unearth and vet yourself, but intelligence given to you by the often sketchy security agencies of other governments.

One rationale for relying on the information of others was its cost-effectiveness. The United States, through its various foreign and military aid packages, was already paying for cooperation from recipient governments. There was no reason not to expect a return in the form of intelligence. An irony no one wanted to contemplate was the real chance that this technique could be not only ineffective but more expensive as well. It costs much more to support a corrupt government than it does to buy a spy. And here's the biggest problem: this intelligence can mask hidden agendas. The agencies providing it might actually be rooting for or helping the other side.

That was especially the case in South Asia, and it made it nearly impossible for the CIA to get a handle on who was behind the new radical jihadi movement. Afghanistan, which had quickly become the headquarters of this new threat, didn't even have a liaison intelligence service to cooperate with. In Pakistan, where much of the jihadi infrastructure was maintained, the host liaison agency was the ISI, which was—and had been for a long time—allied with many of the same jihadi groups that the U.S. wanted to penetrate.

Complicating matters still more was the resentment the Pakistanis and Afghans felt toward what they regarded as the American abandonment of their cause after the Soviet withdrawal from Afghanistan. Once the last tank had rolled out, the CIA and the rest of the American government vanished, almost overnight, and so did U.S. funding. Worse, Washington hit Pakistan soon afterward with crippling sanctions for an illicit nuclear program that it had known about—and tacitly approved of—for years. Not only did the U.S. betray them, the Pakistanis felt, but its abandonment gave the jihadis a safe haven in which to train, organize, and practice using the weapons that America had given them.

When the CIA successfully cultivated sources in these liaison intelligence agencies, including Pakistan's, the information gathered was often innocuous or just plain wrong. Hundreds of millions of dollars were spent on these relationships, and on handing out weapons and cold hard cash, and no one had much to show for it. Countries such as Jordan received millions of dollars and produced a stream of useless reports, yet somehow didn't discover terrorist exploits (such as the millennium plot against the United States, being devised on the doorstep of the king's palace, which would use the turn of the millennium as an occasion for a terrorist attack) until they were nearly under way. In Pakistan, things were far worse, as the ISI's ties to militant groups made them in some cases almost indistinguishable from each other.

These failings were broadly recognized within the CIA, but there were few alternatives. Even in a country like France, with eight million Muslims among its population of forty million, the agency had only a handful of operatives. Its cadre of what were known as core collectors—case officers and reports officers—had dwindled. The network of people who ran logistics and finance for overseas operations—those who rented safe houses, bought property, established cover stories—they were largely gone, too.

On a fundamental level, the United States lacked situational awareness of this particular enemy and its positions and plans. It had almost no ability to know what the hell was going on. The result was that the CIA was essentially flying blind in South Asia from the early 1990s on, at the time when Al Qaeda, and KSM, were plotting, planning, and expanding around the world. This also allowed KSM to continue to travel widely, to become a sort of Johnny Appleseed of terrorism, without anybody in the CIA catching on—except for a very select and controversial few.

## *Tysons Corner, Virginia, 1997*

By 1997, Mike Scheuer had his new group up and running inside a nondescript office building in Tysons Corner, Virginia, a Washington, D.C., suburb. On the organization chart, their little outfit was called the Bin Laden Issue Station, a name that seemed cumbersome to everyone involved, not to mention pretentious. After all, they were only a dozen people working out of a suburban office park. So, more commonly, the group was referred to as the Alec Station, named after Scheuer's young son. The name was chosen more out of protest than anything. Scheuer was tired of waiting for the bureaucracy to finally finish its ridiculously elaborate process of finding an appropriate formal name. When they first set up operations, and sent their first communications cable out to the rest of the agency, they realized they had to put something in the standard FROM field on the message. Use "Alec," Scheuer had said. The Alec Station. He and his wife had just completed the process of adopting their son. And so a name was made.

Alec Station was the only operational station ever established near the agency's sprawling campus headquarters in Langley. Other stations were in the countries they covered—China, Russia, Yemen. Being operational meant that Alec Station was supposed to combine analysis with action. Case officers worked as if they were in a CIA station in Islamabad or Beijing, where people went out and did things. Virtually all the rest of the thousands of CIA employees in Virginia spent their time as consumers of intelligence, reading reports coming in from elsewhere. By whatever method, Alec Station was supposed to generate its own reports, to create its own intelligence.

When Scheuer had taken the helm, bin Laden was not deemed an important target. In fact, the inauguration of a station dedicated to him was almost an accident. A decision had been made to create a virtual station as an experiment to see if such a bureaucratic structure could work. Scheuer suggested it concentrate on bin Laden, mainly because he seemed interesting, not dangerous.

Soon enough, however, the data Alec Station's analysts gathered persuaded them that bin Laden had been vastly underestimated. He was, they concluded, a significant enemy bent on doing great damage to the United States. Exactly no one wanted to hear this. Bin Laden issued his first fatwa against the United States in 1996, telling Muslims everywhere that it was their duty to kill Americans. It was more vague than his follow-up fatwa in 1998, which decreed that "the ruling to kill the Americans and their allies—civilians and military—is an individual duty for every Muslim who can do it in any country in which it is possible to do it." For Scheuer, it was a call to arms nevertheless.

Scheuer's intense focus on a threat that nearly everyone else at the CIA thought was a myth or a misplaced obsession quickly led to derision. One clear benefit of the new organization was that it provided a formal venue through which the FBI and the CIA could work together harmoniously, and some New York agents and prosecutors spent considerable time there. Garcia, the prosecutor, called it a model of the way the agencies ought to cooperate.[1] Agency bigwigs tolerated Scheuer and his small band even though many thought they were off their rockers. The feeling was, "Hey, let them busy themselves chasing their little Islamic fanatics while we do the important work," one top counterterrorism official said. Most of Scheuer's analysts were women. Taking notice of this, someone at headquarters dubbed the group the Manson family. Like many nicknames, it had the effect of denigrating the abilities of those who bore it. It was a way to demonstrate their profound lack of importance, at least in the eyes of their detractors.

The CIA as an institution was confident that Al Qaeda posed no threat to the U.S.[2] As was the case at the FBI, working on the subject was seen as a dead-end choice for a career-minded agent. The only type of terrorism viewed as important was that sponsored by states such as Iran. (This explains in large part why, later, there was so much effort to tie 9/11 to a state sponsor; the belief was so deeply ingrained that the fact of the attack could not by itself dislodge it.) In fact, after the first Gulf War, the agency's top priority in the region was to penetrate Saddam Hussein's inner circle in Iraq. That didn't occur, of course, but it succeeded in diverting resources and attention.

The tug-of-war that had erupted when Scheuer left the Islamic Extremist Branch of the agency's Directorate of Operations to start Alec Station kept KSM out of the station's purview. At the time, the CIA didn't think Khalid Sheikh Mohammed, if it thought of him at all, was associated with Al Qaeda. Scheuer wasn't so sure, but he also wasn't sure what belonging to Al Qaeda even meant, given the literal translation of the group's name as "the base"—a base with which possibly dozens of other militant groups and freelancers could, to a wildly varying degree, join forces.

Scheuer wanted to bring the KSM portfolio with him to Alec Station, but he was denied.

In 1997, the CIA created a separate renditions branch to handle suspects who had been indicted and were thus susceptible to American arrest. Responsibility for KSM, indicted for the Manila Air plot, was transferred to the new branch. One would expect that assigning him to a team with explicit responsibility for him would have sharpened the focus, but it did not. A "branch" was the smallest unit on the CIA organization chart; it is typically a place where the most inexperienced agents are assigned, a place for new managers to get their first chance at a supervisory role. Thus the new branch in charge of a disregarded subject area was not a sign of high priority. Rather, the opposite, as dozens of low-level suspects were on the renditions list. Additionally, the new Renditions Branch was tiny and lacked any analytical capability. Its sole job was finding fugitives overseas. As a result, once the handoff of the KSM case was made, when information surfaced that was more critical for analysis than tracking, no CIA unit had the job of following up on it—or what it might mean.

Alec Station, in contrast, because it was both analytical and operational, had a continuous stream of data coming in from around the world. Analysts are diviners. They sift through the flood of intelligence reporting flowing into the agency and make sense of it in a way that allows policy makers to "do something" about the problem under consideration. They then send this analysis back to those out in the field to help them understand how what they are seeing through their particular soda straw contributes to and is affected by the larger picture. The renditions group didn't have this, so no proactive efforts emerged from it, and little if any analysis flowed to it. It was not much more than a line on an organization chart.

Analysts get far less fanfare than the derring-do case officers that most people imagine as being the face of the CIA. There aren't many movies made about a middle-aged woman PhD sitting in an office cubicle reading cable traffic. But in many ways, it is the analysts who do the important work of the CIA and the U.S. counterterrorism community at large, especially when the enemy is a shadowy, inchoate force like radical Islam.

The analysts do much more than help the operators assess the credibility of their sources by matching their contributions with the larger body of information and intelligence on hand. The good ones gather disparate strands of information, vet them, and put them together to form the pictures that the operators—and their managers—need to see. Barbara Sude, a career analyst who was one of the agency's top thinkers on Al Qaeda, thought of it as trying to build a view of the forest from the descriptions of individual trees observed in the field. The best analysis provides not just a collation of information, but the context within which it ought to be viewed.

What the analysts at Alec Station soon discovered was that if you were consciously looking for it, there was a torrent of information available on radical Islam. Sude described it as a fire hose, coming so hard and fast you could do little more than grab bits of it as it sped by.

Because their efforts focused specifically on bin Laden's organization, Sude and the other Al Qaeda analysts disregarded everything that didn't pertain to it. They had to, or they would drown in information. If there was any intelligence at all being collected on Khalid Sheikh Mohammed, no one at the bin Laden station studied it.

## *Manila, the Philippines, 1996–97*

Pellegrino and Besheer, having lost KSM's trail, did what they could to pick up the pieces of their investigation after the first Basit trial. Generally, they went wherever those pieces told them to go.

They didn't have a grand theory of the case, just evidence that pointed in a lot of directions. They spent the end of 1996 and the first months of 1997 back in Southeast Asia.

Troves of evidence had been uncovered both at the Josefa and at Wali Khan's apartment. Since the last time the investigators had been there, before the trial, a great deal of effort had been spent trying to sort through the telephone records the Bojinka crew had unknowingly left behind. When they returned, Pellegrino and Besheer had an extensive list of addresses tied to telephone numbers, and they methodically set about tracking them down.

This was not as simple as it might seem. As was common in the Third World, some of the phones turned out to be what could best be described as community assets. The phone itself might be paid for by a little old lady in a village north of Manila who didn't have that much use for it and rented it out to neighbors. The phone would be left in a central location—her windowsill, perhaps—and anybody who wanted to could come use it for a small fee. Likewise, incoming calls would be announced by the age-old method of yelling the name of the intended recipient. The villages were small.

The agents tried to track the whereabouts of the outstanding suspects and their acquaintances. KSM had disappeared, apparently into thin air, after fleeing Qatar, but another of the key players was about to reemerge. Mohammed Jamal Khalifa had been freed after his extradition to Jordan, murder charges against him having been dropped when a key witness recanted. He was allowed to go home to Saudi Arabia, where, as an exemplary organizer of charitable works, he received a gracious welcome. No mention was made that some of those works included funding kidnappings and murder in the southern Philippines, and Khalifa was able to live a normal life in Jeddah. He laid low for months, but soon enough, information surfaced in the intelligence community that he was about to resume his business travels.

Pellegrino and Besheer discovered Khalifa's plans and devised an ingenious approach. They consulted with their colleagues at the

CIA on the feasibility of what they wanted to do. The FBI, when its agents go anywhere in the world, are fundamentally reliant upon the CIA for support. The Bureau had little in the way of a foreign infrastructure to speak of, and the CIA, even in a weakened state, essentially is an infrastructure. What if, they asked the agency, we knew where Khalifa was going to be, down to the hotel room he would be staying in? What could we do to surveil him? The answer surprised them. If you know where he is, and if you know ahead of time where he's going to be, we can provide you with the technology you need to essentially wire his location, listen in real time to everything he says, and tape it. Oh, and also get the numbers of any person he is dialing from his phone.

Everything, they asked?

Khalifa liked to travel in style, staying in large multiroom suites, which made it more of a challenge. Even so, they were told, if he farts in the bathroom, you'll hear it.

So Pellegrino and Besheer embarked on a global listening tour, approved by Main Justice as part of Mary Jo White's negotiated compromise. Wherever Khalifa went, they followed. Or, actually, they preceded. They developed a way of knowing where he was going and would travel there ahead of him and rent the hotel rooms above and below his. The agency's gear would be fitted to observe the room in between. Khalifa spent so much time in Kuala Lumpur that he had an apartment there, just a block from the American embassy. So Besheer rented one in the same building and spent weeks at a time there.

They spent months in Malaysia and Madagascar and points in between. They traveled and recorded hundreds of hours of Mohammed Jamal Khalifa's life. They called it Oreoing, with Khalifa being the creamy center between their two rooms full of recording equipment. They tracked others, too, who had been connected to the Manila Air plot—anyone they thought could lead them to the ghost that KSM had become.

Besheer, the more fastidious of the two, became the overseer of the gear and hence of the recordings. He and Pellegrino would use more than a dozen separate pieces of recording equipment—a few pen registers to decipher the phone numbers Khalifa dialed, and several old-fashioned cassette recorders to pick up audio in each room. All the gear belonged to the CIA, but the FBI flew in a sound guy to make sure it all worked. As strapped for funds as the CIA was, it had access to much more ready cash than did the FBI. If they needed a piece of recording gear, the agency could provide it quickly, or would dip into its cash supply and give Besheer the money to buy it, and more for apartments and even furniture on long stakeouts.

Besheer carefully logged and curated all the tapes, always making a copy for local law enforcement, not only for the sake of good relations but also so that it could potentially be used in a prosecution. Then he'd hand-carry the tapes back to New York, sign them over as evidence to the people who were supposed to pass them along for translation, and then...nothing. The tapes languished for months, and even years, without anyone listening to them. The Bureau was critically short of Arabic speakers—the language on most of the recordings—but these delays beggared explanation. What was the point of spending this amount of time and money, then not seeing what you've found? It was inexplicable. Pellegrino—as the FBI agent of the two—complained to management, vociferously and on numerous occasions, but nothing he and Besheer said or did could speed the translation.

When bits and pieces did get translated, Khalifa was revealed as an exceptionally careful man. If someone he was talking to would begin to refer to something he didn't want addressed on the call, Khalifa would say, "Leh, leh, leh." No, no, no. Then he'd guide the conversation back inside more careful bounds.

Besheer almost felt he was babysitting Khalifa. Whenever Khalifa was in the hotel, Besheer was in his room. He wouldn't leave to eat a meal, and only when Khalifa was gone would he race out onto the street to grab a bowl of noodles, then run back to the room. More than once, he made soup with hot water and ketchup packets.

Besheer was a careful traveler, and detail oriented to the point of obsessive compulsion. His bags were always packed to go, and he routinely got to the airport two hours before boarding. Pellegrino was the opposite. Besheer would be in the lounge at 8:30 a.m. waiting for a flight scheduled to leave JFK at 10:00. An FBI rule held that any flight of more than fourteen hours would be flown business class, and most of their trips passed the test. Besheer would board early, stow his luggage, then nod appreciatively when the flight attendant served him his customary glass of tomato juice with a dollop of blue cheese. The business-class travel was one of the few perks afforded them, and Besheer luxuriated in it.

Then he'd sip his juice, nibble at his cheese, and monitor his watch for Pellegrino's arrival. Invariably, at 9:59, the seat next to him would still be empty. Then, just as the door to the plane was closing, Pellegrino would come barreling on board in a commotion, everything shoved in a big duffel, with clothes sticking out around the zipper. He'd fight to cram it in the overhead, then flop down next to the tidy Besheer. Pellegrino, soaking wet from perspiration, would be dressed in jeans, sneakers, and a T-shirt. He'd look at Besheer and his tomato juice and cheese and chuckle, then say, Hey, Bash. How you doing?

Once they got to wherever they were going, Besheer would quickly ensure that the recording equipment was functioning as required. He did his own laundry in the room, washing his clothes in the bathroom sink and hanging them next to the air conditioner duct to dry. Pellegrino would drop by the room, all sweaty from the gym, and plop straight down on Besheer's carefully arranged bed. Besheer was so particular about his bedding and operational security that he wouldn't let the maids change his linens. He did it himself. Pellegrino, of course, knew this and yet there he'd lie. He would grin and say, Hey, Bash. How you doing?

## *New York City, Winter 1997*

As they spent more and more time overseas, Pellegrino and Besheer grew further estranged from the home office. They felt they were making progress on the investigation, but were under constant pressure from New York. What the hell were they doing out there, anyway? Why was it taking so long?

One day, while the two were walking down a street in Manila, where there is no such thing as a comfortable walk—the noise, the humidity, the heat, conspire against comfort—Pellegrino got a call on his cell phone from a supervisor in New York with questions about what they were up to. Pellegrino didn't care much for the suits. The conversation went on for a while and Besheer started to wonder what was up. Pellegrino's voice began to rise and pretty soon he was red faced, sputtering and shouting. Then he stopped midcall and without a word tossed the phone out into the stream of traffic. New York was quickly silenced under the treads of an oncoming truck. There was some comfort on a Manila street after all. Later, asked what in particular had gotten him so upset, Pellegrino couldn't even remember, as it seemed so many of the calls from headquarters were the same.

When they returned to New York, they were inevitably treated as wayward. They were often greeted in the New York office with shrugs and pointed questions about their investigation, as if they were choosing to spend all their time away because they wanted to, not because they felt they had to. "How's the latest boondoggle going?" one agent asked Pellegrino one day as they stood side by side at the urinals. He considered answering for a second, but then walked away. If even his colleagues on the JTTF didn't get it, what was the use in trying to explain?

Above all, there was the expense. Besheer was still beholden to the Port Authority the whole time he was on the JTTF, and even though the FBI was paying his way for the most part, his superiors always questioned him—and within a year or two of his teaming up with Pellegrino, they began requiring prior approval of his travels and detailed time sheets upon his return. He only recorded a small fraction of what he and Pellegrino worked, and still, he got questions. What's more, he couldn't answer many of them, as their investigations were classified, and the "need to know" didn't extend to the Port Authority. He filed one expense report for more than $100,000. He had so much on his government-issued American Express card that Amex canceled it. Besheer was overseas and no one had bothered to pay the bill.

Higher-ups in Washington and New York periodically repeated their efforts to undermine or even derail the investigation, or to shift the duo to other matters that seemed more pressing. Pellegrino probably didn't help matters by going to the New York JTTF office in a Mighty Ducks T-shirt, or, in winter, in a sweatshirt. Besheer at least looked like an agent. Or would have if he had gotten rid of the Yanni ponytail.

John O'Neill, a dapper, ambitious, and charming agent who became head of the FBI's Washington-based Counterterrorism Division the week Basit was captured, was transferred to New York at the beginning of 1997 and placed in charge of all counterterrorism investigations there, including Manila Air. No one knew quite what to expect. He had lobbied at various points to shut down the investigation, or at least to undermine it, deeming it nonessential. By then, O'Neill was focused on Osama bin Laden. The trial of Basit was completed. It didn't seem to O'Neill that there was a lot left to investigate.

If O'Neill was an enemy of the investigation, his transfer proved the adage that you should hold your friends close and your enemies closer. When confronted—and Pellegrino confronted him often—he gave him and Besheer almost everything they asked for in terms of support, even though he seemed perplexed by the two road warriors. O'Neill made his reputation—some would say his career—by networking ceaselessly, holding court with international counterterrorism officials whom he hosted at his beloved Elaine's restaurant on Manhattan's Upper East Side. He was in many ways a throwback to the dashing G-man prototype of an earlier era. He dressed impeccably in hand-tailored suits and expensive silk ties. A few of his agents tried to copy his style and became part of his entourage.

Pellegrino and Besheer were not among them. They worked ridiculous hours. It quickly became apparent that when they returned from overseas trips, they had no hope of sleeping. So they would shower and meet back at the office at 1:00 or 2:00 in the morning. Besheer stopped at the all-night coffee stand outside the office so often that the Pakistani who owned the cart would get the order ready as he walked up—four twenty-ounce black coffees, two for Besheer and two for Pellegrino. A couple of hours later, he'd go back for four refills.

When the two were in New York for an extended period, they made it a habit to get to the office at 6:30 in the morning, far earlier than anyone else. They were on Southeast Asia time. But they'd still be there when the others filed out for the night. They were both music fans, and Pellegrino had a boom box and stacks of CDs on his desk. They'd be sitting there at their desks, writing reports, bouncing up and down in their office chairs to the rhythm of whatever the stereo was blasting out into their headphones. Their tastes differed considerably—Pellegrino liked the popular, literate singer-songwriters of the day like Jewel and Alanis Morissette, while Besheer favored old soul groups like the Platters. But mainly they loved listening. In the early evenings, O'Neill would wander through the squad room, fresh off the cover of *GQ*, with slicked-back hair, shiny shoes, and silk socks, en route to the glamour life way, way uptown. He never said anything at times like that, but he cocked his head and looked at the two agents quizzically, as if he were a biologist trying to determine what species they were. Then he'd shake his head, smile grimly, and walk on through.

O'Neill became an effective advocate for devoting Bureau attention and resources to Islamist fundamentalism. He argued loudly for investigations into radical jihadi networks—except this one. It was too expensive, he would tell people, and there was very little left to discover. The chief culprits were already behind bars, he argued. Plus, he thought Pellegrino was a cowboy, too used to doing things his own way. JTTF head Neil Herman had been a fierce protector of the two agents. When he left, O'Neill assigned a new supervisor to Pellegrino in what many in the Bureau thought was a conscious effort to rein him in. She was a tough and ornery woman who was a stickler for details and chain of command, which weren't Pellegrino specialties. O'Neill and Pellegrino had screaming matches, at times in the office but also on the phone when Pellegrino was overseas. In one particularly heated exchange, Pellegrino accused O'Neill of leaking classified information about efforts to turn Wali Khan into a government informant—including placing his family in some form of witness protection—to a TV reporter friend of his. Pellegrino believed this compromised their efforts to catch KSM and the other outstanding Manila suspects. O'Neill was particularly galled whenever he found out Pellegrino was traveling overseas with assistant U.S. attorneys. O'Neill wanted to control his agents. He didn't want the U.S. attorney's office running his show, and he hated the fact that Pellegrino went to Mary Jo White and her prosecutors for support when he needed it.

At every turn, however, Mary Jo White fought off O'Neill. He was outgunned, and he knew it. Once, in 1999, he was watching the breaking news of the Columbine High School massacre on TV and Pellegrino—always looking for a good opportunity to needle him—sidled up to O'Neill and told him he'd heard that White was angling to bring the Columbine case to New York—a joking reference to the U.S. attorney's well-known proclivity for snatching high-profile cases. "Well, as you know, Frank," O'Neill replied, "what Mary Jo wants, Mary Jo gets." White, for the time being, at least, had the power on her side, and she triumphed in these little intramural battles. She liked her cowboys.

White was so enamored of Pellegrino and Besheer, in fact, that she nominated them for the highest honor the Justice Department can give, the Exceptional Service Award, and on June 13, 1997, the two beaming agents, as well as prosecutors Michael Garcia and Dieter Snell, were personally congratulated by attorney general Janet Reno at a ceremony in Washington, and handed massive glass statuettes. Pellegrino even wore a suit for the occasion.

Thanks in large part to that quartet of agents and prosecutors, the New York JTTF and U.S. attorney's office had become the center of the U.S. government's counterterrorism universe. But it was an unwieldy effort, rife with competing squads, units, and sections, often run by men with large egos, grand ambitions, and, at times, grudges. Some of the teams were tagged as counterterrorism, others foreign counterintelligence, and still others criminal—divisions that institutionally inhibited communication and cooperation. The squads didn't always play well with each other, or, especially, with FBI headquarters, which significantly deepened an already growing rift between O'Neill and FBI director Louis Freeh's inner circle. Neil Herman was one of the few who had been there at the creation of the JTTF in 1980. Every time there was a terrorism event, they'd form another squad and it became more unmanageable. "We started out as two squads and twenty people and when I left there were eight or nine squads and several hundred people. It became very convoluted," he said. "You were all over the map." As a result, Herman said, even within the FBI, "you were fighting different entities. But no one knew the big picture. That was the failing of the government."

Years later, Herman said he had always been haunted by something. Basit had mentioned that he was part of a broader network. But by the late 1990s, that "network" had officially become a cold case. "Some people in higher positions than us didn't think he was important," Herman said of KSM.

Herman and many of the other New York FBI counterterrorism veterans had retired or moved on to other things by then. Pellegrino and Besheer continued to travel—to more than thirty countries—but White's protection became harder to sustain. O'Neill began riding Pellegrino ever harder, second-guessing him and even moving to have the FBI's ethics police investigate him for what he claimed was an obscure procedural impropriety. Such investigations could derail a career even if no wrongdoing was ever found. Once again, White stepped in to protect Pellegrino.

Pellegrino made a special effort to learn everything he could about KSM's sprawling network of family and clan. He asked local governments, especially the Pakistanis, to assist in keeping tabs on family members who were suspected of helping KSM. He was sure that Mohammed would eventually turn to his family for more assistance, and when he did he would be vulnerable. But as had been the case in the past, Islamabad wasn't eager to help.

For nearly two years, Pellegrino and Besheer's pursuit of KSM had been secret because of the decision to keep his indictment sealed. Its unsealing in January of 1998 finally allowed them to publicize his role in the various plots, and the State Department to issue a $2 million reward for him. The next month, however, bin Laden issued his fatwa declaring war on America.

That August, simultaneous truck bombings shattered the U.S. embassies in Kenya and Tanzania. By then, O'Neill's obsession with bin Laden, or UBL, as the FBI called him, was complete. The way he saw it, bin Laden was the target and you were either with O'Neill in recognizing that or against him. That mind-set turned out to be dangerously myopic, not because of what O'Neill and the FBI were pursuing, but because of what they weren't. As Herman recalls, "There was a whole network out there, and we knew it was out there but we didn't know what it was... that it was that big and dangerous, or who besides UBL was in charge."

# CHAPTER 9
# The Plot

*Kandahar, Afghanistan, Spring 1999*

By late 1998, Khalid Sheikh Mohammed's interest in working with bin Laden was revived by the spectacular attacks on the two U.S. embassies in Africa, which had killed at least 224 people and injured hundreds more. He knew, finally, of the seriousness of bin Laden's intentions. KSM had returned to eastern Afghanistan and was working for his old sponsor from the Soviet jihad, Abdul Rasul Sayyaf. How the CIA came by the knowledge is unclear, but the CIA was aware of KSM's presence with Sayyaf, their old ally from the Soviet war, and prepared an internal report noting it.[1] The FBI knew of the CIA report. No one apparently did anything.

Bin Laden had probably been right about KSM's plan to hijack airliners off both coasts at once. It was too complicated. He called KSM back to Kandahar in early 1999 to tell him he had thought more about the proposal and liked its basic premise—to use airliners as weapons against significant American targets. They agreed to slim the plan down, perhaps four or five planes in the United States, more in Southeast Asia if that could be arranged.[2] Bin Laden asked Mohammed to join his organization, to swear *bay'at*—an oath of loyalty. Mohammed demurred. He preferred to keep his independence in case bin Laden changed his mind and decided against pursuing his plan. In that case, Mohammed would find another sponsor and proceed apace.

The essence of the plot was distinguished by its simplicity. It required pilots and teams of men able to overwhelm defenseless air crews. It required money and the ability to move it around the globe. And it required men willing to give their lives. As it happened, there were more than enough people willing to die.

Upon approving the plan and pledging to fund it, bin Laden assigned four men to KSM—two Yemenis and two Saudis, all of whom were experienced jihadis. They were good men and would be the pilots, bin Laden said.

KSM took the men to his apartment in Karachi, his main residence since fleeing Qatar, and gave them basic instructions in how to navigate in America. He gave them English-language phrase books, and showed them how to use Internet chat rooms and American telephone books he picked up in a Karachi flea market.

The two Saudis, Nawaf al-Hazmi and Khalid al-Mihdhar, already had travel visas to the United States. They had thought to get them in case they were lucky enough to be chosen to attack the Americans. The Yemenis, Walid bin Attash, also known as Khallad, and Abu Bara al-Yemeni, applied but were denied U.S. visas. This became one of the recurrent difficulties in KSM's plot—the ability to get willing men into the United States. The Americans didn't ordinarily reject visa applicants because they thought they might be terrorists. In fact, they had a history of admitting known terrorists. But they did reject applicants who were regarded as potential economic migrants. This included almost everyone from Yemen.

Just as KSM was learning of this potential difficulty, four young men from Hamburg, Germany, arrived at one of bin Laden's Afghan camps. The men—an Egyptian, an Emirati, a Yemeni, and a Lebanese—were university students and had been in Germany for years. They had been eager to travel to Chechnya to fight on behalf of their beleaguered Muslim brothers there and had been told that the best way to Chechnya was through the Afghan camps.

A key challenge for bin Laden's organization over time had been the ability to sort out its varied volunteers. Some were nothing more than joyriders, kids looking for an adventure during a summer vacation. Others were troubled misfits who could find no other place to belong. These men from Germany, however, were nearly perfect Al Qaeda candidates. They already lived in the West. They had no criminal records and had done nothing to arouse suspicion. They spoke languages other than Arabic. They wanted nothing but to do right by God. They had not come to their decisions rashly. Indeed, they had spoken with one another about this for years: What should a man do? What is his responsibility as a good Muslim to those who suffer for their faith?

They had answered those questions by presenting themselves for battle. They saw themselves as soldiers and were willing to fight. The men were quickly introduced to bin Laden and asked if they would volunteer for martyrdom missions. Would they be *shahids?* Would they die for their faith? To a man, they said yes.

They must have seemed to bin Laden like gifts from Allah himself.

They had conveniently arrived in Afghanistan at precisely the time Al Qaeda needed men who could train to become pilots. They would become pilots.

They were given rudimentary physical training in the camps, then sent south to Mohammed in Karachi for his crash course on being American—an idea that any one of Mohammed's college classmates would have laughed at uproariously. Mohammed passed his three years in America doing his very best to keep himself separate from Americans.

The idea that using the Yellow Pages was a necessary American skill was curious, too, but Al Qaeda in many ways was a fundamentally unsophisticated organization. Its leaders knew little of the West and understood less. Their complaints about it were often ill conceived or recondite. No wonder American intelligence officials regarded the organization as more nuisance than threat. Its members must have seemed naive, which of course they were. They had a very simple idea and would cling to it no matter what. America was bad, and it would suffer just punishment. To a significant degree, Al Qaeda's greatest strength was its simplicity—in ideas, in infrastructure, even in numbers. It was too small to threaten America.

The men from Hamburg were more sophisticated than the usual recruits, but only just. They had been in the West for years, but had barely adapted. They, too, had held themselves apart.

The four were dissimilar. The oldest, and the putative leader of the group, was the Egyptian, Mohammed el-Amir Atta, Amir to his friends. Atta was a finicky, dour man whose chief attributes were obedience and an extraordinary affinity for detail. He held a part-time job as a draftsman at an urban-planning firm in Hamburg, where he reproduced city plans precisely; his boss later described him as "a drawing slave."[3]

Ramzi bin al-Shibh, the Yemeni, was in personality nearly Atta's opposite. Where Atta was the dutiful striver, bin al-Shibh was an affable layabout who rarely held a job for more than a few weeks and found university study not worth his effort. A friend in Hamburg said Atta was impossible to like, but bin al-Shibh had charm to spare. "Omar," he said, using bin al-Shibh's nickname, "was cool."

Ziad Jarrah was the most worldly of the four, having grown up in cosmopolitan Beirut. He attended Christian schools and enjoyed the Beiruti birthright of good times. He had been in Hamburg for less time, having spent his first year in Germany in Greifswald, a small town in the east. He was also different in that he was in a serious relationship with a woman, a German citizen of Turkish descent.

Marwan al-Shehhi was from Ras al-Khaimah, one of the least wealthy of the United Arab Emirates. He had the deepest Islamic education of the four. His father had been the muezzin for the local mosque and Shehhi was often his companion at the prayer call, sometimes his substitute. He had a ready, easy, relaxed knowledge of his religion. Martyrdom seemed not a burden to him, but a glorious end.

When the men were sent to Mohammed in Karachi for introductions and a basic outline of the plot, he told them they were to become pilots. He introduced them to flight simulation games and software. They then left for the return trip to Germany, although Shehhi had become ill and returned briefly to the Emirates. Once back in Hamburg, they began searching for flight schools and quickly determined that those in the United States were the cheapest. They applied to the schools and requested the visas that would allow them to attend. All were routinely granted the visas except for bin al-Shibh, who, like his fellow Yemenis, was rejected for economic reasons.

Bin al-Shibh applied repeatedly for a visa, but eventually acknowledged it wasn't going to happen. Instead, KSM designated him to be his the go-between—the cutout—with the hijackers. This insulated Mohammed from both the bother and security risk of direct communications. The other three men went to Florida in the summer of 2000. Bin al-Shibh returned to Germany.

Mohammed split his time between Karachi and Afghanistan. He delegated decisions on the details of the plot—which flights, what day, the makeup of the hit teams—to Atta, who communicated his decisions to bin al-Shibh, mainly through coded e-mail exchanges and Internet chat rooms. Bin al-Shibh then relayed the information to Mohammed. While the pilots were being trained, Mohammed continued searching for men to join them in the United States. By far the biggest difficulty was finding volunteers who could legally enter the United States. In two years of searching, which went on almost to the very end, Mohammed was able to insert just nineteen men into the plot. He recruited more than a dozen others. Some backed out, others couldn't get visas. One man, Mohammed al-Qahtani, made it all the way to the customs gate at Orlando International Airport. Mohammed Atta waited outside the terminal for Qahtani to come out, but Qahtani was rebuffed largely because he had no return ticket and did not carry what was deemed enough cash to survive for long in the United States. He also provided no good answer as to whom he was meeting, and a suspicious immigration official sent him back to Saudi Arabia on the first available flight. KSM himself obtained a visa using another name, but there is no record he ever tried to use it. He ordered his nephew Ali Abdul Aziz Ali to apply as well, but his application was declined. Most of those who were able to successfully join the plot were Saudis who, like the pilots, had gone to Afghanistan to volunteer and who carried passports that allowed them easy access to the U.S.

Bin Laden urged Mohammed several times during the plot's preparation to hurry the attacks. Mohammed would not be rushed. He regarded bin Laden as meddlesome and not particularly thoughtful. He blamed bin Laden for some of the choices the Al Qaeda leader had made in selecting the hijackers and wanted to boot at least one of them, Mihdhar, off the attack altogether.

Mohammed waited until the summer of 2001, when Atta told him the attack teams were set; in the meantime, he insulated the hijackers from bin Laden's impatience. He also allowed Atta to overrule bin Laden's choice of the White House as the fourth target. Atta thought it too small and difficult to hit; he substituted the Capitol building, leaving the final list as the twin towers of the World Trade Center, the Pentagon, and the Capitol. KSM approved Atta's decision to push back the plot even further, so that the fourth plane would hit the Capitol dome after lawmakers had returned from their summer recess.

During the planning phase, Mohammed spent most of his time in Pakistan, remaining largely separate from the Al Qaeda leadership as he continued to organize other plots and local terror cells around the world. He recruited people he had known from the Afghan training camps to form small organizations in their areas.

U.S. investigators had no hint of Mohammed's deepening involvement with Al Qaeda, even in the summer of 2001. They wanted him for his association with the Manila Air plot; Pellegrino had tried twice to land KSM on the FBI's most wanted list but failed, though he was on the separate State Department list with a $2 million reward. That would have brought additional international attention and resources to bear on the hunt for KSM. They tracked him—and Khalifa and others they hoped could lead to him—as they tracked bin Laden, but never put the two together.

Not content with organizing this ambitious attack, Mohammed entered a frenzied period of plot design, recruitment, and dispatch. Several dozen recruits and associates stayed at his Karachi apartment or nearby safe houses at different times. One man was there for a two-week training course that ended the day before September 11. Recruits have described the instruction they received as simplistic—how to use the Yellow Pages, Internet chat rooms, and travel agencies. Mohammed would often spend several days getting to know them, assessing them and their viability and motivations, asking them questions about their lives and their beliefs. Those he deemed worthy were given a code to use in their e-mails in which each digit in a telephone number was converted so that the original digit and the coded one added up to ten; for example, Mohammed's Karachi cell phone number, 92 300 922 388, became 18 700 188 722. He gave them simple word codes: a "wedding" was an explosion, "market" was Malaysia, "souk" was Singapore, "terminal" stood for Indonesia, and "hotel" for the Philippines. Thus, "planning a wedding at the hotel" might be planting a bomb in Manila. He used various e-mail accounts, including silver_crack@yahoo.com and gold_crack@yahoo.com. (His password was "hotmail.")

Mohammed refused to respond to e-mail that didn't follow the proper codes. He taught his recruits how to manipulate their identity papers. He explained that while most visas were stamped into a passport, a Pakistani visa was printed on a separate piece of paper and could be removed from the original passport with an iron and reused. The dates on a visa could be removed using bleach. German automobile brake fluid, which is blue in color, was particularly good for this, he would tell his students. KSM also said that Algerian and African students in Islamabad were known for putting their passports up for sale on the black market. There were also well-known and friendly purveyors of passports right there in Karachi.[4]

It wasn't the quality of the instruction that was most noteworthy about KSM's activities. It was the sheer scale of them. He oversaw the 9/11 plot. He was the conduit for the distribution of hundreds of thousands of dollars, much of it in cash, supporting various other plots around the world. He recruited and dispatched several men for a second wave of attacks against the United States. He ordered surveillance of security practices at U.S. Navy aircraft carriers. He prepared and funded men to go to Singapore to bomb commercial and government centers there. He was particularly eager to meet with men who carried Western passports. He dispatched an Australian, "Jihad Jack" Roche, to case bombing targets in his home country and a German, Christian Ganczarski, to blow up a synagogue in Tunisia. He sent Canadians to the U.S. He negotiated a deal for a prospective Al Qaeda program on Pakistani television. He sent José Padilla, the hapless American son of Puerto Rican immigrants, back to the United States to research the possibility of building a dirty bomb and blowing up apartment buildings after filling them with gas. He sent at least one other man to New York to find Jewish targets to strike, and to surveil Wall Street and other financial targets in Washington and New Jersey. He sent others to case nuclear plants, bridges, and buildings. He provided help to a man who wanted to plant bombs in Thailand. He asked one protégé to evaluate the Panama Canal as a potential target. He considered an attack on London's Heathrow Airport. He helped an Indonesian colleague establish a bioweapons research program in Malaysia.

The recruits were an odd lot, almost all idiosyncratic. The experience of Roche, the Australian recruit, was typical in that it showed how easy it was to gain access to KSM simply by showing up in Karachi with a trusted recommendation.

Roche was a drifter who left his home in England at the age of seventeen and ping-ponged from the UK to Germany to Australia, working as a taxi driver and laborer. He became an Australian citizen in 1978. In the 1990s he became good friends with a pair of Indonesian brothers who recruited him into Jemaah Islamiyah and eventually sent him to Malaysia to meet Hambali. Hambali recommended he go to Afghanistan to receive training. He flew to

Karachi in 2000, and within two days of landing was introduced to KSM by the name everyone called him, Mukhtar. After a few days, Mukhtar had an associate hand-deliver Roche to "the Sheikh" in Afghanistan along with a handwritten note vouching for him. The sheikh turned out to be bin Laden, and Roche joined him and some other fighters for lunch. After a brief period of training in explosives, he was sent back to Karachi and spent several more days with Mohammed, who wanted him to return to Australia and recruit more Caucasians to join Al Qaeda.[5]

Mukhtar was an engaging fellow, Roche thought, easy to be around. Roche had no idea who he was, although Mukhtar did tell him at one point that he routinely handled hundreds of thousands of dollars that had been earmarked for various plots. His familiarity with large sums of money, however, did not deter Mohammed from personally dropping by Roche's hotel in his chauffeured taxi and arguing for a refund of a few dollars on Roche's behalf. As Roche watched in amazement, Mohammed spent twenty minutes arguing with the manager, murmuring under his breath in English that he was doing it on principle. Roche didn't get the refund, and Mohammed ushered him back to the cab—and to a hotel he deemed more suitable.

Once back in Australia, Roche went online and checked the State Department's Most Wanted website for bin Laden. He was shocked to find that six of the men he had met on his trip were on it, including KSM. At that point, he decided he was in over his head and started to back away slowly. He said that he kept in touch with Mohammed by e-mail out of fear.

Roche began to make repeated efforts to inform authorities of what he knew. He first tried the American embassy. When that went nowhere, he tried several times to call the Australian Security Intelligence Organization. Agents there eventually listened to his story, they would later confirm at Roche's trial on terrorism charges, but did nothing about it.

By then, KSM was well into planning the 9/11 attacks. He had already arranged a meeting of some of its key participants just hundreds of miles away, in Malaysia.

## *Kuala Lumpur, Malaysia, January 2000*

The first active steps to execute Mohammed's plot nearly caused its immediate end. Late in 1999, the CIA learned that an operative they had identified as an Al Qaeda member and experienced jihadi, Khalid al-Mihdhar, planned to travel from Yemen to Kuala Lumpur for a meeting. They had intercepted a phone call to a known Al Qaeda switchboard in Sana'a, Yemen. Mihdhar and another man, someone named Nawaf, were mentioned in the call. The CIA tracked Mihdhar as he traveled, managing to get a copy of his passport as he transited through Dubai. They noted that he had a valid visa for the United States. They were also able to determine that Nawaf was Nawaf al-Hazmi, another experienced fighter.

They arranged for continued surveillance once the pair arrived in Malaysia. The movement of the two veteran jihadis attracted enough notice that CIA director George Tenet was briefed on it. The U.S. intelligence community was still on heightened alert for turn-of-the-millennium attacks, so Mihdhar and Hazmi, two of bin Laden's hand-selected pilots for KSM's plot, were going to Malaysia mainly because they did not want to enter the U.S. directly from the Middle East. They would also meet with the other two pilots, Walid bin Attash and Abu Bara al-Yemeni, who were going to be in Southeast Asia to surveil security on regional airlines. The Yemenis were assigned to take part in the Asian portion of the plot.

At the CIA's request, Malaysian domestic security picked up the trails of the two men, tracking them to a local hotel and subsequently to a condominium complex in the town of Bandar Sungai Long, outside the city. They stayed at a condo owned by one of Hambali's recruits, a Malaysian who had graduated from an American university and had come home to help Hambali develop chemical weapons.

Malaysian security tracked the men and provided photos to the

CIA. The men stayed in Kuala Lumpur for nearly a week. On January 8, bin Attash, Mihdhar, and Hazmi departed Malaysia for Bangkok, although the security services lost track of them and did not determine what they did in Thailand until later. Two other Al Qaeda operatives met bin Attash in Bangkok and handed him more than $30,000, much of which he passed on to Hazmi and Mihdhar. On January 15, the two Saudis, traveling under their own names, flew undetected from Bangkok to Los Angeles.

The two operatives were not ideal choices to send to the U.S. They spoke little English and had no experience living outside the Middle East. The only English they knew was what KSM had taught them—unhelpful phrases such as "Get down," "Don't move," "Stay in your seat," and "If anyone moves I'll kill you." But the CIA neglected to mention to the FBI that two known Al Qaeda operatives might have arrived in the U.S.

The FBI was hardly blameless in the Mihdhar-Hazmi affair. Not long after the men came to California, they moved south to San Diego, and for a time rented a room in the house of an FBI informant, who didn't think to report the fact that two young Arabs had arrived in the U.S. with no apparent plans other than to learn how to fly airplanes.

## *New York City, Spring 2000*

Pellegrino and Besheer, by now known as Batman and Robin to some within the JTTF, had spent the better part of two years chasing Mohammed Jamal Khalifa around the globe, recording his every utterance. The work-to-information yield ratio was exceedingly small. They pursued others in the Manila network as well, but again the results were less than exciting.

KSM was by far the hardest to track. New signs of him were very faint, and the investigators tried to be creative. By this point, they had assembled a broad mosaic of his family and associates.

They tried to use information as bait in hopes of luring him out of hiding. They monitored his known networks to see if he responded. If he did, they never knew it.

The work was frustrating in the extreme, and was not made any easier by the reception they continued to get when they returned home to New York. Pellegrino continued to face opposition and questions, and Besheer had a tough time dealing with his bosses at the Port Authority, who—unlike the FBI—had never had an officer spend this long on a single case.

Besheer's superiors hassled him more and more about overtime, even though he was required by his union to file it. Finally, he couldn't take it anymore.

When he and Pellegrino had returned from an exceedingly long trip—they had gone literally around the world—late the previous year, Besheer was asked to meet with his boss.

You're kind of high on overtime for the year, his boss said to him.

Besheer tried to explain what he was doing and why—its importance, especially given Port Authority's responsibility for the World Trade Center.

The boss shrugged and said, Still, you're kind of high.

Besheer decided on the spot that was it. He would retire. He was out the door. He was busting his butt for what he regarded as a higher cause, and everyone—his union, his employers—was second-guessing him.

He immediately drove over to 26 Federal Plaza and told Pellegrino, who was devastated. He was nearly speechless. "You can't," Pellegrino said. "We still have to catch KSM." They made one final trip together in January and February, but Besheer stuck to his decision. In his round of farewells, before retiring on February 25 and driving to Florida the next morning, Besheer reminded everyone what was at stake in the work he and Pellegrino had been doing. They'll come back, he said of the people they had been chasing. They'll come back and try to finish the job.

## *Islamabad, Pakistan, 2000*

As KSM plotted and planned from his base in Karachi, he wasn't even on the radar screen of the CIA station in Pakistan, which had been rendered largely ineffectual due to a bitter feud between Washington and Pakistan that had been intensifying for more than a decade.

The Islamabad government, particularly its military and its all-powerful ISI spy agency, hated the United States—vehemently. Many of its top military and intelligence officials had searing memories of how they had spent most of the 1980s working alongside the CIA, covertly training and equipping the mujahideen who had come from far and wide to fight the occupying Soviet army in Afghanistan.

Washington left Pakistan twisting in the wind when it abruptly withdrew after the Soviet pullout. With no money or military assistance to help Pakistan continue what Washington had started, the proud Pakistani military had to watch as its U.S.-made F-16 fighter planes began falling from the sky due to lack of upkeep. Washington, one ISI officer said, "uses us like condoms and then throws us away."[6]

By the time the CIA's new Islamabad station chief, a hotshot named Robert Grenier, arrived in 1999, most CIA operatives in the country left their bunkers in the embassy only infrequently, mostly because they were operating in a hostile country where their intelligence-gathering efforts depended on a host government that was not inclined to provide assistance. Gathering intel in Afghanistan was actually easier, even though the country was controlled by the Taliban, which was a gracious host to Al Qaeda.

As a result, the CIA station in Islamabad was often seen as a backwater deployment, a career derailer, and job opportunities there had few takers. Besides the horrible working conditions and long hours, there was little recognition in Washington that Pakistan was an area of strategic interest, even within counterterrorism, so the chance to use the posting as a way of advancing was virtually nonexistent. The Cold War was long over, the clandestine war against the

Soviets in Afghanistan was done, and the agency was fixated on other threats, including Hamas, Hezbollah, and Iraq. Most careerists stayed away from counterterrorism posts altogether, even with the overtime, hardship pay, and other financial benefits they provided.

That began to change in 1998, with the two embassy bombings in Africa and bin Laden's second and more vehement public declaration of war against the United States, but that did little to improve Islamabad as an attractive posting.

Few, if any, places outside the embassy club served alcohol, and there was little in the way of an expat scene there in which agency operatives could mingle, much less work the room and troll for agents, the CIA term for foreign spies or assets who could be mined for intelligence. The joke was that if you got sent to Islamabad, there was nothing for you to do and nothing to spend your money on, so you socked it away for when you got home. One female case officer bought so many Oriental rugs there that she would later open a carpet store in Washington State.

Despite its size (it would become one of the CIA's largest stations) and strategic importance, Grenier found that the operational tempo of the Pakistan station was slow. Grenier was a rising star in the agency—short, wiry, and athletic, with an unflappable demeanor. He was noted within the corridors of Langley for being a dapper dresser who had a proven record of deftly handling the most difficult assignments, but also one who was unafraid of taking on the most dangerous ones as well. And Islamabad was just that, given CIA director George Tenet's decree that the United States was now on war footing with Al Qaeda.

Soon after Grenier got to Islamabad, it became one of the most productive CIA stations in the world, as measured by the number of reports generated. Grenier presided over a significant expansion of the station, engineered almost entirely to fight the growing threat posed by Al Qaeda, lodged in neighboring Afghanistan. And while bin Laden was virtually untouchable in his fortress at Tarnak Farms, near Kandahar, Grenier soon became fixated on an elusive Al Qaeda operative who had spent years working both sides of the border, virtually with impunity, as one of Al Qaeda's chief logistics chieftains.[7] He was known as Abu Zubaydah.

Zubaydah, whose real name is Zayn al-Abidin Muhammad Husayn, was born in Saudi Arabia in March of 1971. He considered himself a militant Palestinian because some of his teenage years were spent on the West Bank, where he joined in demonstrations against Israel. He moved to Afghanistan in 1991 to join the fight and a year or so later was nearly killed when a mortar shell left shrapnel in his head, causing major trauma and severe memory loss. By the mid-1990s, he had recovered and assumed a key role as a facilitator of foreign fighters into and out of the guerrilla camps—not just for Al Qaeda but for numerous other militant groups from around the world. One of the camps he served, Khalden, was the major Al Qaeda training ground.

The U.S. government was doing whatever it could to gather intelligence on Zubaydah. Grenier told new arrivals at the station that getting him was his—and now their—top terrorism priority.

In late 1999, authorities in Jordan had disrupted a sprawling millennium plot and told the United States that Zubaydah was implicated in the plans to attack U.S. and other Western interests at holy sites in Jordan. On December 14, Ahmed Ressam, an Al Qaeda–trained Algerian militant from Montreal, was arrested in Washington State with a car trunk full of explosives as he drove off the ferry from Canada. Over time, FBI agents wheedled out of Ressam that Zubaydah was not only his facilitator into and out of the Al Qaeda camps but that Zubaydah had encouraged him to blow up U.S. targets and had even facilitated his mission with money and other assistance.

Over the next year, Grenier and others gathered ominous intel suggesting that Zubaydah was living—and plotting—openly in Peshawar. One reason that Zubaydah became an obsession for Grenier was that he wasn't just a member of Al Qaeda but also served as an intermediary between the terror network in Afghanistan and its operations in Pakistan. There, it teamed up with Pakistani militants, including Lashkar-e-Taiba and other groups with deep connections to the ISI. Zubaydah knew these groups well.

Zubaydah's connections to the militants provided the kind of logistical backbone Al Qaeda needed—networks of safe houses on the Pakistan side and ways of moving people and money. This is the meat and potatoes of terrorism operations—logistics, Grenier said. He liked to quote the military dictum that amateurs discuss strategy but professionals discuss logistics.

## *Washington, D.C., Spring and Summer 2001*

Just before the July Fourth weekend, Ressam, the Algerian terrorist, calmly walked into a New York federal courtroom and for the first time described publicly what he knew about the Al Qaeda camps and the group's global network. He had been convicted a few months before, decided to cooperate, and produced a flood of alarming intelligence—on Al Qaeda, yes, but also on Abu Zubaydah.

In his testimony, Ressam said that on his way back from the Al Qaeda camps, Zubaydah had asked him for a bunch of blank Canadian passports, presumably so that he could sneak Al Qaeda operatives into the United States for attacks. In Washington, authorities realized that Zubaydah had gone "operational," and was involved in more than just directing the Jordanian end of the millennium plot.

Soon after General Pervez Musharraf became president of Pakistan in June of 2001, U.S. ambassador William Milam told him the United States urgently needed his help in locating and capturing Zubaydah. This sort of meeting with Pakistani security officials became common. So did the result, which was no action whatsoever. Grenier, who attended some of the meetings, said the pleas to Musharraf hit the wall behind him after going in one ear and out the other.

By that summer, Ressam's information had not only pushed Zubaydah to the top of the list of most wanted terrorists but it caused top intelligence officials to sound a "red alert" about impending Al Qaeda attacks, possibly in the United States. Barbara Sude, the Al Qaeda analyst at the CIA, drew up a classified memo for President George W. Bush entitled "Bin Laden Determined to Strike in U.S."

The memo, known as a PDB, or President's Daily Brief, was personally delivered to President Bush at his Texas ranch on August 6, 2001, and it specifically mentioned that the millennium plotting in Canada in 1999 may have been part of bin Laden's first serious attempt to launch a terrorist strike within the borders of the United States. Until then, Al Qaeda had only struck overseas. It noted that Ressam had said that as early as 1998, Zubaydah was planning his own attack in the United States. And it said that FBI information since that time indicated patterns of suspicious activity in this country consistent with preparations for hijackings or other types of attacks, including recent surveillance of federal buildings in New York.

At the time, the FBI was conducting approximately seventy full-field investigations throughout the U.S. that were considered Al Qaeda–related, the PDB said. It added: "Clandestine, foreign government, and media reports indicate bin Laden since 1997 has wanted to conduct terrorist attacks in the U.S. Bin Laden implied in U.S. television interviews in 1997 and 1998 that his followers would follow the example of World Trade Center bomber Ramzi Yousef and 'bring the fighting to America'.... After U.S. missile strikes on his base in Afghanistan in 1998, bin Laden told followers he wanted to retaliate in Washington."[8]

It also warned that Al Qaeda members—"including some who are U.S. citizens—have resided in or traveled to the U.S. for years, and the group apparently maintains a support structure that could aid attacks."

CIA director George Tenet later described the mood within the intelligence community in these months leading up to September 11 as nearing hysteria. Clues of an impending attack at times appeared to be everywhere. There was, he said, unfortunately little information specific enough to act upon. But there was specific information. In September 2000, a source had reported that someone named Khalid al-Shaykh al-Ballushi was a key lieutenant in Al Queda. Al-Ballushi means "from Baluchistan," KSM's homeland. Recognizing the possible significance, the CIA's bin Laden unit sought more information but dropped the matter. Then, in April, the CIA began analyzing intel that an associate of Abu Zubaydah named Mukhtar was planning terrorist activities. In June, a CIA report said that a man named Khaled was actively recruiting operatives to travel to the United States, where colleagues were waiting to help carry out attacks for bin Laden. Analysts at CIA headquarters presumed from the details of the reporting that this person was KSM, In July, the same source was shown a series of photographs and identified Khalid Sheikh Mohammed as Khaled. In August, the CIA learned that KSM's nickname was Mukhtar.[9]

All of this information was duly recorded and filed away, unacted upon. Any attempts to follow up on it went nowhere. Again, the intelligence community, alarmed though it was, had a nearly laser focus on bin Laden. KSM? The CIA collected information stating that he had plans to attack the United States, but didn't connect the obvious dots. When FBI case agent Pellegrino saw the reports, he was concerned. Was it KSM in full view? He urgently sent off electronic inquiries. No one ever replied, and Pellegrino let the matter drop. The intelligence community was so fixed on Al Qaeda as the threat, it failed to recognize the danger KSM posed.

Sude would later confirm that the bin Laden unit at CIA hadn't given KSM any thought for years.[10] The CIA's own post-9/11 investigators found that while the agency's counterterrorism analysts considered KSM to be a high-priority target for apprehension and rendition, it did not recognize the significance of intelligence received from credible sources in 2000 and 2001 that portrayed him as a senior Al Qaeda lieutenant, and that the agency "thus missed important indicators of terrorist planning."

Even then, with the 9/11 attacks looming, KSM was already looking ahead to the next battles in his war. That summer, he was busy laying the foundations for a second wave of attacks. He approved further payments to Zacarias Moussaoui for flight training and he sent a Qatari computer expert, Ali Saleh Kahlah al-Marri, to Illinois with instructions to lay low, conduct surveillance, and await further instructions while attending Bradley University in Peoria. He did the same with others, most notably the team of nineteen hijackers in the 9/11 plot, who were putting the finishing touches on his grand plan.

# CHAPTER 10
## September 11

*Pakistan, Summer 2001*

One Sunday morning, the U.S. ambassador to Pakistan, William Milam, was enjoying breakfast at the embassy club with a State Department security official when he noted a number of unfamiliar faces. "Those are all Grenier's people," Milam's dining companion observed. "He runs the place."

"No," Milam spat back. "I run the place."

By July, Milam was off to his next assignment.

With support from George Tenet, Bob Grenier had readied the CIA's Pakistan station, and Langley ramped up deployment of officers and analysts to Islamabad, which it called tag-teaming. So many temporarily deployed agency operatives were there that it appeared the agency was taking over the massive embassy.

"The system," Tenet said, "was blinking red."[1] It continued to blink furiously right up to the morning nineteen young Arab men boarded four westbound transcontinental commercial airliners.

Al Qaeda had called its most important operatives back to Afghanistan to protect them. In August, Ramzi bin al-Shibh sent a courier to Karachi to tell KSM that Atta had chosen September 11 as the date for the attacks. Later in the month, Mohammed traveled to Afghanistan to inform bin Laden personally of the date, then returned to Pakistan. Mohammed and bin al-Shibh watched news reports of the attacks at an Internet café in Karachi.[2] When the first plane hit the first target, the World Trade Center, a celebration commenced. Men shouted, "God is great!" and wept with joy.[3]

## *Port Charlotte, Florida, September 11, 2001*

On the morning of 9/11, Besheer, now a health nut and patrol officer for the Punta Gorda police department, had just finished his early morning walk across the bridge between Port Charlotte and Punta Gorda, made a cup of coffee, and gone to his computer room. His wife, Barbara, called out to him to come watch the TV. A plane had just hit the World Trade Center, she said, apparently a commuter plane.

His stomach sank at the mere mention of a plane and the Trade Center in the same sentence. He got up from the computer and walked slowly into the living room. When he saw the smoke pouring out of the North Tower, he knew immediately what had happened. After he watched the second plane come careening in minutes later, he turned, walked to his bedroom, and started packing. His raid jackets—the familiar law enforcement outerwear worn on hazardous assignments—had been hanging neatly in his closet since he left the Port Authority the prior year. He laid them out on the bed. His wife walked in and asked what he thought he was doing.

Besheer, despite his powerful physique, was gentle by nature and habit. Now, however, he grabbed his wife's arms, fiercely. He shook her and wailed, "I told you they were coming back!" Besheer had a long record of warning people that the same group of terrorists who attacked the Trade Center the first time would come back and finish the job, reminding them of what Basit had said that night as his helicopter passed the Twin Towers. He said it at his retirement dinner from the Port Authority in 2000 and numerous times before and after. He told his Port Authority bosses when he abruptly retired, after they once again asked him what the hell he was doing over there on the Joint Terrorism Task Force, racking up so much overtime to chase ghosts around the world.

Still holding his wife, Besheer sank to his knees. Then his cell phone rang. It was Pellegrino, calling from Malaysia, where he had gone to meet a potential informant as part of his continuing hunt for the Manila Air coconspirators. Pellegrino had high hopes for the meeting, which was supposed to take place the day before, but the informant never showed. He had first called his wife in New York, but couldn't reach her. He was not usually an emotional man, but he sounded distraught. He was yelling into the phone:

"Bash, look what they've done! Look what they've done to us! They did the building and the plane all in one!"

They both knew exactly who "they" was. Khalid Sheikh Mohammed was the first name Pellegrino thought of when he saw the news.

Besheer sat on his bed and cried. He couldn't stop. Once he did, he finished packing his clothes, stocked a cooler full of snacks and juice, gathered his suitcase and his raid jackets, threw them in the backseat of his car, and headed north at high speed. He got pulled over for speeding even before he got out of Florida. When the state trooper looked inside the car and saw the raid jackets, he pulled back and looked at Besheer. "Godspeed," he said, and waved him on.

Besheer drove without resting, and first went to the Port Authority offices in New Jersey to officially reenlist. Then he went to "the hole," where the towers had stood. He found his former colleagues from the Port Authority and JTTF and immediately went to work with them. For several days, working out of their makeshift command center on the Hudson River, they clawed through the rubble and wreckage, looking for clues, for evidence amid the bodies, the bonded stationery, the computer consoles, everything the giant towers had contained and pulverized on their way down. He tried to rejoin Port Authority formally, but red tape in a time of crisis got in his way. Then, within a few weeks, the FBI bureaucracy also put its foot down. A supervisor—a former colleague—told him he couldn't stay because he no longer had the security clearance necessary to work with the JTTF.

As he turned and walked away, he saw crowds of people, hundreds, standing near the ad hoc command post. They waved signs that read God Bless You and You're Our Heroes. They held out to the workers whatever food they could scrounge from their own kitchens. One woman offered Besheer half a package of Ritz crackers sealed with a twist tie and two bottles of water. It was all she had to give.

# CHAPTER 11
## Panic

### *On Board, September 11, 2001*

The investigation into the September 11 attacks had begun while the hijacked airliners were still in the air. When the muscle hijackers on the four planes took control of the aircraft, they did so with a suddenness and violence that shocked the flight crews. Using small utility knives as weapons, they stormed past stunned flight attendants and invaded the cockpits. They subdued the pilots by whatever means they needed, in some cases slicing their throats and dragging their bodies back out into the main cabins, then clearing the way for the single pilot in each group to take over the flight. The flight attendants could do little to stop or even slow the hijackers, who, on average, were not large men, but who had the elements of surprise, months of weight lifting, and determination to their advantage.

The flight attendants in several instances did what they could to fight back. This mainly meant making telephone calls to the ground, reporting what was happening, and identifying the hijackers by their seat numbers. Matching the numbers to the names on flight manifests, airline workers on the ground in at least a few cases identified the hijackers before the planes even crashed. It was too late and too little, of course, to spare the passengers, crews, or the people going to work in the buildings that would be the targets of the airliner missiles. But it gave investigators on the ground enough information to begin their search. In the case of United 93, the aircraft that crashed in Pennsylvania, information from the alert attendants lent frightening specificity to the origin of the attackers. Khalid al-Mihdhar and Nawaf al-Hazmi, the two Saudis who had slipped past the CIA on their initial entry into the United States the year before, and Hazmi's brother, Salem, were named on the manifests.[1]

All three were known as Al Qaeda recruits. Thus were Osama bin Laden and Al Qaeda identified as the likely originators of the attacks long before the sun set on September 11.

Investigators also caught a huge break. Mohammed Atta, the pilot of the first plane to strike the World Trade Center, had on the day before the attacks driven from Boston, where he intended to depart on his suicide mission the next day, to Portland, Maine. He and another hijacker, Abdul Aziz al-Omari, had eaten that evening at a Pizza Hut, visited a Walmart store, and spent the night in a Comfort Inn in Portland. They very nearly missed their commuter flight back to Boston the next morning, arriving at the airport just fifteen minutes before their plane was due to take off.[2] But they made it, flew down to Boston, and transferred without incident to their American Airlines flight. Atta's luggage, however, didn't make the transfer. He had checked two bags. Neither was loaded onto American Airlines 11.

The bags were discovered later that day at Boston's Logan International Airport. Atta had left a record of virtually his entire life in them. Included were his last will and testament, his college diploma, and transcripts from both Cairo University, where he obtained his undergraduate degree, and Technical University of Hamburg-Harburg, where he did his graduate work. The hijackers also left rental cars littered with paperwork and fingerprints in three different airport parking garages.

With the identification of Mihdhar and the Hazmi brothers, and with the caches of information in Atta's luggage and the cars, investigators were handed the identity of both the plot's sponsor—bin Laden—and its chief executioners, Atta and his fellow pilots. Within hours, administration officials were searching for potential bombing targets in Afghanistan and directions to Atta's apartment in Hamburg, Germany.

Investigators were deployed immediately, combing hotel rooms and apartments for evidence and trying to find anyone who had come into contact with the hijackers. The web widened with astonishing speed, quickly jumping from the United States to Germany and then to the United Arab Emirates, Pakistan, and Afghanistan.

## *New York City, September 2011*

In the immediate aftermath of the attacks, the panic was everywhere, and overwhelming.

David Kelley, one of the supervisory assistant U.S. attorneys most involved in prosecution of terrorism cases, was in his Manhattan office when Mohammed Atta steered flight 11 into the North Tower. His window in Federal Plaza looked north, so he saw nothing, but he heard a huge bang. Then he saw what looked like confetti floating through the air. He was about to call the police to see what the hell had happened when U.S. attorney Mary Jo White, his boss, called him.

White's office looked south and she had seen the plane hit the building,

"A plane hit the Trade Center; go with Barry [Mawn], he's waiting for you," she said. It was a routine reaction. Any time anything happened, White wanted her prosecutors right there in the middle of it. Kelley, similarly, had been rushed to investigate the attack on the USS *Cole*. He arrived, he liked to say, before the smoke cleared.

Kelley ran out of the building, passing his wife as she was going to work. He joined up with Mawn—the head of the FBI's New York field office—and a New York fire department officer, Joe Dunn, and they ran toward the Trade Center. Other law enforcement officials reacted exactly the same way. In the few minutes it took the three to travel five blocks, others had beat them to the spot. The three men arrived at the site and immediately started coordinating an investigative response. Then the second plane hit the South Tower. No one knew what was going on. Kelley was told to go to three different places. Finally, they were directed to a temporary command post on West Street. They took off again, running past dozens of body parts on the ground. Kelley passed one leg on the pavement—an entire leg, hip to foot, clothed in a kind of harem pant. It was exactly the sort of garment worn by Basit, the original World Trade Center bomber, when he first entered the United States.

"We need to preserve this as evidence," he told Mawn. They stopped and bent over to examine the leg. "We need to tag this," Kelley said.

"I'm not touching that fucking thing," Mawn answered.

Kelley started to argue that, no, we have to tag it, or we'll get someone else to tag it, when the South Tower collapsed. He had no idea that was what had happened, but the noise was overwhelming. They all started running. Kelley was an athlete, exceptionally fit. Mawn was not. The air filled with debris. They ran through it as far as they could. Kelley felt he was about to suffocate. He stopped, exhausted. He looked behind him; Mawn was nowhere to be seen.

Suddenly, the noise ceased and the air temporarily cleared. Kelley resumed his search for the command center. Ken Maxwell, the head of the JTTF, was there when he arrived.

"Where's Barry?" Maxwell asked.

"He's dead," Kelley said. "He didn't make it. He was behind me and then he wasn't."

Then somebody said the North Tower was bound to fall, too. It was the first time Kelley realized the South Tower had come down. Kelley got on the phone to White, who was still back at her office.

"Barry's dead," Kelley said.

"No, he's not," White replied. "He's on the other line and told me *you* were dead."

On the ground at the three impact sites—lower Manhattan, the Pentagon, and a farm field in southwestern Pennsylvania—no one quite knew what had happened or how to respond. Plunging into the rubble and hunting through the carnage for survivors provided an immediate plan of action. Beyond that, things got confusing.

Virtually the entire FBI and Department of Justice was thrown into the 9/11 response. The Joint Terrorism Task Force's offices at 26 Federal Plaza were just five blocks north of the World Trade Center, beyond the blast zone, but the building lost all electricity and telephone service. The JTTF, along with most of the New York field office, was forced to pack up and move north and west to the second floor of a parking garage in Manhattan's Chelsea neighborhood, next to the Hudson River. They built makeshift temporary quarters there, living out of the trunks of their cars, and accommodated a huge influx of reinforcements from the New York police department and other agencies. Those who couldn't fit into the garage were set up on a retired aircraft carrier, the USS *Intrepid*, which was docked upriver.

Even before the strong evidence supporting it came to light, the immediate suspicion among almost everyone who knew anything about Al Qaeda was that Osama bin Laden's group was behind the attacks. Some sensed it immediately. When George Tenet, director of the CIA, was given his first news of the onslaught while at a breakfast meeting at a Washington hotel, he wondered aloud if it was bin Laden. Richard Clarke, the White House counterterrorism coordinator, who had been ranting about bin Laden for years, immediately told top administration officials it was Al Qaeda.

Farther down the food chain, Pellegrino and his former partner, Besheer, had much different reactions. Both thought it was the man they had been chasing since 1994, Khalid Sheikh Mohammed.

In a way, it was surprising how few other people came to this same conclusion. With his nephew Abdul Basit Abdul Karim, Mohammed was known to have been involved in two different plots targeting Americans—the initial 1993 bombing of the World Trade Center and the foiled attempt to blow up a dozen American-flagged jumbo jets in 1995. Basit had been captured, had vowed to take down the towers again if he had the chance, had boasted of a network of associates who could do it, and had been tried and imprisoned. But Mohammed remained at large, an ever more ghostly figure with a phone book full of dangerous acquaintances. Mohammed had not shown in any way an intention to stop attacking. As Pellegrino said in his 9/11 call to Besheer, the September 11 attacks were a clever combination of the two prior attacks—using the World Trade Center as a target and airliners as weapons. Other targets had been added to the list, and the planes were hijacked, not blown up in flight, but the core similarities were unnerving.

Of course, some other people had thought of Mohammed as a potential suspect, including Pasquale "Pat" D'Amuro, a top counterterrorism official in the FBI's New York office who had been promoted to headquarters. There were a couple of early mentions of KSM having something to do with the attacks, but so strongly was the security apparatus wedded to its own beliefs that the thought quickly perished. Security officials had grown impatient with Pellegrino and Besheer over the years, suggesting that the hunt for KSM was an arcane endeavor that grew less important by the day. Some had tried to kill it. Others on the JTTF, even among the true believers, described Pellegrino as "that old guy working that old case," a case that probably deserved to be put into a file and forgotten. Pellegrino was reduced for the most part to periodically sending out notices—including photographs and fingerprints—to U.S. embassies and FBI legal attachés around the world, reminding them that this man remained at large and dangerous. Nobody much cared.

It was an article of faith within the intelligence community that Mohammed and Basit were lone wolves running a more or less ad hoc enterprise. When Mohammed was finally added to the FBI's most wanted list with a reward of $5 million that October, he was described as armed and dangerous and still wanted for the Manila Air plot. Bin Laden's Al Qaeda, meanwhile, had blossomed into a full-blown threat. Since the devastating attacks on American embassies in Kenya and Tanzania, official opinion of bin Laden had undergone a full turnabout. Once dismissed as a poseur, his grandiose public pronouncements the rantings of a madman, bin Laden was transformed from terrorist financier to terrorist mastermind after the 224 deaths at the embassy attacks in Africa were tallied. He was sometimes described as a sort of evil genius. Much was made about the sophistication of those attacks, how they had been long in the planning and were synchronized. A follow-up attack in October of 2000 against a billion-dollar U.S. Navy warship, the USS *Cole*, in the harbor of the southern Yemeni city of Aden further heightened bin Laden's reputation.

Threat reporting during the months leading up to September 11 had been rife with references to bin Laden's activities and likely vectors of attack. The stream of warnings, some referencing KSM directly, had been nearly nonstop. The president had been warned directly about bin Laden's ambitions. But the system, aware of the danger but unprepared and unable to stop bin Laden, was fully prepared to blame him 100 percent. At the moment of his greatest triumph, Khalid Sheikh Mohammed was relegated to history's round file.

Hundreds attended the many funeral services for the fallen, including that of the Port Authority public safety director, Fred Morrone, who had henpecked Besheer about his overtime. Besheer couldn't help but wonder if, in his last moments, Morrone thought about Besheer's warning that "they" would be coming back to hit the World Trade Center again. The biggest turnout was for the funeral of John O'Neill. The toughest of agents, Besheer included, wept as eulogists praised O'Neill as the man who virtually single-handedly tried to take the fight to those who attacked on 9/11. The speakers all noted the irony of O'Neill dying in the very towers he had tried so hard to protect. They were unaware of another, perhaps even more tragic irony—that in his single-minded pursuit of Osama bin Laden and Al Qaeda, O'Neill had at least partially undermined the effort to find the man who had actually ordered the attacks.

In New York, word had come down from on high to ramp up the JTTF—and fast. Dozens of agents were streaming into the makeshift headquarters along the Hudson, and most of them knew little about bin Laden—and less about Mohammed. Many knew nothing about terrorism at all, or knew only what they had read on various wanted posters. FBI director Robert Mueller III had given the order that every single lead had to be run to ground, no matter how unlikely its provenance or probability of value. So they were all thrown into the fight.

Thousands of tips poured in, many of them eventually determined to be from competitors of Arab business owners, jilted lovers, or closet racists. It didn't matter. Each had to be followed to the end. Nationwide, hundreds of Middle Eastern men were detained for "acting suspiciously." If the tip was that somebody was buying chemicals to build a bomb and it turned out that the "suspect" was buying cleaning supplies for his swimming pool, somebody had to talk to the person who sold the supplies and to anybody who knew the buyer. The manpower demands were gargantuan, and exhausting.

The focus was almost entirely on stopping the next attack. In the New York JTTF, this imperative was enshrined bureaucratically. An Al Qaeda squad was divided into two teams. International Terrorism One, IT-1, was designated Al Qaeda New, for new investigations, and IT-2 was designated Al Qaeda Old, for preexisting cases. But for some reason, IT-2 was stuck chasing all the bad leads and most of the others as well. Pellegrino was assigned to IT-2.

"It was a madhouse," said one of the supervisors on the JTTF. "It was like learning a new language, especially for the NYPD guys."[3] The cops couldn't believe how much paperwork the FBI required—the FD-302 field reports; the ECs, or electronic communications; the LHMs, or letterhead memorandums needed to open a case—and how important it was to use specific forms for specific things, and how seriously the Bureau took it if you got it wrong.

"Cops aren't used to doing that. So it was a huge, huge learning curve for [the NYPD] guys. [The] NYPD would just have forms where you check in the box here or there so it was totally different," the supervisor said. "And there was no orientation. [They] were just thrown into the deep end of the water, and at a time that was as unbelievable as you can imagine in terms of stress and pace and people being overworked and understaffed."

Training? Forget it. The new guys were given a computer log-on and told to get to work. Many had no idea where to even start. So some gravitated toward Pellegrino and the other task force veterans for guidance.

In the relentless orthodoxy of the FBI—dark suit, white shirt, spit-shined shoes, dark tie—Pellegrino stood out. He was, the supervisor said, "the most un-FBI guy I've ever seen. He'd wear jeans and a sweatshirt. Short. Wild hair. Frank marches to his own drum."

Whatever he was doing to help out, Pellegrino knew that in the midst of the biggest criminal investigation in history he was being marginalized, as were many of the other old-timers. While the world moved in new and dramatic ways, he was left like a restless polar bear on an ice floe, watching the shore as he floated off into the distance.

Pellegrino tutored the young cops on how to finesse the FBI's paperwork-based culture, and told them who was who in the Al Qaeda firmament. He also showed them a way to behave. He was quiet, a listener, an absorber, so low-key that "he would sit in meetings for forty-five minutes and never open his mouth, even though he knew more than anyone else in the room," the supervisor said—probably more than everybody else in the room combined.

Except, that is, when some stupid supervisor tried to get between him and his investigation, and then computer keyboards went sailing against a wall.

## *Washington, D.C., September 2001*

Mueller, a former San Francisco prosecutor, decided within the first week that the 9/11 investigation would be run out of FBI headquarters in Washington, D.C. That was only his second week on the job, having taken over on September 1. The New York office had been home to nearly every investigation into radical Islam that the FBI had ever undertaken, including all the bin Laden cases—the first Trade Center bombing, the Manila Air plot, the embassy bombings in Africa, the *Cole*. The New York office had the history, the expertise, the investigators, the institutional knowledge, and a well-oiled system in which FBI agents, federal prosecutors, and grand juries worked together to produce indictments and win convictions. It also had one of the most dramatic crime scenes in history at its doorstep—the smoking pile of concrete-and-steel rubble that had been the Twin Towers. Its leaders argued that the investigation belonged there. Mueller didn't care. He wanted to be able to see what was happening on the investigation with his own eyes. Some thought it was because he blamed the New York squad for failing to stop the attacks, and because he thought there were too many cowboys there on the JTTF, people who didn't like to follow protocol. And Mueller was big on protocol. He also wanted to centralize the organization of the FBI, to undo the traditional feudal structure under which every local office was its own little principality run more or less as the special agent in charge saw fit. Aside from the bureaucratic concerns about a structure like this, there was also the plain fact that international terrorism was hardly a problem unique to New York; the threat reporting was coming from all corners of the United States and the world. This was not an argument you have even the slightest hope of winning, Mueller said. I don't care about the history. If those investigators are so valuable to the investigation, they can move, too. Bring 'em along. Many did. Half the New York office came to Washington, it seemed.

Amid everything else going on, moving dozens of agents from New York to headquarters was not the most obvious way to ensure a smooth operation. But the task confronting all the security services overwhelmed whatever complaints were lodged against reorganization. There simply was not enough time to fight about it.

David Kelley had no sooner scrambled out of the debris at the World Trade Center than he received a call from Washington. Attorney general John Ashcroft and Mueller wanted him there immediately. Within hours, he got another call from a top DOJ official. "Do you know about this guy in Minneapolis?" The "guy" was Zacarias Moussaoui, the French Moroccan man KSM had approved for flight training as part of a second wave of attacks. Moussaoui was the first strong link to KSM and his cadre of operatives already in the United States. As the FBI and CIA scrambled to figure out Moussaoui's role, they never found a hint of KSM's involvement. Nor did they suspect there were KSM agents other than Moussaoui already in the U.S.; as usual, the ghost had left few traces behind.

After tracking down his wife, also an assistant U.S. attorney, and ensuring she was safe, Kelley was taken to an FBI car and driven through the night to FBI headquarters, which was about to be inundated with agents from around the country. He showered, changed suits, and was told he would be briefing the nation's two top law enforcement officials shortly after sunrise about a subject that had consumed him for years. During the prior five years, Kelley had been out of the country looking for Al Qaeda as much as he was in. Finally, Ashcroft and Mueller would hear what he had learned.

Kelley didn't mention it in that briefing or others that followed because it was just a random thought, but he had been a supervising prosecutor in New York when the World Trade Center and Manila cases were tried. Although KSM's name had purposely been kept out of the public part of the trials, Kelley was well aware of him.

"Where the hell has *that* guy been?" Kelley asked himself.

Few others were giving much thought to KSM. On October 2, the State Department sent out a classified memo to all U.S. embassies, instructing them to brief world leaders on what the U.S. knew about the attacks, and Al Qaeda. The top-secret briefing memo cited the most up-to-date, sensitive, and classified intelligence, including some from a highly placed Al Qaeda informant.[4]

It listed several key figures involved in the 9/11 attacks, but KSM's name was notably absent—despite several references to the Bojinka plot and to the first World Trade Center bombing. That omission was all the more noticeable to some because the memo specifically implicated Al Qaeda in both of those plots.

For his part, Pellegrino kept his suspicions about KSM's possible 9/11 role to himself and sent out another round of messages to embassies around the world, asking them to be on the lookout for KSM. It had become a matter of routine, but this time, Pellegrino was hoping that with all the attention on 9/11 and Al Qaeda, something—anything—might shake loose on what had now become a cold case.

The secret State Department memo said that the United States was mobilizing as never before to counter Al Qaeda and its global network. "Many of these groups support each other and are supported by states," it read. "Given the extensive nature of this network, the United States has a multi-phase, long-term strategy. We will need cooperation and assistance from around the world, possibly for years to come. As President Bush has said, we are embarking on a lengthy campaign that will combine diplomacy, financial measures, military action, intelligence, and other instruments of power and influence. We want to starve terrorists of funding, and we want to deprive them of refuge."

FBI leadership noted that the memo—the first known blueprint for what would become the Bush-Cheney doctrine in the War on Terror—said nothing about the FBI, even though PENTTBOM already had become the biggest criminal investigation in the Bureau's history. At FBI headquarters, halfway between the White House and the Capitol on Pennsylvania Avenue, agents were arriving from around the country and were squeezed in wherever they could find space. Some were set up in the basement, next to the loading dock and the print shop. They slept at their desks, on couches, or doubled and tripled up at nearby apartment complexes.

The investigation was run out of the FBI's Strategic Information and Operations Center (SIOC, pronounced *sigh*-ock). The multimillion-dollar, 40,000-square-foot complex was made up of offices, suites, computer hubs, and secure video conference rooms that were all connected by gleaming white corridors on the fifth floor of headquarters. By the time the second plane hit the World Trade Center, Dale Watson, the Bureau's assistant director for counterterrorism, was already in the command center conducting a briefing. Mueller placed Pickard, the deputy FBI director, and D'Amuro in charge of the investigation and Watson directly under them. The top executives of the Bureau began meeting at the center twice a day.[5]

As happens in many organizations, the briefings were dreaded by those not involved for the simple reason that every unanswered question raised during the course of the meetings would be sent downstream as soon as the briefing concluded, often prefaced by the words "The director wants..."

Sometimes they went downstream based only on what people *thought* the director wanted.

This drove operations people crazy. Dennis Lormel, chief of the Bureau's financial crimes section, knew there had to be a money trail that led from the crash sites back to the 9/11 plot's organizers. He also knew that despite his best efforts and frequent complaints, the Bureau still didn't have a comprehensive way to pursue that trail. He watched with growing irritation as his investigators were picked off one by one to chase whatever new lead had just come in or whatever question had just been asked. It was exactly the kind of approach the Bureau had taken to tracking terror financing before the attacks. There was no comprehensive, strategic plan.

By the third night, the lack of a plan bothered Lormel enough that he sat up all night writing one. By the end of the first week, he had pitched his immediate supervisors on the idea that his section—which typically investigated white-collar crime—should grab the finance end of the plot, coordinate it, and chase it down from beginning to end. There had to be a money trail, he told them. He had no sooner pitched his idea than his secretary received a call from SIOC. The bosses wanted another investigator to chase the latest clue. Lormel stormed down to SIOC and told a supervisor there that he would take the lead himself. The supervisor, Don Kelly, said, Dennis, you're the section chief, you don't need to do this. We just need an agent to track it down.

I'm going to handle this one; let me see the lead, Lormel said, extending his hand. There was some resistance. Kelly thought Lormel was busting his chops, which in a sense he was.

Kelly handed it over and, as Lormel suspected, it was typical of the requests that were being made—some mope's credit card charge to be tracked down. It was almost random. It confirmed for Lormel that there was no plan, just spasmodic reaction.

At that moment, Mueller and Pickard came out into the foyer. Lormel went up to Pickard and said, This is a crazy way to handle this stuff. If it's all one plot, it's all related financially. We need to know where the money is coming from, where it's going, and who's behind it. We should treat all the financial questions as one investigation, pull it into our shop, and pursue it. Pickard agreed on the spot, and Lormel was suddenly the 9/11 money man.

On the next conference call, Pickard announced that all the money stuff "has to go through Dennis." At the time, all FBI field offices were issuing subpoenas on 9/11-related probes, often literally on the same targets. Lormel, a gruff, no-nonsense former accountant who had spent a career doing big, complicated cases, became a traffic cop of sorts, making sure leads were neither duplicated nor ignored.[6]

Lormel immediately pulled together his entire staff of one hundred people and eventually supplemented them with another two hundred filched from wherever he could find them—including some of the Bureau's youngest and most creative thinkers. They seized a huge, empty space on the fourth floor that was in the midst of a remodel, dropped phone and computer lines out of the ceiling, and hauled in furniture. It popped up as fast as one of those huge boiler-room operations, Lormel recalled, up and running almost overnight.

Within a week, the financial effort began to pay off. The money trail led from the hijackers' bank accounts back to the United Arab Emirates, where KSM had placed one of his nephews, Ali Abdul Aziz Ali, a year before the attacks. He later sent Mustafa al-Hawsawi to help Ali. The two had wired funds to the hijackers, as needed, from local exchange centers, which didn't require much more than a name for identification. Lormel's agents had no idea at the time, but the money trail had quickly led to the plot's virtual doorstep, on the other side of which sat KSM.

## *Washington, D.C., Autumn 2001*

The FBI's computer system was almost worse than one could imagine, with virtually no networking capabilities among the fifty-six field offices scattered from coast to coast. Fax machines, diplomatic pouches, and the U.S. Postal Service were the principal means of moving information. Supervisors literally mailed packets of information on the nineteen hijackers to the JTTFs after the attacks. Many agents could not send or receive e-mail from their offices; they had to use private accounts. Louis Freeh, Mueller's predecessor, boasted about using his computer every day—as a place to put all his Post-it notes; Bureau legend has it that he rarely, if ever, turned it on. He spent most of his time visiting field offices, he would say, not in his office writing memos. The FBI, in many ways the inventor of a sophisticated data-based approach to law enforcement, had slowly become crippled by its inability to access and distribute its own information in useful ways.

It was—in this regard, at least—an organization spectacularly ill-equipped to wage war against a global and shadowy enemy that was better able to employ the technologies of a networked world. What the FBI did have, however, was an institutional knowledge of radical Islam gained from more than a decade of investigation, interrogation, examination, and trial of international terrorists. This history of success was the FBI's best argument for a major role in the 9/11 investigation. Unfortunately for the Bureau, and with long-lasting impact on American legal culture, the White House of George Bush was not much interested in investigation. It wanted two things—revenge for the attacks and an ability to stop the next one.

Bush told any and all who would listen that the United States was at war and new rules would apply. Vice President Dick Cheney went on national television and warned that the United States would no doubt have to venture onto the "dark side" in order to pursue and punish its enemies. Cheney, more than any other individual, was the architect of the new War on Terror. He made it clear that doubt and nuance had no role to play in this new world.[7] The FBI's customary ways of doing business were not a fit for what Cheney had in mind, and perhaps chiefly for that reason the Bureau lost its status as the preeminent antiterror agency.

In the days immediately following the attacks, George Tenet and his deputies made a forceful case to the administration for allowing the CIA and its network of intelligence agents around the world, who could leverage the help of literally dozens of host countries where Al Qaeda was active, to lead the new war. Their argument: the hardest part wasn't going to be killing the enemy but finding it—not just the terrorists but their logistics networks, financiers, and supporters and sympathizers. Bush even noted this in his special State of the Union address to an unsettled nation,

Khalid Sheikh Mohammed attended this high school in Fahaheel, Kuwait. He was radicalized during his teen years, joining the Muslim Brotherhood. *(Terry McDermott)*

Mohammed's father was imam of this mosque near the headquarters of the Kuwait Oil Company in Al-Ahmadi, Kuwait. *(Terry McDermott)*

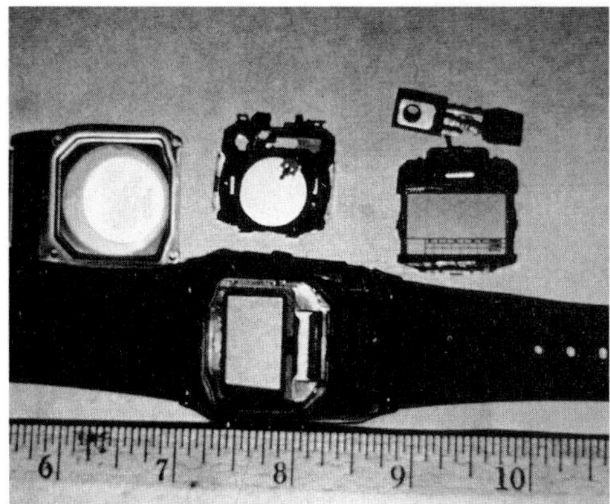


Abdul Basit Abdul Karim, also known as Ramzi Yousef, designed a tiny bomb that could be smuggled disassembled onto an airplane and put together once on board. The design used a Casio watch as a timer. Basit and Mohammed planned to deposit twelve of the Casio bombs on a dozen U.S.-flagged jumbo jets and blow them all up on single day in 1995. *(United States Government)*

This is the room at the Doña Josefa, a transient hotel in Manila that Abdul Basit used as a bomb factory in 1994–95. A chemical fire he accidentally ignited in the room led to the disruption of his plot to blow up airliners. *(United States Government)*

The plans for the airliner plot were stored on this Toshiba laptop, recovered from the sixth-floor apartment where Abdul Basit lived in the Philippines. There were also clues on the laptop that helped investigators identify his uncle and coconspirator, Khalid Sheikh Mohammed, known within law enforcement as KSM. *(United States Government)*

FBI special agent Frank Pellegrino (right), New York Port Authority detective Matthew Besheer (center), and Assistant U.S. Attorney Michael Garcia (left) were among those honored in 1997 by the Justice Department for their role in convicting KSM's nephew Abdul Basit. *(Matthew Besheer)*

Wanted posters and matchbooks offering a $2 million reward for the capture of Ramzi Yousef, aka Abdul Basit, were distributed widely throughout Pakistan, where he was eventually captured in 1995. *(United States Government)*

The room KSM and Abdul Basit rented at the Doña Josefa faced a main thoroughfare where they believed Pope John Paul II would travel during a visit to Manila in 1995. The two plotted to kill both the pope and President Bill Clinton. *(Terry McDermott)*

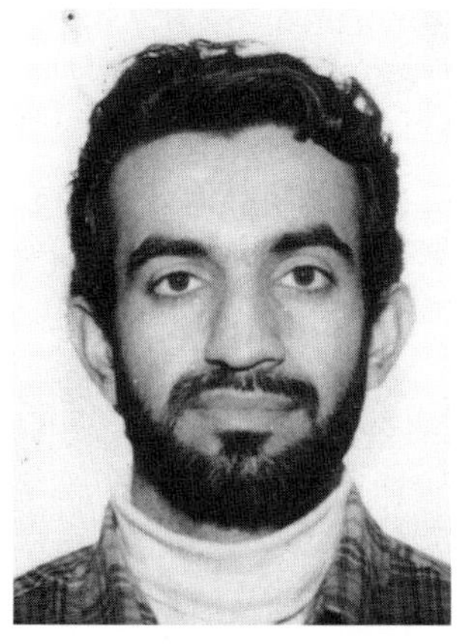

An early photo of Abdul Basit. *(United States Government)*

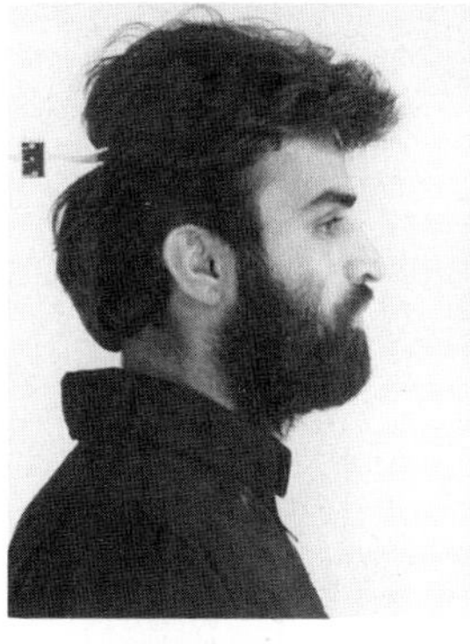

Abdul Hakim Murad was a childhood friend of Abdul Basit who joined Basit and KSM for the airline bomb plot in Manila. *(United States Government)*

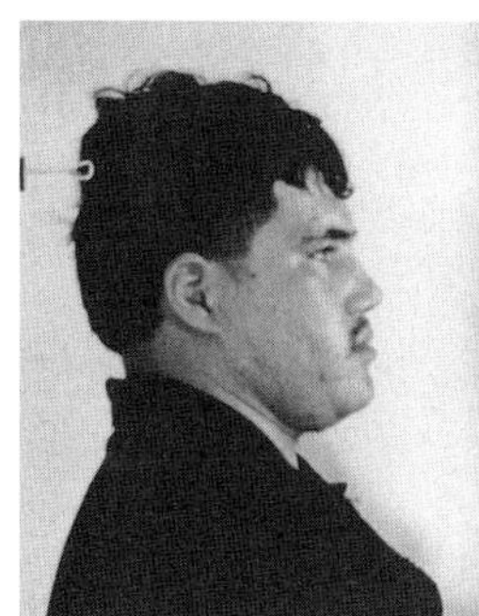

Wali Khan Amin Shah, an Afghan veteran of the anti-Soviet jihad and an old friend of Osama bin Laden, was convicted in 1996 for his role in the "Manila Air" plot to bomb a dozen American airliners. *(United States Government)*

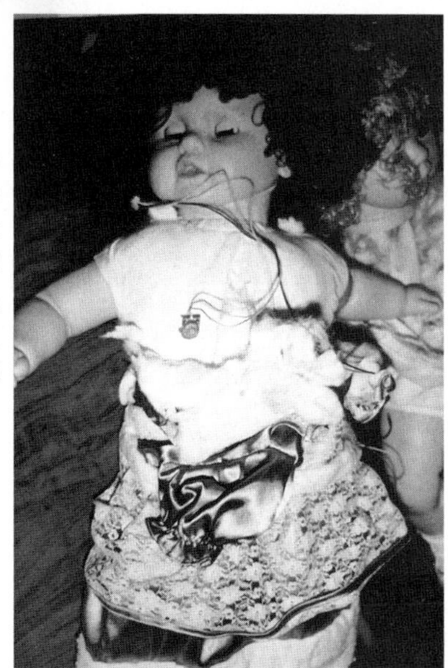

Abdul Basit planned to turn these children's dolls into bombs to be used against Western targets. He had several of the doll bombs with him when captured in 1995. *(United States Government)*

Abdul Basit remains imprisoned at a maximum-security federal penitentiary in Colorado, where he is serving two terms of 240 years each. He has been kept in solitary confinement almost the entire time he has been jailed. *(United States Government)*

KSM often posed as a Middle Eastern businessman when he traveled the world establishing terror cells. He sometimes wore Western business attire, sometimes flowing Arab robes. *(United States Government)*

KSM when he was younger. *(United States Government)*

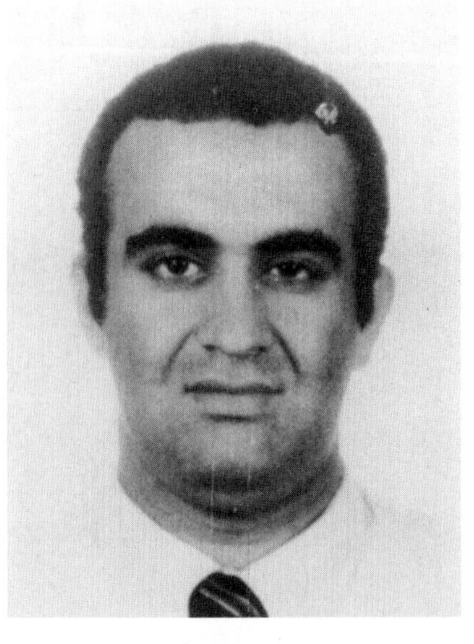

KSM clean shaven. Mohammed altered his appearance and used different names and personas frequently. *(United States Government)*

577

C.R. No — F.P. Classification No. 16 — C.C. No. — Division — C.I.D. No

Name: KHALID SHAIKH MOHD

Nationality: — P. No: 069133 — Address: — Occupation: — Date of Birth: 1965

Date — Classified by / Rank — Date — Impressions taken by

Electronic Classification

RIGHT HAND

R. THUMB | R. INDEX | R. MIDDLE | R. RING | R. LITTLE

LEFT HAND

L. THUMB | L. INDEX | L. MIDDLE | L. RING | L. LITTLE

PLAIN PRINTS

This set of KSM fingerprints was taken in Doha, Qatar. KSM moved to Qatar after the end of the jihad against the Soviet Union. He worked as an engineer in a Ministry of Electricity and Water and used Doha as a staging area for many of his international travels over the years. He was nearly captured there in 1996 but slipped away while an FBI rendition team waited to take him into custody. *(United States Government)*

Ali Abdul Aziz Ali, also known as Ammar al-Baluchi, was just one of many of KSM's relatives who assisted him. This photo was taken by the Red Cross at Guantánamo in 2009. *(Courtesy Mohammed family)*

An earlier photo of Ali Abdul Aziz Ali in Western clothes. *(United States Government)*

Mohammed Atta (second from right on the bottom row), the lead hijacker on September 11, 2001, earned an architecture degree from Cairo University. He's shown here with classmates on a field trip in 1990 in Egypt. *(Courtesy Mohammed Mokhtar el-Rafei)*

FBI special agent Jennifer Keenan was assigned to Pakistan as the assistant legal attaché during the hunt for KSM. *(Courtesy FBI)*

KSM was held in Pakistani custody for three days after his capture in 2003. He was interrogated by both Pakistanis and Americans in those first few days. *(CBS / 60 Minutes)*

# REWARD
# $2,000,000

**KHALED SHAIKH MOHAMMAD**

**ALIASES: KHALED SHAIKH, SALEM ALI, ABU-KHUALA, ASHRAF REFAT NABIAH HENIM**

1993-1994

October 1995

**DESCRIPTION:**
**DATE OF BIRTH:** April 14, 1965 or March 1, 1964
**PLACE OF BIRTH:** Kuwait or Pakistan
**HEIGHT:** 165 cm
**WEIGHT:** 60 kg
**HAIR:** Dark Brown/Black

**EYES:** Brown
**BUILD:** Slightly overweight to medium
**COMPLEXION:** Olive or Light skinned
**CHARACTERISTICS:** Long shaped face, wears a full beard, a trimmed beard and clean shaven. Has been known to wear glasses.

On January 6, 1995, a fire broke out in an apartment in Manila occupied by KHALED SHAIKH MOHAMMAD. The information developed from the investigation into this small fire, ultimately saved the lives of thousands of people.

The investigation revealed that in August 1994 through January 1995 in this apartment and elsewhere, KHALED SHAIKH MOHAMMAD unlawfully and willfully conspired to bomb U.S. civilian airliners by placing explosive devices on twelve airliners flying over the Pacific Ocean during a two day period in January 1995.

Had any of these devices exploded, innocent lives would have been lost. People should not have to live under the fear of terrorism. KHALED SHAIKH MOHAMMAD has been indicted for his involvement in this deadly conspiracy and must stand trial for his crimes.

The United States is offering a reward of up to $2,000,000 for information leading to the arrest or prosecution of KHALED SHAIKH MOHAMMAD. If you have any information about KHALED, contact the nearest U.S. embassy or consulate. In the United States, you may call your local Federal Bureau of Investigation or contact the Department of State Diplomatic Security Service at 1-800-HEROES-1, or write to:

**HEROES ■ Post Office Box 96781 ■ Washington, D.C. ■ 20090-6781 U.S.A.**
**www.heroes.net ■ e-mail: bsmith@heroes.net**

Diplomatic Security Service

The United States offered a $2 million reward for information leading to KSM's capture in the late 1990s. The amount was raised to $25 million after 9/11. *(United States Government)*

KSM spent most of the years prior to 9/11 in Karachi; this is thought to be one of the apartments where he lived. *(Terry McDermott)*

KSM was captured along with Mustafa al-Hawsawi in this house in the sedate Westridge subdivision of Rawalpindi, Pakistan, in March 2003. Rawalpindi is the headquarters of the Pakistani military, near the capital of Islamabad, and many homeowners in the neighborhood were military officers. *(Noveed Ahmed)*

**11. REPLY TO THE MESSAGE**
الـرد عـلى الرسـالة

*Family and/or private news only*
اخبـار شخصـية أو عائلية فقط

USDOOGH00471

I received your first letter. Thanks to God that your letter was the first letter which I received from Pakistan, Lyari
I am alive, in good health and always praying for you all. Thanks for my family news.

12.

Date Feb 28 2007 التاريخ Signature الامضاء
The addressee is my cusin علاقة الصلة بيني وبين المرسل إليه

ISN-10024

B000062 **1. RED CROSS MESSAGE** رسـائل الصـليب الأحـمر USDOOGH00471

**2. SENDER / المرسل**

ICRC nb. US9-003041 رقم الصليب الأحمر
Full name Khalid Sheikh Mohd الاسم بالكامل
Father's name اسم الوالد بالكامل
Grand-father's name اسم الجد
Mother's name اسم الوالدة
Nationality Pakistani الجنسية
Date of birth 14-4-1965 تاريخ الميلاد Sex F M ذ أ الجنس
Place of birth village / القرية district / المنطقة province / المحافظة country / البلد مكان الميلاد
Refugee camp/Detention place معسكر اللاجئين/ مكان الأسر
Street الشارع
Village, District or City القرية/ المنطقة أو المدينة
Province/Country المحافظة/ البلد
Phone الهاتف House nb. رقم المنزل

TRANSFERRED

**3. ADDRESSEE / المرسل إليه**

ICRC nb. رقم الصليب الأحمر
Full name الاسم بالكامل
Father's name اسم الوالد بالكامل
Grand-father's name اسم الجد
Mother's name اسم الوالدة
Nationality Pakistani الجنسية
Date of birth تاريخ الميلاد Sex F M ذ أ الجنس
Place of birth village / القرية district / المنطقة province / المحافظة country / البلد مكان الميلاد
Refugee camp/Detention place Sayedabad 323/3 معسكر اللاجئين/ مكان الأسر
Street Darya Khan Road الشارع
Village, District or City Lyari, Karachi القرية/ المنطقة أو المدينة
Province/Country Pakistan المحافظة/ البلد
Phone الهاتف House nb. رقم المنزل

**4. INTERNATIONAL COMMITTEE OF THE RED CROSS**
اللجنة الدولية للصليب الأحمر
**19, av. de la Paix - 1202 Geneva, Switzerland**

MCR2 EN-AR 10.05 ACR

KSM's first letter home to his family from prison in Guantánamo. *(Terry McDermott)*

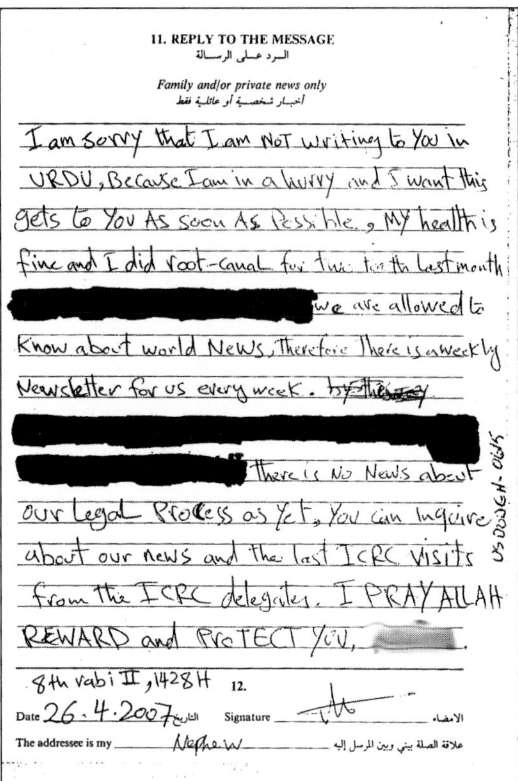

11. REPLY TO THE MESSAGE
الـرد عـلى الرسـالة

*Family and/or private news only*
أخبار شخصية أو عائلية فقط

I am sorry that I am NOT writing to You in URDU, Because I am in a hurry and I want this gets to You As soon As Possible. My health is fine and I did root-canal for two teeth last month [redacted] we are allowed to Know about world News, Therefore There is a weekly Newsletter for us every week. ~~by the way~~ [redacted] there is No News about our Legal Process as Yet. You can inquire about our news and the last ICRC visits from the ICRC delegates. I PRAY ALLAH REWARD and ProTECT YOU, [redacted].

8th rabi II, 1428 H 12.

Date 26.4.2007 التاريخ Signature الامضاء

The addressee is my Nephew علاقة الصلة بيني وبين المرسل إليه

US DODGH-0615

Almost all of KSM's letters home from Guantánamo are written in English. The letters contain mainly inquiries about the health of his family. *(Terry McDermott)*

5. MESSAGE
نـص الرسـالة

*Family and/or private news only*
أخبار شخصية أو عائلية فقط

• in the name of Allah, Most Gracious, Most Merciful

All praise is due to Allah. I praise Him and seek His aid and His forgiveness and I seek refuge in Allah from our evil in ourselves and from our bad deeds.

Asslamu Alaikum Warahmatullah wa Barakatuhu

You was the first man who asked me to send my picture (before two & half years)

Now they allowed us to take & send our picture

Say "Ma sha Allah" & don't forget to pray for all Mujaheen around the world.

The Exalted Allah said: "Nothing shall befall us save that which Allah has ordained for us. He is our Protector. And in Allah then should the believers put their turst."

USDODGH-0199622 6.

Date 25/6/09 التاريخ Signature الامضاء

The addressee is my Cousin علاقة الصلة بيني وبين المرسل إليه

This 2009 letter from Mohammed to his cousin could be read as a plea for absolution. *(Terry McDermott)*

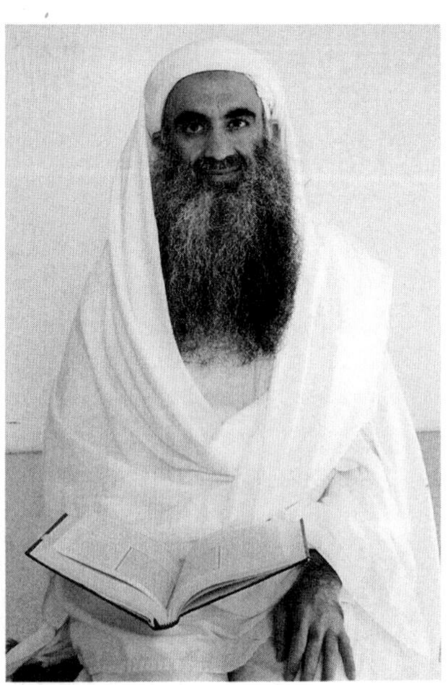

KSM at Guantánamo in 2009. *(Courtesy Mohammed family)*

saying the U.S. would go after those harboring Al Qaeda just as aggressively as it would pursue the terror network itself.

By Friday, September 14, Tenet and Cofer Black, the chief of the Counterterrorist Center, had drawn up a comprehensive plan to take out Al Qaeda and its Taliban protectors in Afghanistan as the opening shot in a global intelligence-gathering, kill-or-capture campaign. Tenet, Black, and deputy director John McLaughlin briefed the president and his War Cabinet the next day at Camp David on their plan, which they titled "Destroying International Terrorism."[8] Black in particular could be a great salesman. He was a passionate, hyperpatriotic man, charismatic to friends, blustery to enemies. He had more than a few of both. He had also won bragging rights by squaring off against bin Laden when the two were in Sudan in 1994, and Black caught wind of—and thwarted—a plot by bin Laden to assassinate him. By the end of the weekend, Bush handed the "get bin Laden and Al Qaeda" portfolio to the CIA. Much of it was immediately delegated to Black. Most of the initial effort would focus on destroying Al Qaeda's safe haven in Afghanistan, using the Northern Alliance and Pashtun leaders in the south to fight the Taliban.

Dale Watson and his successor, Pat D'Amuro, would accompany Robert Mueller to the White House to argue that the Bureau needed to play a central role, but they never had much of a chance. The terrorists would be treated from then forward as enemies in wartime, not criminals. The long-term consequences of this—what do you do with them when the war is over?—were not well thought out, or really thought out at all. But few people were interested in long-term anything then.

Mueller was new to the high councils of government and would probably not have been much of a match for the CIA's Tenet in any case. Tenet was a creature of the bureaucracy and a master at finding its hidden levers. The FBI's main advantage—that it had been the premier agency—was blunted by the fact that Mueller could hardly argue it had succeeded. The evidence of failure—nearly three thousand dead—was indisputable.

The most obvious particular points of failure were much discussed almost immediately after September 11. One of them concerned a memo written in the Bureau's Phoenix office concerning the number of Middle Eastern men training as pilots. The memo had been widely ignored. What could or should have been done about that at the time—mid-July of 2001—was less than clear. The 9/11 pilots had all concluded their training long before that and were in the final stages of preparations for the attacks. It was clear, however, that a piece of insightful, evidence-based analysis had been done on the ground, sent to headquarters, and quickly forgotten.

There were other missed opportunities to learn about the 9/11 plot prior to its execution, and the Bureau bore responsibility for its share of these—notably in the case of Zacarias Moussaoui, who proved to be spectacularly ill-suited to any sort of stealthy operation. The opposite, in fact, was nearer the truth. He specialized in calling attention to himself.

"Hello, Mrs. Matt," he wrote in an e-mail, applying to Pan Am International Flight Academy. "I am Mrs. Zacarias! I contacted you today by phone. Basically, I need to know if you can help to achieve my 'Goal' my dream. I would like to fly in a 'professional' like manners one of the big airliners. I have to made my mind which of the following: Boeing 747, 757, 767, or 777 and or Airbus 300 (it will depend on the cost and which one is the easiest to learn)."[9]

Once enrolled at the school's Minneapolis branch, he behaved erratically from the first day, so much so that officials at the school called the FBI, who came, interviewed, and arrested him. Moussaoui had direct communications by telephone and e-mail with Ramzi bin al-Shibh, KSM's top lieutenant in planning the attacks. The local FBI office in Minneapolis wanted to obtain a special national security search warrant to examine Moussaoui's belongings, but FBI headquarters in Washington declared there was insufficient evidence even to make such a request. Noting that Minneapolis had suggested Moussaoui might be preparing to hijack a plane, HQ accused the local office of overreacting.

This was cast after the attacks as a sign of the FBI's general suffocation by process, a too-rigid adherence on too-strict procedures. The FBI could, and did, argue that those procedures had resulted in dozens of terrorist convictions. The argument held little water now. The Bureau by general consensus had failed to protect the nation. Mueller himself was apologetic, to a degree that many of his subordinates—especially the career folk—felt went too far.

An oddity in this was that the CIA was a full partner, perhaps the senior partner, in the failure. It had at least one indisputable opportunity to learn about the September 11 plot before it was executed—the curious case of Khalid al-Mihdhar and Nawaf al-Hazmi, whom the CIA had followed to Malaysia in early 2000. The agency knew the two Saudis were associates of bin Laden; the agency also knew both men had entry visas to the United States. While it lost surveillance of the pair in Southeast Asia, the agency within a couple of months had determined that both men had flown from Bangkok to Los Angeles, where they disappeared from official sight. The agency, which had as a matter of routine kept the FBI and the rest of government aware of the future hijackers' movement to Malaysia, for some reason failed to alert the rest of government, notably the FBI, that they might be in the country. In at least one instance, they actively withheld information. Pellegrino, the FBI's KSM case agent, happened to be in Thailand in early 2000. When abroad he routinely met with local CIA agents. In Bangkok, a CIA officer showed him photos of the two Saudis and asked Pellegrino if he recognized them, which he did not. When Pellegrino asked who they were, the CIA man was vague: just something we're working on, he said.

The pair of Saudis had flown to Los Angeles in mid-January, then had moved to San Diego, where Hazmi remained for most of a year. Mihdhar grew bored in California and lonesome for his family, leading him to return to Yemen for several months and enter the United States yet again in July of 2001. The CIA hadn't asked that he be placed on a terrorist watch list until August 23, a month after he had returned and just weeks before 9/11. There was no intelligence failure more obvious or inexplicable than this. Two known Al Qaeda operatives with direct links to Khalid Sheikh Mohammed and Osama bin Laden were essentially hidden from the rest of the government.

The CIA was no better prepared for the new post-9/11 world than anyone else, but one crucial distinction favored the agency over the FBI. The FBI, looking at the smoldering ruins in New York, the hole in the earth in a Pennsylvania farm field, and the skid trench outside the Pentagon, reflexively asked: What happened? They would almost certainly do an astonishing job of re-creating the history. To which the rest of government would say, So what? The CIA was far better at looking past the disaster that had occurred and asking the defining question of the period: What next?

Knowing which direction to look did not give the agency special insight. Everything, said one top official, was "seat of the pants." Plots such as the one that had just been executed had simply not been discussed at the highest level of the CIA. "It was just not done," an agency executive said. "I was on Tenet's top staff for a year before nine eleven and no one talked about this kind of thing, an airline attack."[10]

There had, of course, been plenty of warning about *something*. Here, for example, are the titles of a series of reports from the CIA to the rest of the government that were written before the attacks, and were prepared in large part by Barbara Sude and the rest of the Al Qaeda analysts:

"Sunni Terrorist Threat Growing" (February 6, 2001)
"Bin Ladin [*sic*] Planning Multiple Operations" (April 20, 2001)
"Bin Ladin Public Profile May Presage Attack" (May 3, 2001)
"Terrorist Groups Said Cooperating on US Hostage Plot" (May 23, 2001)
"Bin Ladin Network's Plans Advancing" (May 26, 2001)

"Bin Ladin Attacks May Be Imminent" (June 23, 2001)
"Bin Ladin and Associates Making Near-Term Threats" (June 25, 2001)
"Bin Ladin Planning High-Profile Attacks" (June 30, 2001)
"Bin Ladin Threats Are Real" (June 30, 2001)
"Planning for Bin Ladin Attacks Continues, Despite Delays" (July 2, 2001)
"Bin Ladin Plans Delayed but Not Abandoned" (July 13, 2001)
"One Bin Ladin Operation Delayed, Others Ongoing" (July 25, 2001)
"Bin Ladin Determined to Strike in US" (August 6, 2001)

The reports, as Tenet described them later, were maddeningly short on detail, on actionable intelligence.[11] The simple fact was that after the attacks the warnings were easy to see. Before the attacks, hardly anyone had their eyes open. Those few scattered through the government who did were largely dismissed as cranks. There was enough blame to go around; virtually every agency that had a function in protecting the country was due its share. Not wanting to make the same mistake again—that is, not wanting to wait for specific details that might never come and be blamed after the fact for not finding them—the government now regarded everything as high priority. Raw intelligence was coming into Langley and likely as not the next morning was deposited on the president's desk in the form of a PDB. The FBI, seeing how business was to be done in this new era, did the same. If a tip seemed at all feasible, it was passed up the line. There were literally tens of thousands of them. There was little time and little thought given to analyzing them. When direction was needed, gut reactions won the day, most days.

# CHAPTER 12
# KSM Ascendant

## *Pakistan, Autumn and Winter 2001*

The U.S. military response to the attacks was launched on October 7, 2001. It was swift and devastating, unseating the Taliban government in Afghanistan by Thanksgiving. Al Qaeda, without a sponsor, was dislodged and on the run. When the United States declined to deploy enough troops to block their exit, bin Laden and Ayman al-Zawahiri escaped through the snowy passes of Tora Bora into Pakistan. Others weren't so lucky. Mohammed Atef, the military commander of Al Qaeda, was killed in Kandahar—under bombardment from American air forces—in mid-November. Atef had been among bin Laden's most influential aides, and his death left a huge void in Al Qaeda's leadership. Khalid Sheikh Mohammed filled it.[1]

Mohammed had been rising in the Al Qaeda hierarchy even before 9/11. Although he refrained from pledging an oath to bin Laden after bin Laden agreed to the 9/11 plan, he assumed an ever-larger role in the organization. He had begun by assisting with media and computer operations; then, even while running the 9/11 plot, was formally named head of the media committee. After

9/11, with Atef dead and the organization on the brink of disintegration, Mohammed took charge of bringing some order to the retreat from Afghanistan. He convened a meeting of Al Qaeda leadership in December in Zormat, in eastern Afghanistan, to bring some order to the retreat. He and Zubaydah and other bin Laden lieutenants decided their fighters should retreat less haphazardly; they decided who should go where and when. Even before the attacks, KSM had helped organize a collection of safe houses in Karachi and elsewhere in Pakistan, many of them operated by jihadi groups like Lashkar-e-Jhangvi, Harkat-ul-Mujahideen, Jaish-e-Mohammed, Sipah-e-Sahaba Pakistan, and Lashkar-e-Taiba, with whom KSM had had relations for years. He wanted Al Qaeda to be ready for the U.S. response.

The militant groups were a classic Pakistani creation. Most originated in the 1980s with full support and funding from the Pakistan spy agency, the ISI, as frontline resistance to India in the disputed territory of Kashmir. Dozens of different groups were supported by the ISI as they morphed and splintered over the years, and ISI officers established their training regimens and sat on councils to plan strategy and attacks.[2] KSM had been living in Karachi off and on since 1992 and had developed connections throughout this underground, immersing himself in the jihadi world of Pakistan and cultivating relationships among its many branches. It is almost impossible to overstate the importance of such groups throughout Pakistan. Within Pakistan's urban areas they are nearly omnipresent, and in some cities they control entire districts. After 9/11, the groups were indispensable in helping KSM evacuate key operational Al Qaeda members from Afghanistan into Pakistan and helping them regroup, in part by providing money, logistics, safe havens, and a ready army of trustworthy foot soldiers. Those connections and his ties with a network of ethnic Baluch, including his family, formed the basis of KSM's ability to operate throughout the country. The Baluchs numbered about six million within Pakistan, with millions more across the borders in Iran and Afghanistan.

The Baluch comprise the majority in the southwestern province of Baluchistan, but the largest, densest concentration of Baluch in Pakistan is in Karachi's Lyari district, a sprawling, overflowing enclave of well more than a million people where outsiders—including the police—seldom venture. Lyari is a warren of narrow, deeply rutted roads. It is in many ways a city within a city, with private armies substituting for municipal and state security forces. The Baluch are known for their colorful dress, especially women's clothing, which is detailed with elaborate embroidery in vibrant colors. Jingle buses, the main means of travel between Baluchistan and Lyari, have similar dazzling decorative schemes. The buses and dresses, however, are among the few touches of brightness in Lyari. A haze of dust hangs overhead throughout the day, and at night turns the slum into a bleak netherworld ruled at gunpoint by sectarian and ethnic gangs, criminal bands, and drug dealers.

Much of KSM's extended family was in Iran. But those who lived in Pakistan were mainly in Lyari.[3] This provided a safe haven to which KSM could always retreat if the need arose. It was like fleeing to another country, but you could take a taxi across the border.

Much of Al Qaeda's membership seemed panicked by the ferocity of the American response to September 11. Initially, KSM was concerned, too. He later told a U.S. interrogator that he rejoiced until the moment the towers fell down. "Shit," he said. "We've awakened a sleeping bear.... I think we bit off more than we could chew. We had no idea what the cowboy [Bush] would do."[4]

It didn't take KSM long to recover his swagger. In some ways, it was as if he had lived his whole life to prepare for this moment. He arranged passage and shelter for those terrorists who would scatter across the Indian subcontinent, and often helped them through to the Middle East, Africa, Southeast Asia, and the Americas, where they were able to re-form Al Qaeda cells and launch attacks. The exodus was accomplished while the eyes of the world were trained on the region, looking for exactly this sort of activity.

KSM seemed not to notice. He traveled freely, commuting to the Afghanistan border lands over and over in the months immediately after 9/11. At times he and Zubaydah would stay at the border and decide which lucky fighters would be most suitable for bringing back to Pakistan and which would have to return to the battle in Afghanistan.[5] He detailed plans and directives. He dispensed cash by the hundreds of thousands of dollars. But KSM wasn't relegating himself to logistics. He calmed jittery nerves and gave orders for training classes to be established, giving the Al Qaeda refugees something to do while they awaited transit. The instruction, however, was hardly innocuous.[6] KSM wanted his fighters to be trained in assassinations and kidnappings so that they could mount such operations against Americans when they returned to their home countries.

KSM was popular among the Al Qaeda rank and file, who saw him as an effective leader. Coworkers described him as an intelligent, efficient, and even-tempered manager who approached his projects with a single-minded dedication that he expected his colleagues to share. Zubaydah, perhaps a bit jealous of KSM's ascension after his own years of toiling for Al Qaeda, expressed more qualified admiration for KSM's innate creativity, emphasizing instead his ability to incorporate the improvements suggested by others. Another top Al Qaeda commander, Abd al-Rahim al-Nashiri, was similarly measured, alleging that although KSM floated many general ideas for attacks, he rarely conceived a specific operation himself. In any case, as one U.S. intelligence operative would later say, KSM was showing all the signs of a successful leader of a Fortune 500 company—leveraging the talents and skills of others, coordinating multiple projects, building key relationships, and getting things done.[7]

To carry out his plans, KSM still favored young men with Western passports or other connections that would make their transit simpler and safer. The difficulty of getting the hijackers into the United States had been a fresh reminder of the importance of these resources, if one were needed. Customs security, mainly aimed at blocking economic migrants, not terrorists, was virtually America's sole defense against 9/11. In two years of trying, Mohammed had been able to get only the nineteen hijackers into the country to take part in the plot.

Using men already at home in the West eliminated this problem. KSM sent Mohammed Jabarah, a Kuwaiti-born Canadian citizen, to Singapore to study attacks against Western embassies there. He sent Roche, the British-born citizen of Australia, to Australia; he was working closely with Christian Ganczarski, a German national, to launch an attack against a synagogue in Tunisia. Adnan el-Shukrijumah, a Saudi-born Florida resident, and Dhiren Barot, a British citizen of Indian descent, were tasked with casing potential U.S. targets, including Wall Street and the Panama Canal.

KSM was especially fond of those who, like him, had what seemed to be dual cultural identities, with one foot in the Arab world and the other in Asia. He also valued those with his own ability to speak both Arabic and Urdu. That was important, because top Al Qaeda leaders were invariably Arab, but the frontline soldiers, middle-rank officers, and support networks for Al Qaeda were more likely to be South Asian. If they had a grounding in the West, especially in America or the UK, even better. One example was Shukrijumah, who grew up in Saudi Arabia, then Trinidad, then South Florida. Another was Barot, an India-born, London-reared veteran of the Kashmir insurgency who went to terror camps in Pakistan before KSM sent him to Southeast Asia for more training. When he was ready, KSM dispatched him to the United States to surveil targets and help plot attacks. With a group of coconspirators, all Britons of Pakistani origin, Barot plotted to bomb the New York Stock Exchange, the International Monetary Fund headquarters, and the World Bank, among other targets. Authorities later disclosed that Barot had planned to use limousines packed with explosives and radioactive "dirty" bombs for the attacks.

What was extraordinary about KSM's plans, apart from the sheer volume of them at a time when he could have been lying low, was the degree of personal attention he devoted to the recruits he designated to execute them. He was able, somehow, to shield them from the biggest counterterrorism dragnet in history—and not just in Pakistan but in those other countries to which he had sent operatives and support cells. Unlike the 9/11 plot, in which he used intermediaries, or cutouts, to disburse funds and communicate with the pilots and hijackers, he personally directed many of these smaller plots. Jabarah spent an entire week in KSM's Karachi apartment before being sent to Southeast Asia.[8] KSM shepherded Roche back and forth between safe houses in KSM's traditional mode of travel: a Karachi taxi with a personal driver.

He usually introduced himself as Mukhtar, and in at least one instance asked that he be addressed in e-mail communications as Mukh. He so endeared himself to a young Pakistani American, Majid Khan, that Khan referred to him familiarly as Chacha—"uncle" in Urdu.

He was low-key, easygoing, with a sense of humor, self-deprecating and cracking jokes. KSM didn't mind boasting a bit—"big-noting himself," as Roche put it.[9] The two had enjoyed several dinners together at nice Karachi cafés after daytime meetings in which KSM was assessing him to see if he was fit and trustworthy for jihad. KSM deemed that he was, and sent him and a chaperone off to Afghanistan with a note to give to "the sheikh" when he got there. He never told Roche that the sheikh was actually bin Laden, who received him warmly once he read the short handwritten scrawl from KSM.

KSM also told Roche he controlled all the Al Qaeda cash that came through Pakistan, saying that at one point he had received a suitcase stuffed with $400,000. This appears not to have been a fanciful boast. Some months later he gave $500,000 to a Pakistani businessman, ostensibly as an investment but more likely as a means of storing the money safely.[10] Unlike Osama bin Laden, who hinted repeatedly about something major about to happen in the months prior to 9/11, KSM gave no sign to those around him of huge plans afoot and in fact spent considerable time and energy trying to get bin Laden to shut up. KSM confided to associates that he was pulling his hair out in frustration over bin Laden's inept meddling. As bin Laden boasted at the training camps of something big about to happen, KSM simply told a couple of his recruits that they needed to depart Pakistan before 9/11 without ever mentioning why, and summoned others back to the fold.

He was similarly cool after the attacks. He took on the added responsibility of engineering the underground railroad out of Afghanistan, evacuating not only key operatives but their families and providing them with financial support. He oversaw specially trained groups of document forgers and travel facilitators who churned out the documents needed to stay safely in Pakistan, or to travel through so they could help rebuild the network elsewhere. He went about his main business much as he had before. This meant mainly one thing—more plots.

KSM sent Richard Reid, a British convert to Islam, and Saajid Badat to Europe with shoes lined with explosives, the idea in Reid's case being to ignite the explosives aboard a transatlantic flight on Christmas Day of 2001 and blow the airliner and its passengers apart. He sent José Padilla, the Puerto Rican convert from Florida, to Chicago with the idea of causing natural gas explosions in high-rise apartment buildings. He and his nephew Ali Abdul Aziz Ali outfitted Majid Khan, the young man from Baltimore, with a suicide vest to test whether he was sincere in his desire to work for them. KSM then drove Khan to a mosque where Pakistani president Pervez Musharraf was scheduled to appear, and let him out of the car. KSM had told Khan that he, KSM, held the detonator. When Khan proved reliable by not fleeing, KSM tasked him with returning to the United States and studying the idea of blowing up gas stations. When KSM heard that that could possibly ignite massive gas tanks and underground fuel lines, it became one of his favored plots, especially for the heartland of the United States. After an introduction by Khan, KSM sent Iyman Faris, an

Ohio truck driver, to New York to examine the possibility of cutting the cables on the Brooklyn Bridge and derailing passenger trains. He had other sleepers in the United States, too, including Uzair Paracha in New York City and Aafia Siddiqui, a Pakistani woman in Boston who had science degrees from the Massachusetts Institute of Technology and Brandeis University.

KSM directed the truck-bombing of a synagogue on the island of Djerba, Tunisia, Al Qaeda's first successful effort after 9/11. Twenty-one people died. Most of them were German tourists; that got the German government after him.

He directed bombers in a failed attempt to hit the U.S. consulate in Karachi. They followed with a successful attack on the Sheraton hotel across the street. KSM later subcontracted an attack against French engineers who were staying at another nearby American chain hotel, the Marriott, that killed twenty-two. With each attack, the international posse pursuing KSM grew, nation by nation.

New recruits came to Mohammed through various routes. Some were sent from elsewhere around the globe by old comrades like Hambali, the head of Jemaah Islamiyah in Southeast Asia. Others were recommended by friends in the Karachi underground. Still others were Al Qaeda recruits who had been singled out at the camps as potential agents and sent to KSM for both vetting and training. Keeping track of all this required a constant stream of communications, both within Pakistan and beyond. For that, KSM juggled as many as a dozen devices, burning through cell phones, satellite phones, and, especially, SIM cards at a manic pace, always paranoid about operational security.

Communications is a point of vulnerability for contemporary terrorists. Unless they're lone wolves who intend to stay that way, they occasionally have to leave their local lairs and cross the electronic borders into a high-tech frontier that is rigorously patrolled by Western spies and satellites and interception equipment. Technology both enabled these terrorists and exposed them. They were always safest in the no-tech world of nitrate truck bombs and switchblade knives, but their horizons were necessarily limited in that realm. If they wanted to take their plans out into the broader world, to Europe or America or anywhere beyond the neighborhood, they could. But with every step they took into this new, modern digital age, they risked detection.

KSM knew this and took care to minimize his risks. When, immediately after 9/11, the situation was most treacherous, he at times eschewed modern communication systems entirely and sent coded messages into Afghanistan by donkey. When the situation demanded he use telephones, he hid behind the anonymity of prepaid phone cards that could be bought in bulk without identification. Each SIM could be used for whatever brief period he desired, then discarded. In this way, KSM thought, he could prevent sophisticated tracking satellites from finding any pattern to focus on. Every week, every day, even every call could be made under the identity of a new SIM. He instructed recruits to follow his security protocols exactly. In some cases he instructed followers to make a draft of an e-mail, then he'd access the same account and review it in the drafts folder, assuming that if it wasn't sent, it would be safer. When he was forced to talk to someone by telephone or to use instant messaging, he employed codes that were so elaborate that his subordinates sometimes had no idea what he was talking about.

## *Islamabad, Pakistan, September 2001*

The United States and Pakistan, two countries that had barely tolerated one another before September 11, were forced into a shotgun marriage by the attacks. Soon, CIA director George Tenet and his boss, the president, began trumpeting Pakistan's newfound spirit of cooperation. Circumstances on the ground were much different—and much tougher and testier.

For more than a year before the September 11 attacks, Islamabad station chief Bob Grenier had been busy trying to engineer a split between Taliban leaders and Al Qaeda, secretly traveling to remote locations to meet with the leaders of potential splinter factions and exploiting the differences between the often backward local tribal elders and bin Laden and his often arrogant group of Arab guerrillas. The effort ultimately failed.

Grenier had been operating for more than a year with virtually no assistance from the Pakistani security services and quite probably a good amount of subterfuge from them, though he couldn't prove it. After 9/11, changes were promised. Those changes might have been prompted by deputy secretary of state Richard Armitage, who two days after 9/11 arranged a meeting with Pakistani ambassador Maleeha Lodhi and General Mahmood Ahmed, the ISI chief, who happened to be visiting Washington. Armitage's message was brief and blunt: give us your fullest cooperation or we will bomb Pakistan back to the Stone Age. Washington also lifted the crippling economic sanctions against Pakistan. Billions in potential aid were let loose even as Pakistan's military, its powerful Inter-Services Intelligence apparatus, and nuclear weapons custodians were linked closely to religious fundamentalists, the Taliban, and Al Qaeda. In return, besides supporting U.S. military operations and blocking the borders, Washington expected Pakistan to fully support U.S. intelligence-gathering efforts in the region. That never happened.

Musharraf made some gestures; for example, he fired Ahmed, who had been a symbol of recalcitrance. But from the CIA's vantage point, that and other pro-U.S. gestures by Musharraf only made things worse on the ground. The ISI and the Pakistani army were furious with Musharraf for sacking Ahmed, who had been a longtime supporter of the Taliban and Pakistani jihadi groups. They resented the influx of suspiciously athletic U.S. embassy officials, who, it turned out, were part of a massive CIA surge.

The expansion came at a time when the State Department was ordering a drawdown in its embassy staff that left many offices vacant. An army of carpenters descended on the empty space and remodeled it for the growing CIA presence. By the time the buildup was complete, Grenier had more than a hundred people working out of the Islamabad station and from bases in Karachi, Lahore, Peshawar, and elsewhere. The FBI, on the other hand—even after 9/11—seldom had more than six agents in the country, and only two of those were full-time. The others rotated in and out on temporary assignments, often just for one or two weeks. At more than $8,000 per round-trip business-class ticket, it was a curious way to staff a war. Few, if any, of the agents stayed long enough to actually know what they were doing.

The CIA agents, analysts, and case officers came by the chartered planeful. Other jets arrived carrying multimillion-dollar loads of high-tech gear—heavy weapons and handguns, battering rams to knock down the doors of suspected Al Qaeda safe houses, night-vision goggles, and eavesdropping equipment so sophisticated that most of the officers didn't even know what it was. The first task for this new army was to deal with the flight of Al Qaeda fighters out of Afghanistan.

When Jennifer Keenan, the assistant legal attaché for Pakistan—one of the two full-time FBI staff—first arrived in Islamabad in July 2001, she brought with her a massive book of photographs. It was a scrapbook of a kind, but a very particular kind. It contained photographs of every Al Qaeda figure, every radical Islamist she could get her hands on. She had been a member of the FBI's Joint Terrorism Task Force in New York and intended when she received the assignment to Pakistan to continue that work. The book was the pride and joy of the New York JTTF and had been started years earlier by veterans like NYPD detective Louis Napoli. Many of the old hands on the task force had considered her their goddaughter and were protective of her until they realized she didn't need it. Keenan could outrun, outwork, outperform, and probably out-bench-press any of them, even with her wiry 5-feet-3-inch frame.

Keenan had been a stockbroker before joining the Bureau, and spent her early years working on financial crime. She played a key role in a big health care fraud case, and as a reward was offered the chance to join the New York field office's Al Qaeda squad—not her first choice. The embassy bombings had just occurred, and she spent much of the next year deployed to Africa investigating the bombings. When she returned, she took a desk just across a partition from Frank Pellegrino and Matt Besheer—Frankie and Matty, as she called them.

She was amazed by their dedication, the sheer amount of work they did, the hours they worked, their creativity overseas in gathering evidence and intelligence—the fact that they brooked no bullshit from anybody. She made their habits her own. Plus, she loved the work. It was a secret world almost never glimpsed by outsiders, alluring and important. Besheer was so impressed by her commitment he gave her a windup toy—the Energizer Bunny. Keenan was relentless. She was also an adrenaline junkie who jumped at assignments other agents, even on the JTTF, avoided. When a job opened in the Bureau's two-person Pakistan office, she applied, having been there to work sources in the past and liking it. She was relatively young, unencumbered by family, and already traveling so much—why not live overseas? She got the pager text from Pat D'Amuro while heli-skiing in British Columbia—you got the job, if you want it. Pakistan was the center of radical Islam, right next door to the headquarters of bin Laden's network. Where better to be?

Keenan's deployment to Pakistan was a cause for celebration for her colleagues at the New York JTTF; they saw it as a solidification of their place at the center of the U.S. counterterrorism universe. At the raucous going-away party they threw for her, an FBI sketch artist drew her a custom T-shirt that showed her running after the Energizer Bunny that Besheer had given her—which by then had become her nickname. Underneath the sketch, it said: JENNIFER, PLEASE SLOW DOWN. And the Jennifer on the T-shirt was wearing her own T-shirt, which had Osama bin Laden's likeness on it, over which was a red circle with an *X* drawn through it.

Within a few years of joining the JTTF squad, Keenan was one of its most valued and well-traveled members. She was named a team leader on the USS *Cole* investigation in Yemen. She was often the only female FBI agent on such assignments, and the rare supervisor among them. Keenan quickly developed a reputation as a spitfire—very bright, hard-charging, and argumentative to a fault. She was virtually fearless. "She never hesitated to be the first one in the door. Tough as nails. No problem pulling the gun out, kicking in a door, taking someone down," said one colleague from numerous overseas assignments. "I would go in any dangerous situation with her. I trust her in the ghetto or in the boardroom. Her ability to grasp a situation, to say this is what we're going to do, what we should do... She is probably the best FBI agent we've ever had."

Keenan had put in for the Pakistan job because her constant travel overseas meant that an actual posting to a foreign assignment would allow her to be "at home" more, a luxury that might give her a life outside of work. For Keenan, that meant running, so she joined the Islamabad chapter of the Hash House Harriers, a hardcore physical fitness group that describes itself as "a drinking group with a running problem." She cherished the late Sunday afternoon runs, but because Pakistan was so dangerous, she and the others—many of them security types from various embassies—weren't even allowed to know that day's running trail until they were actually running it. It was the only time the self-described control freak ever allowed herself to be at the mercy of someone else's planning schedule. The rare opportunity to get out into the open air made it worthwhile, even if she had to run in long pants, so as not to violate local cultural standards—and run without her Glock semiautomatic, so as not to be weighed down.

After the runs, the Harriers would head to someone's house in the diplomatic quarters, usually the Australians' or the Brits', and they would drink beer and laugh and tell stories into the night.

Soon after 9/11, though, the weekend runs became infrequent. The deteriorating security situation made it harder and harder to run the risk. By the spring of 2002, Keenan's running was restricted mostly to the treadmill at the embassy gym.

Keenan worked seven days a week, from dawn well past dusk, and she forged a wary bond with Grenier, the CIA station chief. They also shared a frustration with the Pakistani security agencies, which refused to do much to help them. FBI agents are not spies. They're far closer to cops and they can't do their jobs abroad without a minimum of cooperation from the host government. In Pakistan, Keenan wasn't getting it. She submitted dozens of requests to the Pakistanis for information, guidance, records, assistance on even the most run-of-the-mill fugitives. They responded helpfully to almost none.

Keenan occasionally took matters into her own hands. When it became apparent that Al Qaeda fighters routinely used a particular phone booth in Afghanistan, she asked the CIA to wire the location with sound and video. The CIA rejected the request out of hand. So Keenan did it on her own, producing a regular stream of intelligence.

After 9/11—and after Armitage's warning about the Stone Age—things changed. Keenan and Grenier were summoned to ISI headquarters along with the deputy CIA station chief and Chris Reimann, the FBI legal attaché. Reimann was Keenan's boss, but given her long background in counterterrorism, he had deferred much of that portfolio to her.

At the meeting, the high command of the ISI—technically a military intelligence agency—suddenly promised full cooperation with the Americans in their war against Al Qaeda. Keenan's problem was that she really didn't have anything she needed help with at the moment. The legal attachés don't originate much work on their own. If someone in Washington wants to know about Mohammed Abdul Mohammed from Gulbai Colony in Sindh Province, the legats make the formal request in Islamabad. After the attacks, nobody in Washington knew what they wanted to know. Sometimes it seemed they didn't even know their own names. Resources that might have been directed against Al Qaeda, resources that might have been devoted to hunting down those responsible for September 11, sat idle while Washington tried to determine what to do. So Keenan and Reimann began this new era of cooperation by recycling all the requests that hadn't been acted upon for the last few years. Suddenly, it seemed, Islamabad knew quite a bit about the Mohammed Abdul Mohammeds of the world. Keenan called the requests from Washington screamers, a lot of noise and very little content.

At that first meeting after 9/11, the Americans had been introduced to the man who would become their liaison. Colonel Tariq* was a seemingly mild-mannered army officer who, like other ISI officers, wore civilian clothes, usually a suit.

Tariq was soft-spoken, very proper, and deliberate in speech. He spoke excellent English, and showed great patience toward his new American counterparts. What he lacked in stature—he was a wispy 5 feet 7 in his wingtips—he made up for in resolve.

Oftentimes in those early months, Keenan and Grenier would arrange an urgent meeting with Tariq, who, once briefed, commonly responded: "You have handed me a grenade; what do you want me to do with it?"

Keenan grew fond of Tariq, and the feeling seemed mutual. The two traveled frequently together, and Tariq helped to arrange raids. Even when it seemed odd that all the places they raided turned up empty, Keenan was sure it had little to do with Tariq, but perhaps everything to do with his superiors.

For the most part, Keenan's and Reimann's efforts were tactical, not strategic: chasing one piece of information or one person after another. To a large extent, they knew they were just biding time, waiting for whatever would come next. They knew there would be an American military response, presumably a ferocious one. What that meant for Pakistan was unclear. Pakistanis once before, in 1979, had attacked the American embassy in fury. The FBI legats knew something was coming; they just didn't know what. They quickly found out.

Once the massive bombing raids started across the northern border in Afghanistan, the old requests were set aside. Many of the militants fleeing Afghanistan were turned in to authorities, often for a bounty, and if they weren't Pakistani, the authorities in Islamabad

*To protect his identity, Colonel Tariq's full name has not been used.

had little use for them. So they asked the Americans to take them off their hands. Most of those presented to the Americans were small fish, but were often dangerous enough to require doing something with them.

Donald Borelli, an FBI agent specializing in weapons of mass destruction investigations out of the Dallas, Texas, field office, deployed to Islamabad in December. He was single and looking for adventure. He was thrown into Al Qaeda interdiction. Almost as soon as he arrived, the Pakistanis reported capturing a bunch of fighters at the border and were bringing them to Islamabad for processing. But the bus carrying the prisoners overturned, and everyone escaped. The Pakistanis flooded the area with troops and recaptured most of the men. Borelli rushed to Peshawar and worked his way through the captives, identifying, fingerprinting, and interviewing them. He then returned to Islamabad and the same cycle repeated itself—absent the bus crashes—over and over. At times the Islamabad FBI agents felt like they were being overrun with fugitives, but from them they began getting information on potential Al Qaeda targets.

They soon began raids on these targets throughout the country. Most raids were led by a single CIA agent, an FBI agent if one was available (and when the CIA allowed it), and an ISI agent. Local police and army forces provided more manpower as needed. The Pakistani involvement was primarily at the point of attack. The U.S. provided almost all the intelligence, the Pakistanis the manpower, and the FBI the crime-scene exploitation—"bagging and tagging" the evidence. There was a raid almost every night.

In a usual crime scene in the U.S., investigators might spend a full day or two combing a site for evidence. In Pakistan, the locations were called Sensitive Site Exploitations and the time spent was usually an hour or less. Agents sprinted through safe houses collecting computers, cell phones, passports, whatever they could grab. They'd haul everything back to Islamabad, record it, and ship it back to the United States.

Keenan was meticulous about photographing and cataloging the evidence. The CIA never really understood this. They wanted to get whatever information they could, then move on to the next target. Keenan wanted to prepare for an eventual trial, and to build a database so she could begin to craft a mosaic out of all the disparate pieces of information.

By January, the intel was flowing in—through detainees at Guantánamo, other human intelligence, and high-tech intercepts. Even so, difficulties persisted. At one raid, as was the protocol, the Pakistani security forces went inside while Keenan and other Americans, all dressed in local *shalwar kameez*, idled outside. The lead Pakistani investigator returned and told Keenan the man they were looking for was not present. She was suspicious. Are you sure? she asked. He was sure. This had become such a frequent scenario that Keenan was expecting it, and was prepared. She pulled out a digital camera and asked the Pakistani officer if he would go take a photograph of the man inside. The Pakistani did as asked and when he returned, she pulled a photo out of her pocket and lined it up side by side with the photo on the camera. It was a perfect match. The Pakistani, either furious at being deceived, embarrassed at being caught protecting a local suspect, or both, went back inside and berated the man, then cuffed him and dragged him outside.

The next day Keenan ordered a bunch of digital cameras and ensured that they were taken on every raid. It was a breakthrough, one of several small victories that helped bring the Pakistani police into the fold. She also bought a scanner and began systematically cataloging every picture of every militant caught and every passport and document seized. This enabled her to begin building her database of bad guys—just as the FBI used to do with the Mafia. By late January, the Pakistanis and the Americans knew their roles and how to fulfill them. The raids became not just routine, but effective—as long as some elements of the all-powerful ISI were kept out of the loop. Their loyalties to the jihadis ran too deep.

The Americans grew reluctant to even brief the Pakistanis ahead of the raids. They'd tell them in the most general possible terms where the raid would be and what was the target—a grocery or a warehouse or whatever.

Grenier already knew that parts of Pakistan's government had deep relationships with local jihadi groups, and he was finding out firsthand how these groups formed part of the infrastructure Al Qaeda fighters used to escape into Pakistan and beyond. He couldn't tell if that infrastructure included the ISI or not, but there were indications that it did, and that made him wary.

The American agents were summoned time after time to process the many fleeing fighters caught at the border and elsewhere. After initial vetting on the ground, the captives—often veteran fighters fleeing Afghanistan—were loaded onto military aircraft and flown back to Afghanistan, to Bagram Airfield, where a huge holding facility was built. In some cases, they were taken to Guantánamo Bay naval base, where the U.S. government had created a makeshift detention center. Pakistan was happy to have any Arabs caught in the web shipped off, but vehemently refused to arrest Pakistani citizens, even when the Americans identified them as Al Qaeda. They resisted, in part, because they were afraid the captured men would reveal their ties to the ISI. One real effect of this was that it hindered the hunt for those who had planned and led the September 11 attacks. The investigators didn't know it yet, as the traditional thinking was that Al Qaeda comprised mostly Arabs, but at least some key players, including KSM and his family, were Pakistanis.

While the CIA bulked up its local forces with recent retirees called back to service—so-called green badgers, named for the color of the identity badges they were given—the FBI supplemented its staff with temporary assignments from its permanent force. Other agencies that were part of some of the bigger JTTFs in the States did the same. Tom McHale, a grizzled Port Authority detective assigned to the Newark JTTF, was one of the guys who arrived in Islamabad in mid-January and stayed for two months.

McHale was lucky to be alive. He had been severely injured while helping to rescue victims of the first World Trade Center attack, searing his lungs so badly he was hospitalized for three weeks. He happened to be just blocks from the Trade Center again in 2001 when the attacks occurred. He plunged inside once more to help rescue the injured, was himself severely injured again, but persevered. A former steelworker, he had spent many weeks working nights on the pile, helping cut through the wreckage to look for bodies, before reporting for a day's work on the JTTF.

Thirty-seven of his friends and colleagues in the Port Authority died in the Trade Center attacks. One of them, Donald McIntyre, perished trying to rescue others from inside the towers. The only son of a New York City cop, the much-decorated McIntyre was last seen on the thirty-second floor of the South Tower, climbing, hoping to find his cousin's husband, a stockbroker. McIntyre was just thirty-nine. He had been stocking up on time off so he could take paternity leave in December, when he and his wife were expecting their third child. His handcuffs, with MAC theatrically engraved on them, had been found in the smoking rubble. When McHale heard about the cuffs, he asked if he could take them with him to Pakistan. McIntyre's wife was honored to oblige—as long, she said, as he put the cuffs to work.

He did more than that. McHale arrived in Islamabad just as the raids were being ramped up. The Americans and the Pakistanis had not yet quite figured out what to think of one another. McHale was a big, bluff man, an emotional, powerful presence with a Marine buzz cut and a mischievous grin. He came to embrace Pakistan enthusiastically, careening around in an ill-fitting *shalwar* and guzzling the strong instant coffee they fondly called paste. He had told the Pakistanis about Mac and the new baby girl he never got to see, and said that whatever else happened in a raid, he wanted to come in and slap Mac's cuffs on the worst of the bad guys. He showed them photos of McIntyre's newborn, Lauren. "You could see it in their eyes—the compassion, the respect, the anger," one of the American investigators said of the Pakistanis. "Once I showed them the photos, it was like they knew Mac, too. After that, it was personal."

Soon, the Pakistanis wanted to touch the handcuffs for luck. And after a while, they began to regard them as a talisman. They would gather just before a raid and, in unison, place their hands on the cuffs in a circle, like members of a basketball team touching hands before the opening jump. "This is for Mac," they would say. Then they would raise their weapons and kick the door in. These were different security officials from the ones the FBI and CIA had grown to mistrust. Most of them belonged to a different part of the ISI, the one charged with protecting domestic security. Even so, the protocol for raids had been for the Pakistanis to go in first and for the Americans to wait outside to be summoned, sometimes hours later. Some Americans suspected the Pakistanis wanted to vet the people inside, to make sure none of them were linked to the ISI's "external operations" division, which handled the militant groups. After McHale arrived, the Pakistanis began to insist that he and the handcuffs lead the charge. It marked a significant improvement—not only in American-Pakistani relations but in the Americans' ability to really see what was behind all those closed doors.

On a broader level, relationships between the Americans and Pakistanis remained strained, neither side completely trusting the other. But Keenan, too, helped build camaraderie over time, in some ways unexpectedly. The Pakistanis admired her bravery and indefatigability, and her willingness to go on even the most dangerous of raids. But she also had a secret weapon. The men respected Keenan, but when their wives found out about this American woman running around Pakistan taking down criminals, they insisted on meeting her. After that, the men never dared come home if they couldn't assure their wives that "Miss Jenny" was safe.

McHale, known as Mr. Tom to the Pakistanis, became nearly inseparable from Colonel Tariq. A decorated war hero, Tariq was said by one of the Americans to be absolutely fearless as a raid leader, possessing "the biggest set of balls in Pakistan." He and McHale developed complete trust in one another.

On one raid, Mac's cuffs mysteriously disappeared. There had been dozens of officers involved in the raid, and even more suspects. Some were shot, others wounded. It was pandemonium, and the cuffs were gone. The normally reserved Colonel Tariq screamed at his men repeatedly: "Who has the handcuffs?!!" His anger frightened even the Americans. "I thought he was gonna kill somebody," one of them later recalled. Tariq declared that no one was allowed to leave the scene until the cuffs were found. Hours later, an ISI officer returned from chasing an Al Qaeda operative out into the neighborhood; he had the cuffs.

Relief washed over the faces of Tariq's men. Tariq himself was overwhelmed. He carefully walked over to McHale, holding the cuffs in his cupped hands before him as if they were holy water. McHale gratefully took them, and then looked into his face. It was only then that McHale saw the tears in the little soldier's eyes.

At times, McHale and others joked that carrying the handcuffs granted a person the same mystical power as carrying the Ark of the Covenant—invincibility. Then they began to wonder if it wasn't in fact true. Maybe, they would tell each other, Donnie McIntyre was up there pulling strings, making sure they all got back home that night.

## *Karachi, Pakistan, January 2002*

Karachi in the best of times is a difficult city. With its "no-go" zones, rampant organized crime, and seemingly perpetual sectarian wars, it has been a kidnapping and murder capital for years. Much as California localities post warnings on what to do in case of an earthquake, bulletin boards in public buildings in Karachi routinely display advice on what to do in case of an abduction.

It is a mark of Karachi's cosmopolitanism that most of its millions of citizens carry on life as if this underworld does not exist. In that regard, it is in many ways no different from any other twenty-first-century metropolis—ungainly, exciting, raucous, difficult. There are hip clubs with DJs, cool new restaurants with enigmatic names, a burgeoning middle class. Kids ride bikes, markets hawk DVDs and digital cameras, the bright shiny silks of upscale ladies-about-town billow in the breeze. It is Pakistan's most progressive city, former home to its first female prime minister, Benazir Bhutto, and thousands of women go about the city unescorted, unveiled, running errands, going to jobs, lunch dates, and prenatal classes. Graduates of its university engineering programs are prized in technology centers and other outposts of the new world economy.

Amid this frenzy, Daniel Pearl, the ambitious South Asia bureau chief of the *Wall Street Journal,* arrived in Karachi in January to pursue a story about the shoe bomber Richard Reid. An earlier news report by the *Boston Globe* had linked Reid to an underground jihadi network led by Sheikh Mubarak Ali Shah Gilani. Pearl wanted to pursue the Reid connections and the murky nexus between the Karachi militant groups and those who carried out the 9/11 plot.

Pearl at that point had likely never heard much about Khalid Sheikh Mohammed. Investigators had by then traced the 9/11 plot's finances back through the Emirates to KSM, but few Americans had ever heard of him. Mohammed almost certainly had never heard of Pearl. But Pearl's inquiries set off small vibrations within the Karachi underground. Word of Pearl soon reached a man named Ahmed Omar Saeed Sheikh, who had built a peculiar career as small-time criminal and large-scale terrorist. He had fought in Kashmir, hijacked airplanes, kidnapped for ransom, and graduated from the London School of Economics. He had deep-rooted relationships with the ISI, Pakistani sectarian groups, and, according to U.S. intelligence, Al Qaeda, especially in Karachi. The Justice Department for years had been seeking his extradition on murder charges, with FBI agents making in-person demands as recently as a few days before Pearl showed up in Karachi. Unbeknownst to Pearl, Sheikh was also—unwittingly—about to deliver a death sentence to the journalist.

Knowing that Pearl wanted to contact Gilani, Sheikh insinuated himself in between the two, contacting Pearl and identifying himself as someone who could arrange the interview. He lined up a crew of local jihadis drawn democratically from the stew of the city's underworld. Pearl never had a chance. Thinking he was being taken to a rendezvous with Gilani, he was instead taken into captivity. Ransom demands ensued, complete with the usual videos of Pearl holding dated newspapers and confessing his sins as a Jew and a spy. The kidnappers failed to anticipate the media storm their escapade would ignite. Kidnapping was routine in Karachi. Kidnapping handsome American reporters with beautiful, young, pregnant wives was not. Caught in the fury, the kidnappers had no idea what to do.

Khalid Sheikh Mohammed, still engaged in the retreat from Afghanistan and busy with the several fronts on which he was advancing terror plots across the globe, didn't need the added diversion of Pearl. KSM hadn't initially even been aware of Pearl's kidnapping. But once informed of Pearl's plight and the growing uncertainty of what ought to be done, he interceded.

"Khalid Sheikh Mohammed got to know of the plot, which he had done nothing to serve," a local police official said. "He got to know of it through the grapevine. And so he said, 'This is a great, a chance to do a spectacular.' So he basically bought Daniel Pearl from them."[11]

The kidnappers, panicked that they had gotten in over their heads, had contacted Al Qaeda colleagues of KSM, offering Pearl to them. Al Qaeda offered $50,000 for him and, because it was in Karachi and Karachi was KSM's territory, asked him to take possession of the prize.

Pearl was being held in a small cement-block building on an isolated property in the remote Karachi neighborhood of Ahsanabad. Sometime in the week following the kidnapping, Mohammed and two of his nephews, Ali Abdul Aziz Ali and Abdul Karim Abdul Karim—KSM's college classmate in America—showed up at the safe house. They weren't there long. They set up a video camera they had brought with them to capture the event. Mohammed also had brought his own knives.[12] His nephews held Pearl down and Mohammed, quickly and with frightening efficiency, slit Pearl's throat. The camera malfunctioned, and after yelling at the cameraman to get it up and running, he reenacted the event. This time he grabbed Pearl by the hair and cut clean through the bone to decapitate him, at the end grasping Pearl's head and holding it aloft for the camera. Then he pushed down on the chest of the dead body, causing blood to spurt from the severed neck, to display for the camera the evidence that Pearl had been alive when the beheading took place. So vicious was the butchery that one of the guards started retching. KSM angrily ordered him out of the room.[13] He then proceeded to carve Pearl's body into pieces suitable for easy disposal, took his knives, and left with his nephews. One witness described it in police reports as *ziba,* the Muslim ritual of slaughter.

Mohammed had not sought out Pearl, hadn't even known who he was until alerted by his Al Qaeda comrades to the already accomplished kidnapping. Once given the responsibility for the journalist, he was brutally efficient in disposing of the problem. Fortunately, he said later, Pearl presented him with an added propaganda bonus—he was Jewish.

## *Islamabad, Pakistan, January 2002*

The Pearl murder occurred just as the American security forces, aided by Tom McHale and the persevering Jennifer Keenan, had begun developing workable relations with the Pakistanis, and even with one another. Pearl's disappearance threw things into disarray. The kidnapping of a reporter from one of the largest and best American newspapers turned Washington's priorities upside down.

The Newark field office of the FBI led the Pearl investigation because the newspaper's headquarters was nearby, and it took the unusual step of setting up a command post right on the premises of the paper. It also deployed as many as a dozen agents to Pakistan from various FBI field offices. This was roughly double the average number of agents already in Pakistan devoted to investigating the September 11 attacks. The disparity was not lost on the FBI agents assigned to Islamabad; they were further aggravated when asked to send temporary duty personnel to Karachi to assist the Pearl investigation. McHale, who was from the New Jersey JTTF, was one of those they insisted spend his time in Karachi. He went briefly, and then refused to go back to Karachi, arguing that he could make more important contributions elsewhere. Keenan and Reimann in Islamabad backed him up. There were already more resources devoted to the Pearl case than to the entire rest of the country, they argued, and McHale was needed for other urgent matters. What more do you want?

Inevitably, however, the pull of the Pearl case was too powerful. It sucked up resources that could otherwise have been used for other cases. A church had been bombed in Islamabad, for example, causing multiple deaths, several of them Americans. People were pulled off that case to investigate Pearl. In addition, the FBI had never had a resident agent in Karachi, even though it is one of the biggest, most crime-plagued cities in the world, or even a working office with basic equipment. With the Pearl investigation, however, a brand-new computer suddenly appeared in the Bureau's tiny part-time work space in the Karachi consulate.

The macabre celebrity aspects of the case—the dashing reporter, his pregnant wife, the powerful publishing empire behind them—were too much. Rather than focusing on who caused September 11, many investigators were trying to figure out who killed a reporter who, many veteran investigators complained, had volunteered for his own death by not heeding warnings about the suspicious nature of the people he was dealing with.

Even without the Pearl case, the hunt for the origins of September 11 was suffering from contradictions in approach between the two agencies handling the investigation. The CIA seemed to bounce from one Langley-based directive to another—look for this person, then that—without a strong idea of where it all might be headed. Its agents were constantly searching for the magic bullet that would stop the next attack. If they didn't find that bullet in one raid, they quickly set their sights on the next. Intel wasn't something to be used to build a mosaic; if it didn't catch someone important, forget about it. Whether right or wrong, that's the way FBI agents saw it. The Bureau, on the other hand, wanted to wring as much evidence as it could get out of every opportunity, methodically gathering information so Keenan could scan it and send it back to Washington for forensic exploitation, safekeeping, and use in future prosecutions. They also hoped that the information they were collecting would eventually lead them to the next attack. Even when the two agencies were aiming for the same result, they had utterly different ways of getting there, and the friction it caused only got worse over time, not better.

At one point in the spring of 2002, the FBI obtained information that KSM's nephew Ali Abdul Aziz Ali, the man who had wired hundreds of thousands of dollars to the hijackers in America, was operating out of Karachi. His role in Pearl's murder had not yet been revealed. Keenan went to the CIA's lead officer in Karachi and told him what she knew. This might be a huge opportunity, she said, to interrupt Al Qaeda's financial supply lines and lead us to its commanders, including KSM, whom Zabaydah had recently identified.

The CIA supervisor wasn't interested. He had never heard of Ali. Maybe you just don't understand, Keenan said. We have two of the Bureau's most knowledgeable agents on the 9/11 plot here temporarily from the U.S. They know this guy inside and out and they're right here, right now. They want to brief you on Ali's importance and what we know about where he might be. He was a key financial link in the whole plot, she said.

The CIA man was not swayed. "We hunt terrorists, not financiers," he said, and ended the discussion.

# CHAPTER 13
# In Plain Sight

*Islamabad, Pakistan, Spring 2002*

By early 2002, the CIA station in Islamabad had gone through its huge growth phase. It was now one of the largest intelligence operations in the world. The carpenters were gone and the station was at work. Station chief Bob Grenier felt he finally had the team he needed in place. John Kiriakou, an experienced case officer and Arabic speaker, had arrived as a TDY to help run counterterrorism. Deuce Martinez, a superb analyst, arrived to provide Grenier with the kind of targeting expertise that had been lacking. The green badgers filled out the duty roster with a depth of experience and expertise Kiriakou had rarely seen. Some of the green badgers were pushing seventy, or had already broken through—it wasn't polite to ask—but were revivified by the mission. One man had been in the CIA for forty years, long enough to have been involved in the Gulf of Tonkin incident. Kiriakou liked to say that the entire counterterrorism support staff wore the badges, and that he thought he learned more from the old folks in a few months than he had in his entire career.

The job that confronted the station was clear. In an odd reversal of historic roles, Pakistan had become the redoubt for Al Qaeda fighters fleeing Afghanistan. For decades—for as long as Pakistan had existed, actually—the situation had been the opposite. Afghanistan had given Pakistan a place for strategic retreat, a place to which it could withdraw and husband its forces against India. Regardless of whether that was ever true on the ground, Pakistan's military strategists had made it a chief component of their war plans against India.

Now Pakistan had become the refuge for Osama bin Laden's fighters fleeing the American assault. The retreat had been ongoing for months, and Grenier finally felt capable of dealing with its consequences. The exodus at times had been a flood, and the pace of work was killing. Some nights, the agents just crawled under their desks to sleep.

By February, Grenier thought he could transition from defense to offense. Rather than reacting to a flood of refugees, he was ready to start hunting.

His first target would be Abu Zubaydah. Zubaydah had been an enigmatic figure to terrorist watchers for a decade. Unlike other presumed high commanders in Al Qaeda, he never appeared with bin Laden in the videos distributed to the Western press. He didn't seem to spend much time with bin Laden at all. But he was always there on the periphery. There was hardly a terror plot in the 1990s to which his name had not been attached. Zubaydah had jumped up the U.S. list of most wanted suspects because of his role in the millennium plots at the turn of the century; the plots had been broken up in the United States and Jordan, but they revealed Zubaydah's ambitions.

Al Qaeda had sometimes seemed as though it were not just the face of radical Islam but radical Islam itself. This had never been true. It was one of many groups of similar ideology. Bin Laden obviously knew this. In fact, Al Qaeda itself began as an amalgam of many militant groups with which bin Laden had formed alliances. It differed mainly in its public profile and its resources. Bin Laden was wealthy from his family's business fortune, and he had always been a terrific fund-raiser. As a result, his group had simply been more prosperous and better able to fund its goals, and bin Laden became a unifying force, in part through his reputation as a leader. He cemented his position by merging Al Qaeda with al-Zawahiri's Egyptian militant organization.

Zubaydah had never formally joined bin Laden. In some ways, he saw himself not as a subordinate but an equal, someone in the same line of business—and someone who had a far broader network of contacts. He had for years run his own training camp, Khalden, just across the Pakistani border in Afghanistan. He had also acted as a gatekeeper for the Islamist cause in general, and for the war camps that were training many other jihadis in addition to those in Al Qaeda—including Chechens, Uzbeks, and Algerians. New recruits were often directed his way when they first arrived in theater to join the jihad. Some recruits he sent on to other camps, to other groups; some he sought to keep under his control at Khalden. Some of those who trained at his camp later sought his support for their proposed plots. Some of these he nurtured; others he sent on their way.

Because Zubaydah was a gatekeeper to Afghanistan and because Khalden was so near the border, he had been a presence in Pakistan—in Peshawar, especially—for years. Much more than bin Laden, he had developed lines of communication through the Pakistani jihadi networks. He was virtually unknown to the broader public, but for all these reasons he had been an intelligence target even longer than bin Laden. As recently as the summer of 2001, American security services had sent out warnings about Zubaydah's activities. "[R]eporting has indicated that Al Qaeda operatives, including Abu Zubaida, have been involved in operational planning in several different geographic locations....Also in early March, Abu

Zubaida engaged in apparent operational preparation with colleagues in Europe and Saudi Arabia. In particular, he planned and facilitated the production of photographs of operatives to be used in high quality European passports.... One limiting factor which seems to be evident is funding. Intelligence suggests that preparation is slowed by lack of available funding to support the operations[s]."[1]

Given this history, Zubaydah was an obvious focus for Grenier, and the reason why he and the ambassador had gone straight to Musharraf with their concerns about him before 9/11. When coalition troops found the bombed-out home of bin Laden's longtime military commander, Mohammed Atef, in Kandahar in November of 2001, they unearthed still more evidence pointing to Zubaydah's importance. Zubaydah surfaced again when Grenier started receiving intelligence about Al Qaeda fighters infiltrating Pakistan. Faisalabad, in the province of Punjab, was the source of many of the reports. Punjab was rife with Kashmiri jihadi groups that had begun to broaden their focus. The influx of Al Qaeda fighters fleeing Afghanistan led to an explosive cross-pollination with native Pakistani sectarian groups, and Lashkar-e-Taiba, Jaish-e-Mohammed, and Harkat-ul-Mujahideen in particular were ambitious and ready to make alliances.

Men with prior relationships to the sectarian groups, most notably Khalid Sheikh Mohammed and Zubaydah, were best positioned to take advantage of this. Grenier knew little about Mohammed. Not many people beyond a small squad of FBI agents in New York did. Zubaydah became their target.

In the past, Al Qaeda had more bountiful resources than any of the sectarian groups. Now the tables were turned. The local jihadis had the resources and Al Qaeda, in retreat, needed help—logistics networks, shelter, transit, foot soldiers. The locals and Al Qaeda made common cause. This posed a security risk for Al Qaeda, or somebody like Zubaydah, in that they had been much more selective in choosing partners in the past. Now they had little choice.

On the run, they took help where they could find it. They were exposed.

If determined, well-equipped people with huge technical resources are trying to find you, it doesn't take much—just little wrinkles in the web—to give them clues. Once they have the clues, technology gives them a ruthless advantage. If the target remains active, engaged in activity, the advantage multiplies. This was especially so when Al Qaeda had moved from backward Afghanistan to teeming Pakistani cities brimming with telecommunications capabilities. So it was with Zubaydah. Had he simply gone to ground, or left the region entirely, he might never have been found. But he continued to plot attacks, to train and recruit, and to oversee an effort to get passports and other travel documentation for jihadis, something he had done his entire career.

Once signals intelligence—telephone intercepts, mainly—indicated his general location, Zubaydah really had little chance. The overwhelming technical advantage the Americans held was inexorable. If raids on Lahore and Faisalabad in late March had not succeeded, the next ones, or the ones after that, likely would have.

Capturing Zubaydah in March in Faisalabad—and more, keeping him alive long enough to be spirited away and interrogated—was a huge triumph for both the CIA and the FBI. And as soon as Zubaydah was gone, Grenier and Kiriakou turned their sights to the next targets, as did Keenan and her small band of FBI TDYers. While the CIA worked its intel sources and liaison relationship with Pakistan, the FBI agents did what they do best: they exploited evidence seized in previous raids. As soon as Zubaydah was in custody, in fact, the FBI agents took charge, scouring more than a dozen raid sites for evidence, and identifying and interrogating the other men captured that night. Before Zubaydah ever landed in Thailand, Keenan and the FBI were processing a huge collection of intelligence—cell phones, computers, notepads, day planners, Zubaydah's voluminous personal diaries—and a cache of bomb-making materials and document forgery tools. They assessed each detainee to separate the Al Qaeda operatives from the unwitting facilitators. While some of the CIA irregulars—many of them flown in just for the raids—were stowing away their SWAT gear for the night after the raids, Keenan was overseeing the effort to photograph and fingerprint each detainee. She had her precious scanner working overtime to make copies of all the passports and other records. The CIA guys had a sound night's sleep and breakfast while she was still making copies and interviewing and assessing the detainees. By the time she was done, the station had to arrange for a chartered plane to take all the evidence back to Washington, and the U.S. team in Pakistan had a bunch of fresh leads.

It was in many ways a model for how the two agencies ought to work with one another. The CIA had collated bits of intelligence, made sense of it, and identified a specific set of targets, and the two agencies teamed up to attack them with their Pakistani hosts. They got their man and the FBI moved in and got its evidence. Nobody had to scream at anybody. There were some minor conflicts, of course—Kiriakou wanting to crack open the evidence seal to see who kept calling Zubaydah's cell phone, for instance.

The two U.S. agencies were hitting their stride, and the mosaic of Al Qaeda's operations in Pakistan was beginning to take shape. Unfortunately, the frontline working relationship formed over the previous months wouldn't last. Grenier and Kiriakou were pulled out of Islamabad soon after the Zubaydah capture. They were to be given a new target: Iraq. They left just as things were about to get really interesting.

## *Karachi, Pakistan, Spring 2002*

Two weeks after *Wall Street Journal* reporter Daniel Pearl went missing, Pakistani police had identified Ahmed Omar Saeed Sheikh as the man who had ensnared him. On February 5, as they were closing in on him, Sheikh turned himself in to Ijaz Shah, a retired Intelligence Bureau official and former ISI operative. Sheikh had been a longtime ISI asset, cultivated for the Kashmir fight, and knew Shah from those days. Shah was also from the same village as Sheikh's mother. For whatever reason, Sheikh, at his father's urging, delivered himself to Shah and remained in ISI custody for a week before he was turned over to the police. U.S. investigators on the ground in Karachi had no idea. In fact, despite their increasingly forceful demands, they had to wait another month before they were allowed to interview Sheikh.

FBI special agent Ty Fairman, from the Newark field office, finally got a chance to talk with Sheikh at a local police lockup on March 10. By then, the hunt for Pearl had lost its urgency, as they knew that he was dead. The FBI agents were now working a homicide investigation, and Fairman fed Sheikh and the Pakistani police tea and cookies as a way of easing the tension. Sheikh started out by questioning why Fairman, an African American, was working on behalf of a racist colonial power like the United States. The two debated black history and militancy and Fairman developed a rapport with Sheikh. In later meetings, Sheikh talked in some detail about the kidnapping and why he had done it. He was proud of what he done, he said, and would do it again. But he insisted that killing Pearl was never part of his plan. Once the Pakistani media published speculation that Pearl was Jewish, Sheikh said he lost control of the situation. This was a significant admission coming from Sheikh, an imperious and egotistical man. In veiled language, he told Fairman that the only reason Pearl was killed was that someone extremely high in the Al Qaeda–jihadi hierarchy had ordered it. Otherwise, he said, they would have had to consult him, given his status within the powerful Harkat-ul-Mujahideen militant group. He didn't know who had made the decision, but someone he described as "the fat man" moved in and took control.[2]

Despite their best efforts to get details, the FBI agents couldn't ascertain who the fat man was. Two weeks earlier, they had gotten the videotape of Pearl's brutal decapitation through a shadowy intermediary. Agents and forensic experts had been poring over it for clues. They went through the video frame by frame, stopping at some points to take high-resolution still photos of the hand holding the knife and grasping Pearl's head by the hair because they afforded them a good view of the veins on the back of the hand—a way of identifying possible suspects and eliminating others.

After each raid, they would photograph suspects' hands in the same positions as the still photos and compare them. When they did so with Sheikh, it seemed as though he might be telling the truth, Fairman thought. At least, it appeared that neither Sheikh nor the others who had been taken into custody had wielded the knife. Maybe he was telling the truth about the fat man, too. Fairman was struck by something else in the video. It was so graphic that even the most veteran FBI agents could barely watch. But viewing it over and over, he noticed that at one point, the killer wielding the knife expertly put two fingers to Pearl's freshly slit carotid artery and then took them off, to show that the blood was pumping out—proof that the journalist was still alive, even if unconscious. After letting the blood spurt out for a short while, the killer, with a few forceful and precise cuts, cleanly severed the head and quickly snatched it up and brought it closer to the video camera. "Whoever did this was a professional," he said in describing Pearl's slaying to other Americans working the case. "He was slaughtered like an animal."

Fairman sent a memo off to Washington asking that the FBI and CIA both report back to the investigation team as soon as possible and let them know whether any senior Al Qaeda operatives had grown up on farms or had other experience slaughtering or butchering animals.

But the mystery remained: Who was the fat man? Whoever it was, the tape showed no trace of his face, only his hand holding Pearl's head aloft for the camera—and for the propaganda videos of it that were already beginning to circulate.

Sheikh never identified KSM as the actual killer, but he did give the FBI and their CIA and Pakistani counterparts another crumb. Whoever the fat man was, he wasn't someone holed up in some faraway lair. He was, Sheikh suggested, a prominent and well-respected man in both jihadi and Al Qaeda circles in Karachi.

Investigators had no idea it was happening, but their two urgent investigations in Pakistan—into 9/11 and the Pearl slaying—were becoming one. As Sheikh's accomplices were found, arrested, and interrogated, they filled in further pieces of the puzzle. The fat man was addressed by those who knew him as Mukhtar, some said. He and his two accomplices who showed up to kill Pearl were generally described as Arabs, but one of those arrested for being at the scene said they might have been Baluch or even Makrani—descendants of African slaves. Ironically, despite the controversy surrounding the deployment of so many agents to investigate a single kidnapping, all the attention paid to Pearl and his abductors would have given the American authorities their first glimpse of KSM had they known what they were seeing. They didn't, of course. KSM remained on the streets of Karachi, hidden in plain sight.

At least, however, investigators had begun to look at Karachi as a place of interest. KSM had lived there for most of a decade without anyone apparently noticing. For much of that time he had lived in the same apartment,[3] even though, thanks to a U.S. indictment, he was theoretically the subject of a worldwide manhunt. There was little indication that the Pakistanis had ever looked for KSM at the request of the Americans, or that Washington had ever made a formal request forcefully enough for it to be acted upon. The FBI's KSM case agent, Pellegrino, had continued to make numerous trips to Karachi, but especially before 9/11, cooperation there was virtually nonexistent.

Another faint arrow pointing at Karachi was uncovered in April. On the morning of April 11, Christian Ganczarski, the young Polish-German Muslim convert, placed a cell phone call from Duisburg in southern Germany to a number in Karachi. The call lasted nearly a minute, yet no words were exchanged. It was a signal. Moments before, Ganczarski, a protégé of KSM, had given the final go-ahead to a young Tunisian to drive a truck fitted with a propane bomb into a synagogue on an island off the Tunisian coast. He was letting KSM know the plan was under way. Twenty-one people died in the attack.

Ganczarski had been conspiring with KSM since at least 2000, when he was an occupant of the same guesthouse where KSM hosted Jack Roche, the Australian jihadi. It was Ganczarski whom KSM had asked to shepherd Roche through the mountain passes to bin Laden's camp, and who handed "the sheikh" the note saying that Roche had KSM's seal of approval. By the spring of 2002, Ganczarski had been under surveillance by German authorities for some time. The silent call was monitored in real time, and two weeks later, after Ganczarski had been arrested, police found a log of phone numbers, one of which was the number he had called the morning of the attack. The number was registered to a SIM card manufactured by the company Swisscom.[4] Swiss authorities investigated and determined that a large number of previously identified Al Qaeda suspects had been using SIMs from the same manufacturer.

Once again, they didn't know it, but authorities—in this case, the Germans and Swiss—had, in a sense, caught KSM in the act.

## *Udorn Royal Thai Air Force Base, Thailand, April 2002*

By mid-April, Abu Zubaydah had been in Thailand undergoing intermittent interrogation for more than a week. He had revealed that KSM and Mukhtar were one and the same, and that KSM had been the mastermind behind the September 11 attacks. The initial reaction was bafflement—KSM isn't even Al Qaeda, right?

But once that connection was made—KSM was Mukhtar, the man bin Laden himself praised as the 9/11 mastermind—the puzzle pieces fell into place. Soon enough, KSM's role seemed so obvious and the 9/11 plot so similar to the Manila Air plot that people wondered how it had remained hidden for so long. Almost overnight, the number of people looking for KSM went from one man to almost the whole damned government. It seemed the only person not then looking for KSM was Pellegrino, who, after a cursory consultation, was sent off to follow other, less pressing, leads.

As Zubaydah's health gradually improved, he grew more and more coy with his interrogators. And his interrogators had a falling-out among themselves. Steve Gaudin and Ali Soufan, the two young FBI agents who had elicited KSM's identity from Zubaydah, were quickly demoted from their initial role as the principal interrogators. Once Tenet learned that the information about KSM had been delivered not to agency personnel but to FBI agents—he was furious, given the president's personal vow that the CIA was the lead agency taking the fight to Al Qaeda—the agency rushed a team of its own interrogators to Thailand. Upon arrival, team members told Gaudin and Soufan that they would take over. They didn't seem particularly interested in KSM. In fact, they said they thought the KSM information could well be a feint by Zubaydah, something to throw them off the trail. It was a legitimate concern. This happened all the time in interrogations—a prisoner would give up something little or false to conceal the thing that needed concealing.

Instead, the CIA team said, we are after one piece of information—when is the next attack? The team allowed the FBI men one more meeting alone with Zubaydah, but its purpose was to hand off the interrogation to "their boss," the CIA, because under the new rules of engagement, Zubaydah needed to see his future in one person's eyes.[5] Once they had done this, Gaudin and Soufan watched as the new team took over and, true to its word, repeatedly asked Zubaydah to tell them what was next. This was, FBI agents said later, more a difference of method than a difference in the desired result. Of course everybody wanted to know about the next attack. But the FBI way was more conversational, one built on decades of success in building rapport with the most hardened of criminals. Get your arms around the conspiracy and you'll stop whatever it is that they are conspiring to do. Once Gaudin and Soufan had KSM identified as the mastermind, they would begin to draw out more information—Where is KSM now? Who works with him? What's his phone number? Whom might he use for an attack in, say, Indonesia? They would use those answers to achieve the same purpose. They would seek to find KSM and stop the next attack that way. It might have worked. Pat D'Amuro, their former boss in New York, who by then headed all counterterrorism for the FBI, made that argument at the highest levels of the Bush administration until he was blue in the face, but no one outside of the FBI agreed. They never got a chance to ask the right questions. The FBI, essentially, was written out of the script. The script was one that called for pursuit of that single overwhelming question and, to get the answer, far more harsh treatment than American investigators had used in the past—treatment that seemed to many to be beyond what American or international law allowed, and likely to produce fiction rather than fact.

As the interrogation continued, the CIA organized what amounted to a schedule of questioning with varying methods and interviewers. Gaudin and Soufan were part of this new regime, sometimes together and sometimes individually, or partnered with a CIA agent. In some of those talks, Zubaydah described KSM's rising role within Al Qaeda, ratcheting up the level of angst among his U.S. pursuers even further.

One day, before the CIA had intervened, Gaudin and Soufan asked Zubaydah to tell them just one thing that might help stop another bombing. To their surprise, he told them about José Padilla and Binyam Mohamed, the two men Zubaydah said he had sent to KSM so that he could give them missions in America.

Zubaydah had first met the two men when they were fleeing Afghanistan in early 2001. They accompanied him through a circuit of safe houses in Pakistan, winding up in Faisalabad and telling Zubaydah about their idea to set off a dirty bomb in the United States.[6] Zubaydah thought the plan too difficult to execute, but finally sent them off to Karachi with a letter introducing them to KSM. They left Faisalabad just a day, perhaps mere hours, before the American raids.

In Karachi, they worked through Ali Abdul Aziz Ali, KSM's

nephew, seeking a meeting. When they made their pitch, KSM told them he agreed with Zubaydah—the plan was too complicated. Couldn't they instead adopt a plan first proposed to them in Afghanistan—use natural gas from appliances to blow up apartment buildings? Ali and KSM gave the pair $15,000, e-mail codes, and a cell phone, and sent them on their way.

Zubaydah didn't know, or recall, Padilla's real name, just that he was a "South American" who used a Muslim name. A mad search through customs and passport records in Pakistan and back in Washington produced an identity and a photograph to go with the story. Zubaydah confirmed the photo was Padilla.

This was exactly the kind of ticking-bomb scenario the Cheney doctrine was created to address: a plot, a dirty bomb, millions at risk. Except that, in a lot of ways, it was a bomb that had never ticked. There was no bomb—and no plot, really. It was, as investigators would say later, aspirational. For a time, there wasn't even a suspect. Padilla turned out to be a terrorist with other priorities. Following a send-off dinner in Karachi with KSM, Ali, and Ramzi bin al-Shibh, he had left, purportedly for the United States but actually for Egypt, where he stayed a month, visiting his wife.

Unaware that he was being sought, he finally departed for the States in May, leaving much of the money he had been given in Karachi with his wife and two young sons in Egypt. He was tracked all the way. When he arrived at O'Hare International Airport in Chicago, FBI agents met him at the gate, arrested him on a material witness warrant, and took him back on the next commercial flight to New York. They were in the process of debriefing him there and offering him a possible plea agreement in exchange for information on what attacks might be coming when the Department of Defense, on orders from the Bush White House, took Padilla in the middle of the night from a federal lockup in New York and put him in a military brig, designating him an enemy combatant. Once again, the FBI was blocked from interrogating an Al Qaeda suspect who might have led them to KSM and, potentially, to his network of operatives around the world.

## *Washington, D.C., Spring 2002*

Every May, Washington, D.C., hosts a celebration and appreciation of law enforcement personnel from across the country. It's called National Police Week and generally serves as an excellent excuse for a lot of people to get really drunk. There are some dinners and official receptions, but National Police Week is nothing fancy.

As thanks for their assistance in the new war on terror, U.S. counterterrorism officials arranged for a few law enforcement agents from several countries to attend the 2002 festivities. Emotions ran particularly high. The large number of police, fire, and rescue people killed on September 11 was fresh on everyone's minds. A huge tent—three blocks long—containing a makeshift bar made out of blue-painted plywood was set up at the corner of H and Second Streets. Several Pakistanis were among the foreigners invited. They included Tom McHale's running mates, Colonel Tariq and another ISI colonel he only knew as Mr. K. Mr. K. always wore Texas cowboy boots.

McHale went to Washington to escort them around and make sure they received what he regarded as appropriate thanks. They visited the White House and the CIA out in Langley and even got the red-carpet treatment up in New York from McHale's Port Authority, including a helicopter ride around Manhattan, where the Twin Towers used to be. The Pakistanis aroused some suspicious stares. Who are these foreigners in suits, people asked McHale. It got worse when he said what country they were from. McHale assured everyone that the two men held a special place of honor in the annals of U.S. counterterrorism efforts. The Pakistanis were given a police escort to the massive tent, where thousands of law enforcement officials were gathered.

Knowing that both men were devout Muslims, McHale explained to them, "Over here, we salute our dead by drinking beers and whiskey." McHale was a bit embarrassed by what his guests would think of all the rowdiness, but he wasn't going to let that stop him from drinking. He was a cop—one who had just spent a few harrowing months kicking down doors in Pakistan. How else do you honor your dead?

When another cop toasted one of the departed, Colonel Tariq and Mr. K. nodded and said nothing. Then one of the colonels grabbed a Budweiser off the plywood and raised it aloft. "To Mr. Mac," he said.

The Americans roared their reply. "To Mac!"

There were toasts all night, to the many cops who had fallen and to those who had not. And the two Pakistanis raised a drink for every one of them. They got stewed.

McHale later arranged for the Pakistanis to be there when McIntyre's handcuffs were returned to his widow, Jeannine, at the National Law Enforcement Officers Memorial, where the names of fallen police are inscribed on a wall.

Then he decided to go one step further. McHale gave the cuffs to Colonel Tariq and Mr. K. They, in turn, gave them to Jeannine. The one thing all the U.S. agents who fought alongside him in Pakistan said about Colonel Tariq was that he was about as sentimental as General George Patton. But with Jeannine, the two men gently took her hands, bent and kissed them, then thanked her for giving them the honor of using her late husband's handcuffs. It was only when they raised their heads that McHale could see the tears once again pooling in Tariq's eyes.

## *Washington, D.C., Spring 2002*

In early June, FBI director Robert Mueller confirmed that KSM was the mastermind behind 9/11. Since then, details about KSM had completely saturated the media. His face was everywhere, and so were descriptions of—and speculations about—his exploits. Overnight, a man who had been virtually invisible to all but the small army of security officials chasing him had become public enemy number one to some and a folk hero to others, especially in Pakistan. Ramzi bin al-Shibh became a lesser sensation as KSM's trusty sidekick and intermediary with the hijackers. Within a few weeks, information from the Zubaydah capture had been processed and fed into the U.S. intelligence-gathering machine. The information was the most important thus far gathered against Al Qaeda.

More information was coming in from a frenzied effort to review every mention of "Mukhtar" that had been collected and intercepted over the past decade. This effort was for some uncomfortable in that it revealed how much information the intelligence community, especially the CIA, had collected on KSM over time without realizing its significance.

Zubaydah himself was still talking, too. He described plots against the Brooklyn Bridge and other New York landmarks. His claims about Padilla and his dirty bomb plot, and KSM's connections to it, took on a life of their own, even though Zubaydah portrayed the American operative—correctly, it turns out—as a bumbler. Suddenly agents around the United States and around the world were looking for some kind of catastrophe without really knowing anything more than that.

On May 20, vice president Dick Cheney warned it was "not a matter of if, but when" Al Qaeda would attack the United States. Defense Secretary Donald Rumsfeld said well-trained Al Qaeda operatives were hiding out in the U.S., and looking to use weapons of mass destruction. Tom Ridge, the new homeland security secretary, and FBI director Mueller both said more suicide bombings were inevitable. Domestic intelligence bulletins were issued sometimes twice or even three times a day about Al Qaeda operatives targeting U.S. banks, rail and transit systems, apartment buildings, financial complexes, and landmarks.

When the New York police department found out about the alleged plots, the city went on red alert. On June 10, 2002, reporters were summoned to Justice Department headquarters in Washington for an urgent matter, and watched on a big screen as Attorney General John Ashcroft, interrupting high-level meetings in Moscow, spoke gravely about how the authorities had uncovered an unfolding plot by Padilla, "a known terrorist who was exploring a plan to build and explode a radiological dispersion device, or 'dirty bomb,' in the United States."

The FBI was panicking. In a secret bulletin that same day, FBI headquarters issued an urgent call to field offices for information on the activities of KSM and his nephew Abdul Karim while they were students in the U.S. in the 1980s, information that had been readily available for years. The bulletin underscored how the Bureau's inability to process, analyze, and share information it had already compiled had left giant gaps in what it knew about the man it was now hunting with unprecedented urgency.

Zubaydah's identification of Mohammed as a key orchestrator of the September 11 attacks had been corroborated in significant ways, although some senior officials said they were still trying to understand Mohammed's role. "He's one of the people believed to be behind it. It may be a stretch to say he's the mastermind," one U.S. intelligence official said. "It's not clear at this point what role he played."[7]

One thing everyone agreed on was that KSM was now at or near the top of the list, and raids in and around Karachi looking for him that spring and early summer became a regular occurrence. Pellegrino flew to Pakistan twice for raids, but they proved inconsequential and he returned to the U.S. The increased American presence provoked a response from the militant groups that were increasingly merged with Al Qaeda. On the morning of June 14, 2002, a suicide bomber drove a creaky old truck to the U.S. consulate in Karachi, parked it, and detonated a powerful fertilizer bomb. At least twelve people were killed and dozens more injured, all of them Pakistanis. The bombing, and other attacks, brought even more U.S. agents, CIA and FBI alike, to Karachi.

## *Karachi, Pakistan, Spring 2002*

KSM wasn't going to stay in the shadows for much longer. The day after sending José Padilla and Binyam Mohamed off to bomb apartment buildings in the United States, Mohammed and Ramzi bin al-Shibh received another visitor. His name was Yosri Fouda, a reporter for Al Jazeera, the Qatar-based pan-Arab television network that had quickly established itself as the most essential news source in the Arab world.

Fouda, based in London, was one of its stars. Early in April he had received a call asking what he had planned for his program, *Top Secret*, on the first anniversary of the September 11 attacks. The caller asked for a fax number and four days later a proposal for a three-part series on the attacks came across the machine—a proposal that supposedly had the full cooperation of Al Qaeda.[8] That evening Fouda received another call, inviting him to come to Islamabad for an important interview. The caller didn't say with whom.

On little more than a hunch that this could amount to something, Fouda flew to Islamabad. Half a day after his arrival, the same voice called again and asked him to fly to Karachi. Again he did as instructed. Over the course of another day, with more calls and blindfolded taxi rides, Fouda was finally delivered to a fourth-floor apartment in Karachi. Khalid Sheikh Mohammed opened the door.

"Recognize us yet?" KSM asked him. With that, Fouda said later, Mohammed announced himself as the head of Al Qaeda's military committee and the leader of the 9/11 attacks. He freely admitted what he had done, even boasted that 9/11 had been his idea.

Ramzi bin al-Shibh, who was also in the apartment, pronounced himself KSM's deputy. What KSM told Fouda was chilling, including the revelation that when he had begun his planning two and a half years before September 11, the first targets Mohammed had considered were nuclear facilities. "[We] decided against it for fear it would go out of control," Fouda, in a newspaper article at the time, quoted Mohammed as saying. "You do not need to know more than that at this stage, and anyway it was eventually decided to leave out nuclear targets—for now."[9] When Fouda was preparing to leave after forty-eight hours, during which the men's roles—and egos—were confirmed, KSM walked him down the stairs and out onto the street to bid him farewell. The journalist was taken aback by KSM's nonchalance. He seemed utterly unconcerned to be outside and exposed.

Weeks later, Fouda flew to Doha to brief his editors on what he had been up to. Once his editors heard about KSM and bin al-Shibh, they insisted he tell the Al Jazeera chairman, a relative of the Qatari emir, what he had experienced. Everyone was sworn to secrecy, and they planned a two-part program for September. The station's chairman, Sheikh Hamad bin Thamer al-Thani, unbeknownst to Fouda, soon afterward called the emir and briefed him on what Fouda had found. The emir, Sheikh Hamad bin Khalifa al-Thani, in turn called his old friend George Tenet, director of the CIA.

Tenet was effusive when he walked into his regular 5:00 p.m. meeting the next day and giddily described to his top command how his personal friend the emir of Qatar, with whom he had had many differences, had given the CIA "an amazing gift." He said that Al Jazeera had the general location of the building where Mohammed was hiding, and that they knew who else was there and what KSM and Ramzi had discussed with Fouda. Fouda had told his bosses that he had a good idea of where the apartment was in Karachi, and even what floor he had been on, Tenet said. "In other words, the fat fuck came through," Tenet said.[10] After all that hunting, the best intel that the CIA had to date was something that a reporter had given his bosses, who had shared it with the director of the CIA.

The net was drawing tighter.

## *Karachi, Pakistan, Autumn 2002*

Everything the Americans could rustle up pointed to Karachi. Ganczarski, Zubaydah, Padilla, and Fouda—every source and bit of information said Khalid Sheikh Mohammed was operating out of the capital of Pakistan's Wild West. Back at Langley, the newly formed "KSM targeting team" had assembled a massive file on him that included all the disparate dots that the U.S. government had previously failed to connect. By then, a congressional joint inquiry was already cataloging those failures. Once the Pakistani security services started looking in earnest, they found the same thing. Almost every Al Qaeda suspect they picked up in the last year had some connection to Mohammed. Some had provided even more information about his role in the slaying of Danny Pearl. Many of those arrested had no links to one another, but they all knew Mohammed.

From their experience with the Pearl investigation, the Americans knew Karachi was a much tougher target than almost anywhere else in Pakistan, perhaps the world. Especially after the Pearl murder, it seemed a woolly, scary place to do business. Agents routinely felt they needed to run what they called surveillance detection routes, SDRs, when they went to and from their living quarters.

Raids, even when they were able to mount them, didn't seem to produce much. Karachi was terribly overbuilt. Much of the construction industry was controlled by the military, and much of the military's money was illicit.[11] It couldn't just sit around; it had to be put to use. It built buildings whether the market existed for them or not. So even a city that was growing an average of 5 percent a year had a perpetually high rate of vacant buildings. It made Karachi an easy place to hide. You could slip in and out of empty places—a new one every day if you wanted; you could rent them for almost nothing. A series of raids in the spring and summer of 2002 had found a lot of empty flats.

The investigators worked from clues gleaned on previous raids, and from tips. They had gotten plenty. Many of them were amorphous, but finally one came in that seemed promising. Pakistani intelligence got the call. There was nothing vague about it. Someone had actually seen KSM. The caller had an address.

Investigators mounted a raid with the usual array of personnel—

a small team comprising one agent each from the CIA, the FBI, and the ISI, with a few Pakistani security officials thrown in for good measure. There had been no information about likely armed resistance from the house, so the Pakistanis simply rang the bell. It was early evening. Khalid Sheikh Mohammed answered the door. Or, rather, someone who was an absolute double for Mohammed except for the fact that he was half a foot shorter than the 5-feet-6-inch KSM.

"We're looking for Khalid Sheikh Mohammed," Jennifer Keenan said. They were met with silence. "You look just like him," she continued. "Can we check your ID?"

The man's ID was checked, and the team went on its way.

In August, the FBI caught a break when it questioned a brother-in-law of KSM, Abdul Samad Din Muhammad, who had been arrested and questioned in the United Arab Emirates in November of 2001 and extradited to Pakistan in 2002. Muhammad told FBI agents that Ali Abdul Aziz Ali was in constant contact with his uncle KSM. He also said Ali received a constant stream of Arab visitors from Pakistan at the airport and that Ali had suddenly bolted from the UAE a day or two before the September 11 attacks. He didn't have his belongings together, but insisted on leaving. When Muhammad asked Ali why he was in such a rush to leave, he didn't get a satisfactory answer.[12] Keenan was now certain that the way to get to KSM was through his nephew.

More raids initially yielded nothing, but in early September, the Pakistani police got lucky. Neighbors had pointed out that there was an awful lot of traffic through a house in the Gulshan-e-Iqbal neighborhood. Police nabbed a man leaving the house on his way to pay utility bills. Agents of the ISI investigated and detained the man, a Saudi native, who said he managed the house. His name was Mohammed Ahmad Rabbani. Rabbani's driver proved to be quite talkative. He said Rabbani and his brother managed several similar guesthouses, all of which had a constant stream of guests. He helpfully gave police the addresses of the houses.

One of the houses was nearby, on Tariq Road. Authorities raided it and found the brother there, along with two other men, two women, and three children. They also found twenty carefully wrapped passports and almost two dozen SEGA game consoles that had been modified for use as detonators for explosives. The passports were for members of Osama bin Laden's family. The police interrogated the children to determine if they were bin Laden's. One of the women was a caretaker, and one child was hers. Two of the children were brothers. The other woman was a nanny to the brothers, and the man was her companion. The two boys, ages seven and nine, were named Omar and Abdullah. No, they said, their father's name was not bin Laden; it was Khalid Sheikh Mohammed. The women were caretakers and nannies. They couldn't say where Mohammed was, but they knew there were large parties of Arab men at guesthouses in the Defence Housing Authority, a generally upscale part of the city. The intelligence agents also learned that the men staying in the house were well armed, and cautious. Rabbani had rented out the house two months earlier. The men had come one by one over a period of two weeks and had taken precautions to avoid detection. Once inside, they hadn't left for a month, while food, weapons, and supplies were brought to them.

The ISI retreated for the day. They contacted the Americans and organized for operations the next morning. They moved in overnight with a large assemblage of ISI, local Sindh police, and Pakistani Army Rangers for backup. The American embassy in Islamabad had gotten a call at about 8:00 a.m. that morning about a possible big fish in Karachi. The new FBI legal attaché, Chuck Riley, dispatched Don Borelli, the WMD expert from Dallas, and another agent TDY'd from Kansas City, Dave Cudmore. "Grab an overnight bag, head to Karachi, and haul ass," Riley told them. It took until 2:00 p.m. to get there.

When they got to Karachi, the two agents were told to sit tight. The Pakistanis babysat the house through the night.

The immediate neighborhood was just beyond the nicer sections of Defence; it was a commercial-industrial tract full of five- and six-story buildings, most with low-rent light-industry tenants:

textile plants, zipper and button factories, and small machine shops. The streets were paved but the buildings were separated by bare dirt; they were shuttered in the front with metal roll-up doors. The streets were empty and dark.

After dawn, they stopped the caretaker coming back from morning prayers. He told them that the entire top floor, the fourth, was filled with Arabs. They'd been there for two months, he said, and overpaid on the rent. The soldiers moved in at sunrise and all hell broke loose. Hundreds of rounds, hours of shooting and grenade throwing, and two dead men later, the authorities secured the building. They searched room by room, and in a storage space under a stairwell they found the man who just weeks before had declared himself the coordinator of the September 11 attacks, Ramzi bin al-Shibh. He and another man held knives to their own throats, threatening to silence themselves before they could ever be made to talk. But Pakistani agents jumped them, and wrestled them down.

They raided the second building as well, with much less incident.

When the dust settled from the massive shootout at the Defence address, Borelli and Cudmore were taken to ISI headquarters in Karachi. They had put on their *shalwar kameez* before noticing that many of the ISI officers wore Western clothes, some of them jeans.

"We don't need to blend in; you do," the Americans were told.

The combined team of Pakistanis and Americans swept the houses. They went to the location of the first shootout and found the place badly damaged. They entered to find an unexploded grenade, IED components, and a large cache of documents, including passports. It was late, so they called it a night and hit the next location in the morning. By then, FBI and CIA agents were on the lookout for Mukhtar. They were looking for other Al Qaeda operatives, too, including Walid bin Attash. At the Tariq Road location, they had found a prosthetic leg they thought was his. They didn't know if it was a spare, or if he'd left in such haste that he had abandoned it.

The Americans processed the men who had been detained. They fingerprinted them and asked them to hold up a piece of cardboard with their names on it—the closest thing to a mug shot they could muster. Like Zubaydah before him, Ramzi bin al-Shibh was much bigger than the Americans had expected. He, too, had gained a lot of weight in his months of hiding in Pakistan.

Most of the others were sullen, even angry. But bin al-Shibh had a smug look on his face. As Borelli took his picture, a CIA officer asked him if he had made a video—a reference to the martyrdom tapes made by Al Qaeda fighters that were being found regularly on raids, including one that was believed to have been his.

Bin al-Shibh didn't say anything. Then "he got this weird goofy smile," one observer recalled. "A shit-eating grin, actually."

The Pakistani officers questioned the men caught at the various locations, including Rabbani. It was all very civilized. An ISI colonel served Rabbani tea as they talked. It was more like a chat; nothing like the rumored tales of ISI beatings of detainees. Rabbani described how he paid the bills, and was sort of an administrator. On further questioning, he said he was also watching KSM's children. At one point, the kids were brought into the room. They were scared, but brightened up after being given Coca-Colas.

"You have to help us out for the sake of the kids," the ISI colonel said. Most of the questions focused on KSM's whereabouts, and why it was that he wasn't at any of the locations when the raids occurred. Rabbani didn't know. Neither did his children, they said. KSM had vanished.

The FBI men combed through the buildings. They found automatic weapons, grenades, ammunition. They found cell phones, address books, laptop hard drives, desktop computers. KSM was not there. They had apparently just missed him at the first house the previous raid—again possibly by just a matter of minutes or hours. They found a letter he had signed "Mukh," for Mukhtar, advising a subordinate about a future attack on a pair of hotels.

If you were on the ground and asked, you could collect an address for KSM from almost every person you talked to. He was here in Defence, in a mansion. It was an apartment in Sharifabad, a mud hut in the swamp flats of Korangi, in the Baluch colony of Lyari, in a third-floor walk-up in that Arab neighborhood full of money changers and bucket shops. A man who was arrested had a phone number for Mohammed that was traced to the other end of town, a middle-class preserve of single-family homes with clean modern lines, behind pale stucco walls.

Suddenly, the man who had been nowhere for a decade was everywhere.

# CHAPTER 14
## Betrayal

*Karachi, Pakistan, Autumn 2002*

Everybody wanted to own the Ramzi bin al-Shibh capture. It was a huge score by nearly every measure—the numbers of people arrested, the cache of materials recovered, the cooperation between the Pakistanis and the Americans. There had been hundreds of previous raids, but none had yielded the young children of an Al Qaeda captain or passports for a large part of Osama bin Laden's family.

As much as everyone involved wanted some credit for its successes, no one wanted even a small piece of the Khalid Sheikh Mohammed escape. The Pakistanis, in particular, were confounded by Mohammed.

"Karachi can never become a control center for Al Qaeda," one high-ranking ISI officer said. "We have informers on every street. Our total concentration is on Karachi, followed by Lahore, Faisalabad, and Peshawar, Quetta. That vendor on the street? He can be working for us. We are covering every street, every nook and corner. Let me tell you, you people have the habit of overexaggerating the importance of these people. This KSM, I don't care a hoot about him. Their mobility has been brought to zero. We have this highly sophisticated electronic gadgetry, we have the [National] Crisis Management Cell center, we have PISCES [the U.S.-originated Personal Identification Secure Comparison and Evaluation System]...and can tell anybody going in and out."[1] The obvious question, of course, was that if the ISI had Pakistan so well covered, how had KSM been allowed to build the Al Qaeda network there before September 11 in the first place—and then rebuild it once again afterward?

Belief in their own infallibility was so deep that several top Pakistani military and intelligence officials maintained for months afterward that, in fact, KSM had been captured—or, if not captured, killed. There were news reports that he was lying in state in a morgue; one senior government official told a journalist that KSM's "widow" had been returned to Egypt.

Pakistan as a society was accustomed to dealing with imperfect information about almost everything. It was often supposed that much public discourse was intended to mislead or obscure. Analysts routinely assumed as a starting point that a piece of public information was untruthful and proceeded from there, trying to discern in what way it was a lie, why it was told, and what it meant. In this case, one conclusion that could be drawn was that although the authorities had nearly caught KSM, they now had no idea exactly where he was.

KSM wasn't, of course, dead or captured; once again, he had somehow gotten away. No matter how close the call—one Pakistani intelligence officer likened it to a Hollywood Western in which the good guys arrive to find the campfire coals still burning but their quarry gone—the raid was a failure in that sense. But every raid told KSM's pursuers something, and this one had validated the broader notion that KSM had been in Karachi and that he had built a substantial infrastructure there.

All the evidence that had pointed to the sprawling city—Yosri Fouda's interview and the resulting satellite intercepts; raids on other safe houses, one of which yielded copies of several 9/11 hijackers' passports; evidence from Ganczarski, Zubaydah, Padilla, and Guantánamo detainees—had been correct. Connections to every Al Qaeda plot ran through the city. The ISI's claims notwithstanding, Karachi was a hub. In fact, Karachi was *the* hub.

No one could say how Mohammed escaped. Some American agents believed the presence of the children at the house suggested he'd been tipped off and fled in haste. Why else would he leave the children there? But there were other indications that Mohammed had set up a system of care for the children so he could pop in for playtime with them whenever possible. A woman caretaker found with the children indicated she was hired by KSM to provide them with an education.

KSM's escape stoked already considerable U.S. fears that he was being protected by elements within the Pakistani police, military, and intelligence agencies. Such fellow travelers, Keenan and others surmised, had probably been harboring KSM—in Pakistan and elsewhere—even as the FBI had racheted up its efforts to find him. His wanted posters had been up all over the world for years, and he had been on dozens of watch lists. Yet he seemed to wander with ease, and without fear.

In photos found at the house with his children, KSM was dressed in traditional Muslim tunic and kaffiyeh. He was shown with "at least one wife" and several more children besides the two sons. In many of them, the children were smiling, and KSM was, too.

To those entrusted with finding him, KSM remained a cipher. "We know less about him than any of the others," a senior FBI official said at the time. "He was under everybody's radar. We don't know how he did it. We wish we knew."

One of the prizes in the bin al-Shibh raid was a large suitcase that contained a virtual road map of Khalid Sheikh Mohammed's life, including bank records and his neatly framed diploma from North Carolina A&T. That piece of paper became another battle in the turf war between FBI and CIA agents, with the FBI wanting to keep it as evidence and accusing a senior CIA officer of putting it on the wall of his Karachi office as some sort of trophy or conversation piece. The disagreement spoke volumes about the rapidly deteriorating relationship between the two U.S. agencies after station chief Grenier's departure, a time when the CIA increasingly tried to keep its raids and seizures away from Keenan. Her confrontations with the agency were growing ever more bitter.

Grenier and Keenan had trusted one another and built a relationship, albeit a guarded one. The CIA veteran appreciated the value of keeping the FBI in the loop and bringing a law enforcement agent on each raid team, if for no other reason than to gather evidence for possible prosecutions. His replacement, Vance,* had a far less inclusive view of the role the FBI should play in the war on terror. Keenan's difficulties were exacerbated by the fact that Reimann's replacement as FBI legal attaché in June of 2002, Chuck Riley, for the most part went along with the CIA's plan. Riley operated from a position of some weakness, as he had virtually no counterterrorism background; his last post had been in Sacramento.

The situation boiled over when Keenan pushed to travel from Islamabad to Karachi to participate in the interrogation of bin al-Shibh. When Vance refused, Keenan appealed to Washington and his decision was overturned. The veteran Al Qaeda expert was allowed to attend. But when Keenan got there, she was told to sit and be quiet while a CIA interrogator asked questions. Keenan fumed to headquarters that because the CIA was running the show, efforts to follow up on KSM's bank records and other documents that could lead to him were ignored. That was especially frustrating given the treasures that agents found in Mohammed's huge, tattered, taped-together suitcase. Besides the photos and bank statements, authorities found Al Qaeda operational records. "It was his life's stuff," said one agent on scene. "Anything that was important to him was in there."

---

*Not his real name.

One great value of the luggage was as evidence that KSM was in touch with bin Laden and his family, and on the move. He wasn't fixed, but mobile. To transport and shelter the Al Qaeda exodus through Karachi, KSM had built a network of safe houses. One estimate put the number as high as fifty.[2] That network now gave him a lifeline.

As a blow to KSM's ambitions, the capture of bin al-Shibh turned out to be insignificant. Bin al-Shibh was a key figure in the 9/11 plot, relaying instructions to the hijackers and passing their information back to Mohammed, but he was a functionary, not a mover in that plot or any other.

What his pursuers didn't know yet was that at the very time their hunt for him was at its most intense—and, in some respects, at its most promising—KSM was busier than ever plotting and orchestrating attacks in Pakistan, Saudi Arabia, the UK, and the United States.

Far more damaging to the Al Qaeda cause than the bin al-Shibh capture was the October capture in the United Arab Emirates of Abd al-Rahim al-Nashiri, who had been in many ways KSM's equal in the immediate post-9/11 Al Qaeda organization. Nashiri played almost exactly the same role as KSM but within a more circumscribed geography—the Arabian Peninsula. He had overseen the 2000 attack on the USS *Cole* in Aden harbor in Yemen and a virtual carbon copy of it against the French commercial ship MV *Limburg* in the fall of 2002.[3] Nashiri's capture was yet another instance of an Al Qaeda operative tempting fate. He had used a satellite phone to communicate with the foot soldiers executing the *Limburg* attack. The phone was tracked by the U.S., and Nashiri was found and arrested by the Emiratis.[4]

Nashiri had been in and out of Karachi frequently. He and KSM consulted and shared operatives with one another. His disappearance from the battlefield left KSM without much in the way of experienced colleagues upon whom he could rely. Instead, he found readily available supplies of younger Al Qaeda and Pakistani militant operatives to tap.

So many plots were being uncovered that authorities didn't know what to do. A secret Pakistani intelligence report described the time as one in which the ISI had helped disrupt Al Qaeda–affiliated terrorist plots so ambitious that it had "helped avert colossal damage to humanity not only in Pakistan but the world over." One of the alleged networks of foreign nationals linked to KSM "was engaged in development and operationalization of Al Qaeda anthrax capability," the Pakistani report said.[5]

In December, bin Laden named KSM the chief of all Al Qaeda external operations. This was significant in part for its acknowledgment that Nashiri had disappeared. KSM's options may have been diminished by the capture of some of his senior cohorts, but if the expectations were that, having narrowly escaped capture once again, he would go dormant, those expectations were sadly, tragically dashed. What he still had available to him in addition to his personal network of militants was his trusted family and clan, and that was where he turned. He had used his nephew—his sister's son Ali Abdul Aziz Ali—to arrange logistics for the 9/11 hijackers. Ali, also known as Ammar al-Baluchi, was as far from a battle-hardened jihadi as you could get. He was born in Kuwait, but left with his mother when she separated from his father.[6] He was raised mainly in Iran. He was a teenager attending boarding school in Zahedan, a Baluch town on the Pakistani border, when his first cousin Abdul Basit Abdul Karim visited him to receive care for the eye he had injured while making a bomb.[7] Ali spent time with Basit, aka Ramzi Yousef, during his convalescence, and for the first time was introduced to the concept of jihad. Basit was a charming and persuasive man, and his talks with the young Ali had a long-lasting effect.

After completing high school, Ali moved to Karachi for training as a software engineer. There, he spent time with his uncle Khalid Sheikh Mohammed. He began to think about devoting himself to jihad. His father, a muezzin at a mosque in Kuwait, had other ideas, and directed him to find work in the United Arab

Emirates, then the booming economic hot spot of the region. Ali took a job with the Modern Electronics Corporation in Dubai, but before moving there he told KSM that he wanted to join the jihad. He thought himself unfit for military training, but suggested he could work for KSM instead.

Not long after he resettled in Dubai, his uncle took him up on his offer and asked him to facilitate transit for the 9/11 hijackers as they traveled from Pakistan to the United States. Over the next two years he did exactly that for almost all the hijackers. He apparently hadn't anticipated how much of his time this would entail, and told KSM he needed help. KSM sent an Al Qaeda accountant, Mustafa al-Hawsawi, to assist him.[8]

Ali returned to Karachi just before September 11, 2001. He worked side by side with his uncle after that, at first not doing much more than running errands. He grew into his role as a financial facilitator. Money to fund their operations arrived irregularly, always by courier and in cash, and often in large amounts. It was not unusual to have $100,000 on hand. Ali helped KSM find ways to store and retrieve the money, sometimes laying it off with cooperative businessmen then retrieving it when needed. One man, Saifullah Paracha, the wealthy founder and owner of a Karachi-based conglomerate that included a newspaper, television production studios, and a textile manufacturing business, held as much as $600,000 for months in shrink-wrapped stacks of American bills.[9] KSM relied on his Baluch network as well. His core cell in Karachi included a pair of in-laws used as couriers and facilitators when the need arose, and another nephew, Abdul Basit Abdul Karim's brother and KSM's college classmate, Abdul Karim Abdul Karim, more familiarly known as Musaad Aruchi. Abdul Karim had assisted KSM and Basit as far back as the early 1990s, providing housing for Basit and his associates when they were preparing for the Manila Air plot.[10] The two nephews had assisted KSM in the murder of Danny Pearl and other activities in Karachi.

What KSM gained in trustworthiness from using relatives he

sometimes lost in efficacy. None was an experienced terror operative. They were fine handling money and logistics, but inexperienced otherwise. Ali had recently taken the initiative to begin planning an attack of his own. He and Hamza Zubayr, a veteran Al Qaeda operative and former instructor at the al-Farouq training camp near Kandahar, had begun developing a plan to attack the American consulate and hotels in Karachi when Zubayr was killed in the bin al-Shibh raid. KSM immediately put a halt to the planning.

This was not retreat, however. He had other, more accomplished allies. Walid bin Attash, even minus the prosthetic leg he left behind in the September raid, was one of Al Qaeda's most experienced and capable operatives and one of KSM's most trusted allies. They had known one another since the Soviet jihad in the 1980s; he had been present when KSM's brother Abed was killed. He and Abu Faraj al-Libi formed the veteran core of KSM's Karachi operation. Bin Attash had commanded troops in battle to much praise, and Libi had worked directly with bin Laden, establishing and administering camps. Both had wide experience operating abroad, too, but neither could operate in Pakistan with the kind of ease that KSM did. They were Arabs, from Yemen and Libya respectively. They could neither converse with nor gain the trust of the powerful Pakistani sectarian groups that KSM and Al Qaeda now relied on to survive.

Whatever happened, KSM never lacked the resolve to do more. His war was nowhere near done. Certainly no one on the ground in Karachi felt that it was. Other plans were in effect. KSM had been sending men and money out from Karachi into the world and just a month after bin al-Shibh's capture one of those emissaries had sent an encouraging report back to the home office. On October 12, a man wearing a bomb in a backpack detonated it in a crowded nightclub in a beachside bar in Bali, Indonesia, killing 202 people and maiming dozens more. KSM had helped fund the attack nearly a year before, sending thousands in cash to his trusted Southeast Asian comrade Hambali. KSM had kept up other relationships with militants in Southeast Asia as well, for plots that included a second-wave attack on the West Coast of the United States.

The Bali attack was the most deadly since 9/11 and was yet one more indication that the threat was nowhere near eliminated. KSM rewarded Hambali by sending him couriers bearing a total of $130,000. The money was intended for use in Hambali's next attacks, against the Marriott hotel in Jakarta, and included a bonus for the successful Bali massacre. The courier for a portion of the money was the young Pakistani American Majid Khan, whom KSM had earlier assigned to study the possibility of blowing up gas stations in the U.S.

Karachi remained in many ways a more dangerous place for his pursuers than for KSM. He could hide; they could not. American investigators there felt overwhelmed. They were so few and the place was so overwhelmingly large, chaotic, and dangerous. The average tenure of an FBI agent was measured in weeks or even days, not months. Even the most confident of agents wondered what they could do in such a short time. Few spoke Arabic; none spoke Urdu. They had no idea what Pakistan was like—its customs, history, or even the backgrounds of the people they were hunting. One agent favored the comfort of McDonald's so much and so often that he earned the nickname Happy Meal. The TDY agents had no rapport with their Pakistani counterparts. Most didn't even try. They were essentially bodies being offered up for raids, as if they were busting drug rings in South Central Los Angeles. They couldn't carry guns or identify themselves as law enforcement. And while the Pakistanis were less than overly hospitable, the reception they got from "the sisters" at the CIA was often worse. These were impossible conditions, and a lot of the agents did not want to be there. One supervisor from Newark showed up one day, got wrapped into all the infighting and security concerns, and went home the next.

Many of those who stayed felt they could barely leave their hotels or the consulate without endangering themselves. Sometimes they didn't have to go that far.

One night an FBI agent heard a knock on his hotel room door. A voice announced, "Room service," which the man inside hadn't ordered. He approached the door and looked through the peephole to see two men in the hall with no food tray in sight. He kept the door shut; investigators in Afghanistan later recovered a videotape showing an Al Qaeda exercise in which assassins posed as room-service waiters to gain access to hotel rooms and kill the inhabitants. The city felt like enemy territory for a reason—it was.

Both sides, the hunters and the hunted, went on about their business. KSM concentrated on operations far from his Karachi base—Indonesia, the United States, England. One new plot involved concealing chemical explosives in shipping containers manifested by one of Saifullah Paracha's companies to contain children's clothing, then loading them onto cargo ships and sailing them into busy American harbors. Another plan was a variant of 9/11. KSM envisioned hijacking several airliners and crashing them all into London's Heathrow Airport, one of the world's busiest. He placed a Karachi computer engineer, Muhammad Naeem Noor Khan, known as Abu Talha al-Pakistani, in charge of the plot.

The raids continued, too. In the end they would number in the hundreds throughout the country. In classic investigative fashion, whether the CIA would acknowledge their value or not, the raids contributed to solving the puzzle. Each raid produced one piece, maybe more, sometimes a lot more; as the pieces were assembled, an image of KSM's broad and hidden network emerged. His reach sometimes astonished his pursuers.[11] The effect was cumulative. Today's raid often led to tomorrow's. Whatever the value of any one raid, when taken in sum, as the FBI had argued from the beginning, they proved valuable. Investigators were beginning to see movement in the dark world of Karachi. Despite her dustups with the CIA, Keenan kept feeding passports, photos, and other documents into her FBI scanner and sending them home, and a massive "document exploitation" effort back in Washington was putting the puzzle pieces together.

In January, acting on a tip that KSM would be there, they

raided a house in the Karachi suburbs. Again, he was not there. They moved on.

Investigators found traces of KSM all over the country.[12] In the thick of the hunt, a senior ISI official marveled to a reporter that he was coming to know the two sides of KSM: the one shown in pictures seized in Karachi, in which he is happily playing with his two young sons, and the other, in which KSM—even while on a dead run—was aggressively directing Al Qaeda terrorist cells. "Despite being so much in danger, he has not gone into hibernation," the official said in an interview at ISI headquarters in November of 2002. "He is trying to protect what they have. He would like to consolidate first and then rebuild on the same edifice. And he is doing that. He remains active."

That official and other Pakistanis showed a grudging admiration for KSM, marveling at his uncanny ability to stay one step ahead of unprecedented dragnets. So much so, in fact, that U.S. authorities continued to question their resolve, especially within the parts of the ISI that were responsible for handling the militant sectarian groups with which KSM was aligned.

"The way he is managing their affairs, the way he is controlling things, he is not an ordinary man," the Pakistani intelligence official said. "He is very sharp and brave—an unusual combination."[13]

In February of 2003, after U.S. authorities picked up a suspicious intercept, a team crashed on a house in Quetta, the capital of Pakistan's Baluchistan province. Pakistani agents had grown suspicious of the house after tracking Al Qaeda operatives there from the nearby border with Iran. Again, they seemed to narrowly miss KSM, but the raid had its rewards. Mohammed Omar Abdel-Rahman, one of the sons of a bin Laden spiritual adviser known as the Blind Sheikh and himself a senior member in Al Qaeda, was captured along with another trove of documents, disks, and information. All of which was welcome, but agents had to wonder how many times KSM could get lucky. Or whether he was being tipped off. Were they getting closer, or would he at some point disappear forever? The FBI had come close to catching him way back in 1996, but once they missed, they never got another chance. The agency needed to get lucky.

## *Rawalpindi, Pakistan, Spring 2003*

KSM was far more careful than most of his comrades about operational security. He seldom risked exposing himself. Others wired money on his behalf. He used cutouts for critical communications. Others sent and received e-mails for him. He seldom wrote anything down, believing that important information was better delivered face-to-face. When he did write, the language was allusive.[14] Other operatives succumbed to the allure of the quick and easy satphone call. Just one call, just this one time. Then they were targeted, caught, and taken off the field of battle.

One group of Arab fighters had been captured on the run because they kept going outside the house they were hiding in to smoke cigarettes.[15] They couldn't help themselves. They wanted smoke breaks and took them, often outside. Neighbors eventually became suspicious, a team was dispatched, and they were taken away. KSM was irate. He lost not just the fighters but their safe house and several others, as well as the man who arranged them.

As time went on and more and more of his associates were captured, KSM relied even less on modern communications. "These guys were lying low. They were not using electronics. They were not being detected by electronic eavesdropping," an ISI officer said.[16] KSM instead sent trusted personal couriers. Others could cast their fates into the ether, where electronic detectives roamed. He stayed down on the ground, in the very human muck that was Pakistan. So in the end it was almost inevitable that it was a human who would betray him.

For more than a year, the CIA had been cultivating an asset who had contacted the agency out of the blue. The man was a longtime acquaintance of KSM's. Mohammed's family thought they might have met as far back as the anti-Soviet jihad in Afghanistan. He was from Iranian Baluchistan, as was KSM's family. They might have been distantly related, perhaps not, but were fellow Baluch—an extremely strong tie—in any case.[17]

The agency was patient in cultivating the walk-in, whom we'll refer to here as Baluchi. He spoke Dari, a dialect of Farsi, the principal language of Iran. The CIA had very few Farsi speakers accomplished enough to communicate with Baluchi. His initial handler was an Iranian American agent who was posted elsewhere overseas and flew to Pakistan whenever Baluchi or he wanted to meet. He was vetted over many months, and had passed polygraph tests. He seemed to be the real thing, maybe even capable of doing what he offered—delivering KSM.

Baluchi was paid regularly and provided useful information from time to time. The money was delivered to him in cash during his meetings with his handler. Fewer than a handful of the agency's burgeoning Pakistan staff were allowed to know the man's identity, or his purpose. The case was being run directly out of Langley under what were referred to as "restricted handling" rules, which mainly meant limited exposure on a strict need-to-know basis. When his case officer left the agency in 2002, his new handler—we'll call him Gino—also flew into the country just to meet with him. The Islamabad station residents were responsible for arranging safe houses for the meetings and sometimes for delivering money—thousands of dollars in bills in a paper bag—but they were not invited in to meet him. One agent caught a glimpse of him through a crack in the door at a safe house, sitting on a bed. He looked short and somewhat frail, much like virtually every other Baluch of his age and economic stature.

Baluchi sought to reconnect with KSM in person for months. The agency devised a plan to lure KSM to him; the bait was information that agents fed to Baluchi, who in turn passed it on to KSM. Finally, in late February of 2003, KSM agreed to meet Baluchi in Rawalpindi, a military garrison town southwest of the capital, Islamabad. He didn't tell Baluchi the precise location, but said it would be that night, February 28. The CIA readied an attack team, made up primarily of its own agents and select members of the ISI who were not told whom they were going after.[18] The FBI was not invited. The Americans still didn't know where or if the meeting would occur, and they didn't tell the Pakistanis the name of the target.

Marty Martin, the voluble head of the agency's Sunni Extremist Group within the Counterterrorist Center, couldn't contain himself at the 5:00 p.m. meeting of the executive staff gathered around George Tenet's conference table on Friday. "Boss," he said to Tenet. "Where are you going to be this weekend? Stay in touch. I just might get some good news."[19]

Aside from information about bin Laden himself, there could be no bigger news. KSM had risen dramatically in the agency's estimation from the days when—except for assigning a single agent in the minuscule Renditions Branch to the task—they couldn't really be bothered to track his whereabouts. Since then, so much effort had been spent with so little result that a potential breakthrough had begun to seem far-fetched.

KSM had been on the road with his nephew Aziz Ali and had met with Al Qaeda's number two, Ayman al-Zawahiri, the day before, near Peshawar.[20] He arrived at the Rawalpindi safe house, a private residence, by car at about 9:00 p.m.[21] The home, a large, comfortable, single-family residence at 18A Nisar Road in the Westridge district of Rawalpindi, one of its nicer areas, was owned by a prominent local couple. The husband was a scientist; the wife, Mahlaqa Khanum, was a politically active supporter of the Jamaat-e-Islami, Pakistan's largest religious political party and one that had suspicious ties to Pakistani militant groups and even Al Qaeda. The couple claimed utter innocence later, but Mustafa al-Hawsawi, the Al Qaeda accountant, had been in the house since January.[22] Baluchi was brought to the house not long after KSM arrived. They talked for more than an hour. KSM, who was vigilant about the use of cell phones, for some reason allowed Baluchi to bring his phone into the house. Sometime later in the evening,

Baluchi went into the bathroom and quietly texted his agency handlers: "I am with KSM."

Not long afterward, Baluchi left the house and, once he was by himself, contacted the CIA agents again. This time, he knew how to bring them back to the home. After taking them there, Baluchi was quickly bundled off to the Islamabad airport by CIA officials, who put him on a plane. He was in the air and on his way out of the country before KSM even knew he was in danger.

The attack team took up positions outside 18A Nisar Road. By this point, the Americans and Pakistanis had cooperated on scores of similar raids, several of which were aimed at capturing KSM. This was, in that respect, just another day at the office. The team waited outside in the dark until it felt certain that KSM, a night owl, would be asleep.

The team waited until past 2:00 a.m., then the Pakistanis broke through the gate, through the front doors, and charged through the house, herding the family into a back bedroom. They found KSM sound asleep. They encountered only minimal resistance. KSM, groggy from an apparent dose of sleeping pills, offered to pay his Pakistani attackers to let him go free. When that failed to move them, he asked them if they'd like to cross over and join his team. "Why are you doing this for the Americans?" he asked. "If it's money, we'll give you what you want."[23] That didn't work, either. KSM, al-Hawsawi, and the owners' adult son, Ahmed Qadoos, were taken into custody and spirited away.

Later, the legend of KSM's capture would grow. There were tales of how he boldly wrestled with his pursuers, grabbed a Pakistani security agent's rifle, and shot one of the Pakistanis in the foot before finally being subdued. It was said that when the authorities burst in he yelled, "Don't shoot, there are women and children here."

But the reality of it is that, in the end, KSM was caught completely unawares, and in his pajamas.

Marty Martin woke George Tenet with a phone call in the middle of the night. Tenet was at Camp David for weekend meetings with President Bush and his senior advisers. There was enough of a ruckus raised during the attack that neighbors were awakened, and the local media swarmed to the scene the next morning. The Pakistani government was forced to respond and acknowledge that three men had been taken into custody; one of them seemed to be a high-ranking Al Qaeda officer. By noon, the Pakistani press was reporting that KSM had been captured. The accounts varied wildly, but the fact of Mohammed's capture was central to them all. Many ran photographs of KSM taken from wanted posters. Several of the photos showed him as a handsome, rugged young man. One pictured him in a Western coat and tie.

Back at Langley, Martin saw these early press accounts and was distressed at the accompanying photos. "Boss," he said to Tenet. "This ain't right. The media are making this bum look like a hero."[24] He asked Tenet for approval to release a somewhat less flattering photograph. Tenet agreed. A member of the CIA team had taken photos of KSM right after his capture, including one in which he looks into the camera, with his eyebrows raised nearly to his hairline. Still, Martin thought, that initial photo did not make KSM look sufficiently unattractive. Martin asked if there were any other photos available. The agent messed up KSM's hair and then took another photo. The result was the famous image of KSM—thickset, glowering, wild-haired, half dressed in his nightshirt—his first introduction to most of the rest of the world.

# CHAPTER 15
## In Captivity

*Rawalpindi, Pakistan, March 2003*

As was often the case, confusion reigned supreme in Pakistan after KSM's capture. Islamabad government ministers gave interviews saying the raid was a Pakistani operation through and through. Some said they had been following KSM for months. One official said that KSM had flown into town the day of the capture, and that one or two ISI officers were on the airplane with him. Another said that KSM had been taken to the local police station, where a case had been opened against him. Some officials said Pakistan would not hand over any Pakistani prisoner in its custody to the United States or any other country, while others denied that KSM was even Pakistani. Kuwait also insisted he was not a Kuwaiti. The ISI, for what was apparently the first time in its history, staged a media briefing at which a grainy videotape, purportedly of the raid, was played. It was so obviously a staged reconstruction that some within the roomful of reporters burst out laughing.

Far less humorous were the questions that began to swirl almost immediately around the KSM takedown. The house where the arrest occurred belonged to the Qadoos family. Ahmed Qadoos's parents were away for the evening at a wedding when the raid took place. Ahmed, his wife, and his two children were at home. The family insisted that they never saw any strangers in the house and that they thought Ahmed had been kidnapped. But the authorities insisted he was arrested there, along with KSM and Hawsawi. The next day Ahmed's parents were put in the odd situation of affirming in public that their son couldn't be a terrorist because he was a simpleton. His mother produced a doctor's certificate attesting to that fact. A neighbor, an army colonel, agreed. "He's a goof, simple in the head," he said.[1] Ahmed spent most of his time playing with his beloved caged parrots and staring at the dogs in the Pakistani army training center right next door. Pakistan's army headquarters, in fact, was less than a mile away, and the community was essentially closed to anyone but the military. Ahmed's parents did not mention that their other son, Adil, an army major who was arrested in Kohat the next day on suspicion of connections to Al Qaeda, might have been using the house to provide safe harbor to one of the world's most wanted men whenever he came to Rawalpindi.[2]

## *Washington, D.C., March 2003*

The long hunt to find KSM was over. It had lasted nearly a full decade. Intelligence officials declared his capture a lethal blow against Al Qaeda. Taking KSM out of service was a rare bit of good news in Washington, where the Bush administration had been heavily criticized for turning its attention away from Al Qaeda to the impending invasion of Iraq. Tenet flew to Pakistan to personally thank the informant, who claimed the reward money—by then raised to $25 million—and now lives with his family under protective custody somewhere in the United States. The CIA trumpeted one intercepted communiqué from Al Qaeda that said, "The loss of Khalid Sheik Mohammed was like the melting of an iceberg. We can never replace him."[3] Chairman of the House intelligence committee (and later CIA chief) Porter Goss likened

KSM's capture to the liberation of Paris in World War II. A new hunt would now begin: What did he know?

The race to exploit the information gleaned from computers and other gear captured with KSM began instantly, especially the effort to identify individuals who U.S. authorities believed might be poised to launch attacks in the United States. While KSM's initial interrogators worked to pry information from the terrorist network's operations leader, FBI agents in the United States and CIA operatives overseas ran down leads pulled from computers, computer disks, paper documents, cell phones, and other electronic paraphernalia seized in the raid.

Authorities said they believed the seized items could prove to be a breakthrough in that they could contain the names of Al Qaeda members, details of past and present terrorist plots, and the locations of "sleeper" cells in the United States and overseas. Much of it was loaded onto a jet and flown straight to Washington.

The good news was tempered by intelligence reports indicating that Mohammed had been coordinating and planning attacks in the weeks before his arrest. Some of them appeared ready to be launched.

"He was an active fellow," a U.S. official said.

A U.S. intelligence memo dated February 26, 2003, immediately before his capture, had warned that Mohammed was overseeing an effort to have Al Qaeda sleeper cells in the United States attack suspension bridges, gas stations, and power plants in major cities, including New York.[4]

Asked if counterterrorism authorities believed that the plotters were somewhere in the United States, an official said, "We don't know."

Investigators thought they had a very brief time—days, not weeks—to exploit the information or risk losing the trails of those implicated. Within thirty-six hours of Mohammed's capture, U.S. forensic experts had found "operational detail, names...including Al Qaeda operatives around the world, including here" in the United States in the documents and computers caught with KSM and Hawsawi. One key official in Washington exulted at their good fortune. He described the cache as "the mother lode of information that leads to the inner workings of Al Qaeda. How they work, where they work, who they are, what their financial structure is."[5]

Officials at the National Security Agency listened attentively to their global array of electronic eavesdropping satellites, waiting for an expected flurry of e-mails and cell phone calls among Al Qaeda members. Other authorities watched for the movement of cell members seeking cover.

Frank Pellegrino, the FBI special agent who had invested nearly seven years in the search for KSM and his accomplices in the Manila bombing campaign, heard about Mohammed's capture in a phone call Saturday afternoon from a friend at FBI headquarters. The news hadn't broken yet. "Turn on the TV," analyst Brian Antol told him. Pellegrino had been largely ignored in the post-9/11 search for KSM, and he felt both shame and anger about his marginalization: shame for not having caught KSM in time to prevent 9/11; anger for having so many roadblocks thrown in his way before the attacks and having been pushed aside after. Not a day had passed in which he hadn't beaten himself up over that. "It was my case," he'd say. "He was my guy." He wasn't the sort of man to display emotions in public, but it weighed on him; he hadn't slept well in years. "Get your bags packed," Antol told him. "They want you down here asap."

Pellegrino welcomed Mohammed's capture—and his summons to headquarters—as a chance for redemption. The FBI had played virtually no role in KSM's capture. It was "the sister's" big score. The Bureau felt sure, however, that once KSM was in custody its agents would have to be called in to help extract whatever information he had. The lobbying effort began even before KSM left Pakistan, and from on high. Pat D'Amuro, now the FBI's number three, waged a forceful campaign to get Pellegrino in front of KSM before the coercive interrogations could be started, insisting that the KSM situation was different from that of the other high-value detainees because KSM had been indicted by a federal grand jury. Besides, D'Amuro argued—to George Tenet and to anyone who'd listen—nobody else knew KSM like "Frankie" Pellegrino did. "Our guys, by far, knew more than anyone about Al Qaeda and its organizational structure, its history, everything about it," D'Amuro said. "You have to know what to ask them."[6] Pellegrino was at home in New York when he got the call from Antol, who had been working with Pellegrino since the days when they were hunting Abdul Basit. Pellegrino was so certain he would be deployed that he told his wife, Maeve, that he would see her and their young children when he could. It might be months, he said. "Do what you need to do," she told him, knowing how much he wanted, and needed, another chance.

The next day, Sunday, Pellegrino, brimming with emotion, drove down to Washington, expecting to be escorted quickly to wherever the interrogation would take place. In some ways, this was a moment he had prepared for his entire career. He went to the J. Edgar Hoover Building early Monday morning and discovered that Andy Arena, the FBI official who had asked that Pellegrino be brought in, was suddenly gone, replaced by Art Cummings. Arena was moved out because he refused to go along with orders from the Bush White House to keep looking for an Al Qaeda–Saddam connection as a pretext for war when there wasn't one. And Cummings, on his first day on the job, wasn't able to send Pellegrino anywhere. The FBI, despite urgent pleas from executives like D'Amuro to let its agents "get in the box" with captured terrorists, was still shut out of the process. In part, this was a result of a choice the Bureau had made the previous summer.

FBI agents Ali Soufan and Steve Gaudin had described to their bosses the aggressive techniques that CIA contractors employed against Abu Zubaydah—techniques that would be further enhanced later; they weren't yet simulating drownings. Soufan called the techniques he had witnessed borderline torture.[7] In the summer of 2002, D'Amuro argued to director Robert Mueller that the Bureau should not get involved with this new program. Torture, he said, was ineffective: prisoners would sometimes admit to anything just to make the torture stop; it was shortsighted—how would any court of law, civilian or military, ever accept evidence obtained by torture?—and it was morally wrong. He also argued that it would taint any FBI agent who ever participated in it, effectively rendering him unable to do his job because his credibility would be challenged any time he testified in court—on any matter. In effect, D'Amuro was both the most aggressive advocate for the FBI taking charge of the interrogations and the one who was mostly responsible for his agents not taking part in the CIA-run program.

Mueller agreed, and ordered his agents not to participate so long as the CIA was using aggressive techniques. The idea that the CIA would suddenly succumb to the FBI's wishes and let the Bureau run the KSM interrogation was never seriously considered. "We lost," one FBI supervisor, Chuck Frahm, told a glum group of FBI agents after one particularly testy confrontation over KSM. Pellegrino was shut out once again. In the hallway at headquarters one afternoon soon after he arrived, Cummings asked him if he would sit down and write one hundred questions that the FBI could put forward so that KSM could be asked them by others. Pellegrino looked at Cummings and said: "Art, I don't write questions. I ask questions." Then he turned and walked away.

## *Vicinity of Rawalpindi, Pakistan, March 2003*

Two days after his capture, KSM sat in a spartan interrogation room across a small table from a Pakistani security official, with an American off to the side. The prisoner was dressed in baggy white pants, a white shirt, and a vest, and his appearance had been cleaned up significantly from the infamous photo of his capture. He looked far smaller and less imposing. If he had been allowed to sleep in the time since then, it wasn't apparent. A thick stubble of black whiskers covered his face. He rubbed his eyes constantly. He slumped dejectedly in the chair, a blanket around his shoulders; his head fell to one side and then the other as he fought sleep. Sometimes he gave in and just put his head on his shoulder and closed his eyes. At other times he put his two hands together, as if in prayer, and held them next to his ear as a cushion.

As a camera videotaped[8] from above, KSM was wobbly. His interrogators, polite as they were, nonetheless persisted in asking him questions. KSM spoke fractured English in short, guttural sentences, at times only a word here or there. His legs twitched incessantly; he would lift his heels and then slam them down again and again. He swayed from side to side, too, then rocked back and forth, and leaned forward with his elbows on his knees. He was passive, bowing his head often, crossing his arms to the degree that his handcuffs would allow. An ashtray full of cigarette butts was on the table, and so was a notebook and a bulky, old-fashioned clock. KSM covered his face with his hands wearily.

"You say you are going to do something. Maybe you can..." he said to the American. KSM was in Pakistani custody and had been since his capture, but the Pakistanis had allowed a CIA officer to participate in the questioning.

The American interrupted him. "I haven't promised you anything," he said.

It was a polite conversation, conducted in quiet, even hushed, tones. KSM had told his captors that Al Qaeda had a code that all must obey: if you get caught, do not talk for forty-eight hours, to give the brothers time to go deep underground and destroy any trail that might lead to them. He appeared to be waiting for that time to pass, and his interrogators, it seemed, were doing nothing to force him talk.

"Same thing, different night. Maybe go to sleep until night, you come back the next night," KSM said. "I cannot make sure you make sure..." He nodded off in midsentence again.

The American laughed quietly. "I cannot make sure you make sure?" he said, mockingly repeating KSM's exhausted gibberish. The American pointed to the clock on the table.

"It's one twenty," he said. He pointed at the Pakistani officer. "He said you would be talking by one twenty. It's now one twenty."

KSM, his head getting even more wobbly, quickly stole a

glance down at the clock. "Yes," he said softly, almost inaudibly, looking downward. Then he leaned forward, his elbows back on his knees as he tried to focus his attention on his questioners. He looked across the table at them, almost expectantly, waiting for the questions to start. The American's hand moved to a notepad on the table, and he pointed to a word that had been written on it. He asked KSM what it meant.

KSM again tried to focus and squirmed in his chair, adjusting the blanket draped around his shoulders. He said nothing.

"Do you want to talk to him [the American] alone?" the Pakistani interrogator asked. KSM shook his head no, cockily, almost defiantly. After a long pause, KSM said, "Other people know about the matter.... The word is out already, on BBC... CNN."

His interrogators saw this as a sign that KSM was rationalizing that it was okay now for him to talk. Whether he would actually give up anything of importance was another matter.

"Somebody was talking—yesterday, actually—about Hazem," the American said. And there the grainy footage went dark.

KSM was held in Pakistani custody for three days. He was then transferred to U.S. control and taken on a three-year tour of the secret prisons the CIA had established in Asia, Africa, and eastern Europe, most of it blindfolded. Dark side, indeed.

The agency ceded its interrogation program to outside contractors who had reverse engineered a torture resistance program developed by the army decades earlier. The contractors knew little about interrogation. They also knew so little about Al Qaeda and KSM that they wouldn't have known what to do if their prized captives had suddenly agreed to tell them all about the workings of Al Qaeda and its ongoing operations. The man who, by any measure, knew the most about KSM, Pellegrino, was not allowed to go anywhere near him. Pellegrino spent most of his time in Washington, spinning his wheels or commiserating with other agents at Harry's Pub, down the street from headquarters. Then he drove home to New York and went back to his other casework.

As was often the case, the materials captured with KSM were

of more immediate importance than anything they were going to get quickly from him. In particular, the laptop computer and portable hard drives contained a wealth of data. The Qadoos family claimed that the raiders took a desktop computer that belonged to the children in the house. The laptop belonged to Hawsawi, who seemed to be a paymaster. His computer contained bank ledgers, scores of phone numbers and safe house addresses, and the identity of a web of financiers and couriers. There was so much financial information that when Alice Fisher, the deputy assistant attorney general overseeing counterterrorism, saw Dennis Lormel in the foyer outside SIOC, she nearly hugged the FBI chief money tracker. "You're going to be the happiest guy in the whole place," she said. At least one of the portable drives appeared to be KSM's. And it contained something that confirmed the worst fears of the U.S. counterterrorism community: a list of contacts for people KSM had deployed, or was planning to deploy, abroad. It was a road map to many of his sleeper cells, dozens of them, including some who may have been in the United States for years.[9]

## *Washington, D.C., March 2003*

On the morning of March 5, Art Cummings wasn't yet midway through his first week in his new job as head of the FBI's International Terrorism Operations Section I. Dale Watson, who as an assistant director had been head of all FBI counterterrorism on 9/11, knew Cummings and called him on the afternoon of the attacks to tell him that he was being transferred, effective immediately. Cummings, a gung-ho ex–navy SEAL with a penchant for handkerchiefed suits and wingtips, arrived at HQ that night and never left. He was just eighteen months removed from working in a Virginia field office. Now all of a sudden he was coordinating Al Qaeda investigations worldwide.

That morning, his deputy—a CIA officer temporarily deployed to the FBI—burst into his office with news that the agency was about to bust Majid Khan in Pakistan. Khan, the son of a Baltimore businessman, had made several trips back and forth to Pakistan in the previous three years and had come to the attention of the FBI. He was suspected of being connected to Al Qaeda and KSM, but the details were murky.

Khan was a burly young man whose family came to the U.S., to Baltimore, just in time for him to attend Owings Mills High School. Khan was a normal kid who listened to hip-hop and played video games. Like many other KSM acolytes, he was computer-savvy, volunteering to teach computer classes at the Islamic Society of Baltimore. He began to take more of an interest in religion and attended secret prayer meetings at the society. On a trip home to Pakistan, after spending time with an uncle who was a religious fundamentalist, he became further radicalized. Both the uncle and a cousin were members of Al Qaeda, and in early 2002, they introduced the young man to KSM, and he became quite attached.[10] Mohammed was fascinated with the possibilities of using the impressionable young man, who spoke excellent English. After learning that his father owned a gas station, KSM began thinking of ways they could blow it up. He sent Khan off to be trained in the construction of explosive timing devices. KSM further tasked Khan to conduct research on poisoning U.S. water reservoirs.

None of this, obviously, was known to the FBI, who saw Khan as a young man who was perhaps a bit too fascinated with Pakistan. In the post-9/11 era, the Bureau nonetheless had invested substantial investigative resources trying to figure Khan out. They had pieced together his network of friends and family in the United States. The CIA wasn't good about sharing information, so it gave little explanation about why the arrest was occurring then and even less about what it had on Khan. Presumably, Khan's name had turned up in KSM's electronic pocket litter.

Whatever the case, Cummings knew an opportunity when he saw one. More important, he saw a potential *missed* opportunity.

"Holy shit!" Cummings said. "How and when are they going to do it?"

"They're going to do it quick," the deputy said.

"How much time do I have?" Cummings asked.

Cummings needed to get agents in position to surveil Khan's network of acquaintances in the U.S., to see how they reacted to news of his arrest. If Cummings got lucky, some of them would betray themselves by their actions. But that kind of surveillance effort takes a tremendous amount of time—not just to get the people in place but also to get the legal approvals needed to use electronic devices to augment the human "net" being placed over the suspects.

"I'm just not in a position to do that," Cummings told his deputy. "I need some time." The deputy placed a call to Langley, then reported back to Cummings that they could only delay the takedown by so much.

"You have four hours," the CIA agent told Cummings.

This set off a mad scramble. Cummings went into overdrive, issuing orders to his team of lieutenants, to supervisors in the FBI's Baltimore field office, and calling Justice Department legal officials to see about getting expedited wiretap warrants.

In the time Cummings had been at headquarters, he had become known for his mantra: the FBI was no longer a law enforcement agency but an intelligence-gathering operation, one in which agents watched terror suspects like hawks, following them for days, weeks, months, even years before taking them down—if they ever did—so they could understand the entire universe of bad guys in their purview. Terror suspects were no longer persons to be handcuffed. They were "collection platforms" to be exploited as much as possible—as long as agents could guarantee they didn't lose sight of them. With Khan, Cummings and his agents were operating virtually in the dark. Cummings's biggest fear was that "we didn't know what we didn't know." In other words, they didn't even know who—or what, exactly—they were looking for.

They were helped by Khan's carelessness. On his previous trip to Pakistan, he had let his U.S. visa lapse, and in trying to reestablish his residency he had been assisted by a young New Yorker, Saifullah Paracha's son Uzair, and the Boston scientist Aafia Siddiqui. Siddiqui posed as Khan's wife when she rented a post office box, an attempt to show that Khan was living in the United States. She gave Paracha a key to the box, and he began impersonating Khan, making phone calls to what was then the Immigration and Naturalization Service. Their attempted ruse was, until March of 2003, unknown to authorities. But it would soon give investigators a ready-made set of clues to follow.

At some point in the eighteen months after September 11, Cummings and others had begun to suspect that an apparently substantial number of operatives had been sent to the United States. Evidence came from virtually every significant arrest—Zubaydah and José Padilla both yielded information on plots that were aimed at the U.S., and as hundreds of men were captured in Afghanistan, or in Pakistan, their interrogations provided more information. It was almost always sketchy, but sometimes investigators got lucky.

That happened with the Khan case. Cummings's agents were in place, and the wiretaps approved—by the White House, no less—half an hour before the takedown took place in Pakistan. Then they waited. The new FBI supervisor slept on the couch in his office, and awoke to an early-morning fax informing him that an interesting call had indeed been made and intercepted.

FBI agents had listened in on the telephone call between Khan's father in Baltimore and a house in Columbus, Ohio, where three suspicious men lived. They soon determined that one of them was an Ohio truck driver named Iyman Faris, who had already come up on their radar screen but who seemed fairly innocuous. But now the FBI agents heard the elder Khan tell Faris that the money he had given him was strictly for business. It seemed an odd call.

One investigator described it: "That was one of those moments where you say, 'What the hell are they talking about?' We knew it was code, but not for what. But we knew that it was something bad. We knew that it connected two bad dudes, and we were thinking—this can't be good."[11]

The FBI agents, in part through the capture of KSM, realized that Faris had been part of a plot to surveil the Brooklyn Bridge dating back to 2002, that he had been to Afghan training camps—and that he was one of KSM's sleeper agents in the United States, connected somehow to an Al Qaeda plot of unknown size, scope, means, and location. "The pucker factor was through the roof," one law enforcement official said of that realization. "Everything that came out of KSM was on fire; we had to track it immediately." And a fire hose of information was coming from KSM, at least from the computers, phones, and other gear caught with him. FBI agents, in the words of one of them, were going "batshit crazy" in their urgent effort to run down leads.[12]

The New York Joint Terrorism Task Force had known about Faris separately. Now suddenly they had a connection between Khan and Faris. And they already had one between Saifullah Paracha and Khan. They needed to find the younger Paracha, Uzair, and fast, so they raced to the home of his father's American business partner, an Orthodox Jew who lived in Brooklyn. He had a home address for Uzair back at the office, he said, and he offered to go with the agents to get it. When they got there, around midnight, they found the young Pakistani in the back of the office, typing away on a laptop. They arrested him on material witness charges and hauled him away.

Then Saifullah's name showed up in the KSM materials. Investigators interviewed him in Karachi and learned that he knew and did business with several Al Qaeda operatives. They learned, too, that he shipped goods to the United States all the time. Suddenly, it seemed they had evidence of a potential shipment of explosives into American harbors, especially Newark, where Paracha senior sent his exports for transport to his business in New York. In New York, JTTF officials had another oh-shit moment when they realized that Faris was the suspicious man who had taken surveillance photos in and around New York. Now they were connecting the dots to a terrorist conspiracy in which Faris could have already driven his eighteen-wheeler to the port, picked up a container with explosives, and taken it who knows were. It didn't help that Faris's tractor-trailer was registered under Kashmir Trucking, in what they read as a reference to the Pakistani jihadi groups waging war against India over Kashmir, and that they weren't sure where he was.

With as much secrecy as can be mustered at one of the nation's busiest ports, the JTTF started intercepting containers from Pakistan destined for Newark. After hours, they hauled the containers to a secluded high-security warehouse, unloaded them one by one, and inspected their contents. Then they reloaded them overnight so they could be shipped on their usual schedule with no one knowing the difference.

Of course, they had no idea what they were looking for, or whether it would explode on contact as they unloaded the containers.

The exchange of information between the Pakistanis and the Americans, between the CIA and everybody else, and between FBI headquarters and the New York JTTF was imperfect in almost every instance, but eventually, investigators arrested most of the known suspects—including Saifullah Paracha, whose partner lured him to Thailand at the FBI's request under the pretense of meeting him to discuss concerns about his son. Faris was flipped by the FBI and spent weeks talking to jihadi associates from a safe house in Virginia while the tape recorders rolled. Khan was whisked off to an undisclosed location by the CIA, only to surface at Guantánamo with KSM and others in 2006, proclaiming his innocence all the way. It wasn't clear what, exactly, the conspirators had been planning, and who else was out there. Siddiqui had disappeared into Pakistan, and there were indications of others involved in the scheme, but no proof—in part due to the CIA's reluctance to share information, according to a senior supervisor who oversaw the operation. "We stopped something, but we don't know what it was," he said. "And we can't be entirely sure we got it all."[13]

# CHAPTER 16
## The Black Sites and Beyond

*Bagram, Afghanistan, and Beyond, 2003–2006*

KSM was flown to Bagram Airfield in Afghanistan for three additional days, after which he was again moved, this time to Poland. The Polish prison, near the town of Szymany in the country's northeast, was located on a military air base, as were many of the CIA's other secret prisons. KSM remained at the Polish site for approximately six months and moved to Romania. In total, he was held in at least five, and perhaps more, black sites before being deposited—along with all the other high-value detainees—in a newly constructed jail at Cuba's Guantánamo Bay in September of 2006.

The black sites were spread across Asia, Europe, and Africa. Transporting prisoners among the sites on privately chartered Gulfstream jets cost tens of thousands—and sometimes hundreds of thousands—of dollars per trip, including fruit plates and $39 bottles of wine for the flight crew. The crews filed fraudulent flight plans to disguise their destinations and deliveries. The planes often stopped on three or more continents in a matter of days. Why there was so much movement is unclear.

What is clear is what happened within the prisons. The Central Intelligence Agency, under pressure from the Bush administration to produce immediate results, hired private contractors to extract information from its prisoners. The contractors sought and received approval to employ harsh interrogation measures drawn, at least in part, from manuals of torture. The manuals had been produced decades earlier as a means of instructing American troops on how to resist torture. The contractors turned that on its head, presenting a plan to use the manuals as instructions for what were euphemistically called enhanced interrogation techniques. The CIA, with explicit approval from the Bush White House and Department of Justice,[1] adopted the plan and put it into operation.

The contractors were purported experts in psychology and not Al Qaeda; they often had little idea what sorts of questions to ask, or what to make of the answers, including whether they had any semblance of truth to them. So the contractors frequently appealed to Langley for guidance. People with genuine expertise on Al Qaeda were seldom, if ever, consulted on lines of inquiry. There was, instead, a vague but constant push for information about coming attacks. In fact, three organizations with specific knowledge of KSM desperately pushed for inclusion in the process—the FBI, the 9/11 Commission, and a multiagency Criminal Investigation Task Force (CITF) overseen by the Department of Defense. Barred from actually interviewing him, all three organizations did take the additional step of composing lists of questions they thought KSM should be asked. None of them received much of a reply. "It was like sending questions out into the ether," said a senior investigator from one of those organizations. Investigators in all three organizations felt that getting specific questions to KSM, and having him answer them, was not only key to uncovering the next attack but also to understanding the broad outlines of the sprawling terrorist network he had pieced together over the years, which they believed still had tentacles extending deep into the United States.

In the case of the FBI, the CIA's indifference might be explained—if hardly excused—by the historic antagonism between the Bureau and the CIA. The lack of cooperation with the 9/11 Commission may have been a result of the fact that it was investigating potentially embarrassing lapses by all government agencies, including the CIA's failure to catch KSM before the attacks; some of these mistakes had by then been identified by a separate congressional joint inquiry. The CITF, on the other hand, was brand-new and had been created specifically to gather evidence against those suspected of perpetrating 9/11. The evidence was intended for use in the very military tribunal system that the Bush administration had created through executive fiat.

Mark Fallon, for twenty years a special agent and supervisor with the Naval Criminal Investigative Service, was the deputy commander of the CITF. Almost from the time the first captives arrived at Guantánamo, Fallon and his group butted heads with the army's Joint Task Force 170, which actually ran the prison and had overall authority for the prisoners. The dispute was a mirror image of the fight between the FBI and the CIA. Fallon and his people were veteran investigators with experience on numerous terrorism cases—the bombing of the USS *Cole*, the Khobar Towers attacks, and the Blind Sheikh case in New York, among others. Many of the Joint Task Force 170 interrogators, on the other hand, had never been in the same room with a terrorist before arriving at Guantánamo, and knew little of their history. The general in charge, for instance, gained most of his experience as a small-town family court judge in Pennsylvania.

It wasn't long before Fallon had barred his investigators from working with Task Force 170 because of concerns that its interrogators were using coercive methods that he believed to be illegal and counterproductive. His complaints went up the chain of command and eventually curtailed the Joint Task Force 170 methods. But long before KSM was captured, Fallon had figured that the terrorist would eventually end up at Guantánamo, and had begun an investigation on him. When KSM was finally captured, Fallon sought to include his team in the interrogations. He was rebuffed.

By early 2002, the CITF efforts at Guantánamo were paying

off, and threads of intelligence about KSM and his rise within Al Qaeda helped the larger counterterrorism community to connect the dots. The emerging picture showed KSM to be even more involved than investigators had believed; he was rebuilding Al Qaeda and launching new attacks. At one point soon after KSM was caught, Fallon and Colonel Britt Mallow, the commander of CITF, went to Langley for a meeting of the Near East Division of the CIA. Most of the CIA station chiefs from the Middle East were at the briefing, and Fallon was taken aback when he and Mallow were asked to tell the group what they knew about KSM. He had been asking the CIA the exact same question, with no success.

"You're interrogating him. Why are you holding out on us?" he asked them. "Are you thinking two steps ahead? Given what you're doing to him, enhanced interrogations, waterboarding... we need direct access, because you can't try him, and we're gonna inherit him.... We want direct access now, not just for intel but also so that we can participate in this process and keep open the possibility of gathering evidence and trying him later."[2]

The meeting turned into a heated argument, and eventually Fallon and Mallow left unceremoniously—and empty-handed. They joked about being thrown out of the CIA, but their concern was serious. It didn't seem as though anyone had a plan, or even a thought, about what to do with the detainees in the long term. That was especially the case with KSM, whose trial, if there was ever going to be one, was supposed to be the centerpiece of the entire military commission effort.

The FBI continued to express similar concerns, and so did the 9/11 Commission, especially the team headed by Dieter Snell, the former federal prosecutor in New York who had chased KSM through South and Southeast Asia as part of the Manila Air and World Trade Center investigations. His team had been reading the transcripts from the interrogations of KSM and noticed gaping holes in what was being asked—and what was being answered. It was clear that KSM was lying, and that his interrogators were simply accepting his claims and moving on to the next question on the latest list sent to them from Langley. The appointed leaders of the 9/11 Commission went to the White House and stressed the urgency of having their investigators and other knowledgeable authorities interrogating KSM, but their requests also were denied.

No one was as frustrated as Pellegrino. Late one afternoon, agent Stephen Gaudin, his former colleague on the New York JTTF, was walking through the basement of FBI headquarters and noticed Pellegrino hunched over a desk looking at photocopies of e-mails and pocket litter.

"Frank, I don't understand. What are you doing here?" Gaudin asked him.

Pellegrino looked ashen, and embarrassed. The veteran agent had finally been given a role in the FBI's involvement in the KSM case. But instead of being in a room with KSM trying to pry out information about pending attacks and the others in his network, he was going through documents that many others had already been through, double-checking to see what they might have missed.

When Pellegrino didn't respond, Gaudin again said, "Frank, I don't understand."

There was a long, strained silence as the two old friends just looked at each other. Pellegrino didn't know what to say. So he didn't say anything.

In the course of his three-year tour of the black sites, KSM was subjected to an escalating series of coercive methods, culminating in seven and one-half days of sleep deprivation and 183 instances of waterboarding. He was hog-tied, stripped naked, photographed, hooded, beaten, kicked, suffocated, exposed to extreme cold and noise, denied food and sleep, sedated with anal suppositories, placed in diapers, and hung by his wrists until they bled.[3]

KSM spoke voluminously during these years. The torture and interrogations produced more information than investigators could competently track down. Much, if not most, of the information was bad—made up, KSM would later say, so the torture would stop. From the outset, in fact, the written reports of his interrogations that were sent back to Langley contained a warning at the top that the detainee had a history of lies and fabrications. KSM talked about Al Qaeda's nuclear and chemical war ambitions, about how he built his network. He gave what amounted to lectures on how to conduct terrorism. He wrote letters to President Bush and CIA director George Tenet and poems to the wife of one of his interrogators.

He admitted almost everything, or so his interrogators thought, giving up information that led directly to an impressive series of arrests—including that of Mohamad Farik Amin, one of Hambali's Malaysian operatives; Hambali himself; Hambali's brother, Rusman "Gun Gun" Gunawan; and Ahmed Khalfan Ghailani, an African Al Qaeda facilitator and forgery expert involved in the 1998 U.S. embassy bombings in Kenya and Tanzania. The hunt for KSM associates played out around the world, often in secret. Exploiting information found on KSM and gleaned from his initial confessions, authorities moved particularly quickly in Southeast Asia to shut down KSM's network there. After his capture, Hambali was told that seventeen of his operatives had also been captured; he admitted under interrogation that they were being groomed at KSM's behest for attacks inside the United States, probably again using airplanes as weapons against skyscrapers. During questioning, KSM also provided details of other plots. He described the design of planned attacks on buildings inside the United States and how operatives were directed to carry them out. In some cases, he instructed his operatives, Padilla among them, to ensure that the explosives went off at a point that was high enough to prevent the people trapped above from escaping out the windows. KSM also detailed the Heathrow airplane plot and the operative assigned to it, Naeem Noor Khan.[4] It has been presumed that he gave information on these men because he believed the information would not be new to his captors. Khan, for example, had worked on the Heathrow plot with Ramzi bin al-Shibh, who had been in American custody since September 2002. In all, KSM and other al Qaeda detainees helped the CIA identify at least eighty-six individuals whom the terror organization deemed "suitable for Western operations." Most of them remained at large. Of even more concern was whether KSM was giving up the small fish in an effort to protect the bigger ones, including bin Laden himself.

The CIA noted how cooperative KSM was almost immediately.[5] Others were not so certain, or were outright suspicious that he was being far too helpful from the outset. One senior intelligence operative said KSM turned the torture sessions into a contest. He had intuited that the interrogators, although they were willing to inflict great pain, behaved as if they had limits beyond which they wouldn't go. He noticed that the waterboarding sessions never exceeded a certain length.[6] So he simply steeled himself and counted the time off in his head—or, at times theatrically, by ticking off the seconds with his fingers.

KSM was always stripped of his clothing before the waterboarding began. On one occasion, a senior female CIA officer who helped supervise the interrogation program from her office at Langley flew in to witness a session, even though she wasn't officially assigned to do so. KSM was irate that a woman would be in the room to view him in the nude. And he told his interrogators so. He glared at her for several minutes, and held out especially long that day. His interrogators said that even though he talked when he wanted to, KSM's resistance to physical and psychological punishment was almost superhuman.[7]

KSM did not hide the fact that he was trying to game the torture protocols. He did it flamboyantly, being sure his interviewers knew what he was doing. "To him, it was a challenge, a competition with his interrogators and his competitors, and even in something as otherworldly as this, it became a game and competition to KSM, a way to master those who were trying to master him," said one operative. When interrogators threatened to track down his female relatives and have them raped, he shrugged, saying, in effect, Really? Is that the best you can do?[8]

Mohammed ultimately confessed to more than three dozen

plots and attacks around the world. Many of these were hardly fully formed. Some seemed like little more than teatime chatter. Most were aspirational. No one knew the aspiration business better than KSM, who had imagined hundreds of plots, most of which never got beyond the imagining.

KSM bragged later about sending American agents scurrying around the globe on the impossible task of trying to distinguish the truths from the half truths and the lies. "During the harshest period of my interrogation I gave a lot of false information in order to satisfy what I believed the interrogators wished to hear in order to make the ill treatment stop. I later told interrogators that their methods were stupid and counterproductive. I'm sure that the false information I was forced to invent in order to make the ill treatment stop wasted a lot of their time and led to several false red alerts being placed in the U.S.," he told the Red Cross.[9]

This web hasn't been untangled even now, but the range of his contacts around the globe was stunning. Investigators believe parts of it remain in place, waiting for another day. "He had us chasing the goddamn geese in Central Park because he said some of them had explosives stuffed up their ass," Ali Soufan, the FBI counterterrorism agent, said. He was exaggerating, he conceded, but not by much. KSM's claims of Al Qaeda's nuclear and WMD capabilities had the CIA and the FBI especially spun up, but after frantic and intensive deployments around the world, it was determined that KSM was making up almost all of it.

What KSM said under interrogation was valuable; what he did not say might have been more so. Describing plots that were later discovered to have been in the planning and operational stages when KSM was captured, some of them supervised by direct lieutenants of his, Soufan said, "KSM had to know about the Madrid bombings [which occurred in March of 2004], about Al Qaeda cells throughout the world, and especially [about cells] in Europe, where there were many plots under way, including the ones in the UK. He didn't ID the Madrid cells. He didn't give up the London subway plot."[10] And he said nothing about the deadly terrorist attacks that some of his operatives would soon launch in the kingdom of Saudi Arabia, killing many Westerners, including some Americans, and shaking the foundations of the Saudi royal family. The intel from raids, intercepts, and interrogations was enough to prompt homeland security secretary Tom Ridge to issue an unusually broad warning soon after the Riyadh bombings. "The U.S. intelligence community," he said, "believes that Al Qaeda has entered an operational period worldwide, and this may include terrorist attacks in the United States."

One senior investigator said KSM kept to himself the most important things he knew—the locations of Osama bin Laden and Ayman al-Zawahiri and the ways in which they might have been found, notably the courier system by which they communicated. This last part was especially important because so many of the couriers were Kuwaitis and Baluchis who had been part of KSM's own personal network, and whom he had relied on himself. He obviously knew something of Zawahiri's whereabouts, having met with him the day before his own capture. He probably knew, too, how to find bin Laden. He denied this, then when tortured, said he did indeed know bin Laden's whereabouts. Then he would make up a story: "Where is he? I don't know. Then he torture me. Then I said, 'Yes, he is in this area.' "[11]

Despite repeated questioning on the point, KSM explicitly denied knowledge of the Kuwaiti-Pakistani courier who eventually led the CIA to bin Laden in Abbottabad, Pakistan. He was so strenuous in his denials that some believed KSM was protecting the courier because of his operational significance. They were right. It was later learned from other detainees that the courier had been, in fact, a protégé of KSM's for years.

The CIA boasted from the start about its handling of KSM, saying its "enhanced" interrogation methods had not only saved lives but led to the arrests of countless terrorists. In the fall of 2003, agency officials were planning to give a presentation at FBI headquarters, in the massive Bonaparte Auditorium, about their successes with KSM. It was billed as an educational opportunity for the Bureau's agents and brass to hear all about how the agency had figured out KSM, and how it had gotten him to open up. By that time, Pellegrino and most others at the FBI believed that KSM was feeding the contractors one falsehood after another, in part to protect active plots and plotters. The FBI agents who had been trying to track him knew that KSM knew the location of most, if not all, of the members of Al Qaeda's leadership council and covert cells around the world—and that he hadn't given them up. Unbeknownst to them, the CIA had acknowledged as much in a top-secret internal report months earlier, in April of 2003, entitled "Khalid Shaykh Muhammed's Threat Reporting—Precious Truths, Surrounded by a Bodyguard of Lies." It concluded that protecting operatives in the United States appeared to be a "major part" of KSM's resistance efforts.[12] Worse, it indicated that the interrogators often didn't know enough to confront KSM over what appeared to be blatant falsehoods. In response to questions about U.S. zip codes found in his notebooks, for instance, KSM said he was planning to use them to open new e-mail accounts. Pellegrino ended up attending the CIA briefing, and watched as CIA officials went on and on about their techniques and their purported successes. He sat through about half of it, then got up and walked out. He kept going until he reached the bar at Harry's, a few blocks away.

In some respects, the capture of KSM and then of his lieutenants was the beginning of the end for Al Qaeda, at least in Pakistan. Without his relationships with the Pakistani militant groups and command of Urdu, the mostly Arab fighters felt uneasy and vulnerable. So they moved north into the far more remote tribal areas, where they received protection but also found it hard to do recruiting, training, and plotting. It severed Al Qaeda's ties to much of its network.

## *Guantánamo Bay, Cuba, September 2007*

When the coercive interrogation regime was finally revealed to the world, the question of what to actually do with KSM and other high-value detainees—how to exact justice from them—was posed publicly for the first time. It had, of course, been percolating for years at the highest levels of the Bush administration, provoking heated battles. Top officials in the Justice Department and even Condoleezza Rice, the national security advisor, had repeatedly instigated discussions about what the ultimate plan was, and had asked how these men would finally be disposed of. Justice feared that the military, which had ultimate control over Guantánamo, wasn't sufficiently experienced to run the court system it had established.

Top Justice officials offered to send prosecutors to the detention camp, but the offers were ignored—willfully, it seemed to some—by Donald Rumsfeld, the secretary of defense.

"The people running the process at Guantánamo had no real trial experience," one senior Justice Department official said at the time.[13] "My proposal was, why not get DOJ prosecutors who know how to try big cases like Moussaoui—we have a bunch in New York and eastern district of Virginia—why don't you use them? They never took us up on it.... You can't understate the emasculation of Condi Rice in all of this, especially by Cheney, which freed up Rumsfeld to ignore her as well. I sat in a bunch of meetings where Condi wanted to move the process along, and Rumsfeld wanted no part of it, he wouldn't even attend the meetings. He did not want to engage in Gitmo.... I saw her break down in tears over Rumsfeld's disrespect for her. At a meeting over Gitmo, he stood up and said, 'I have another meeting.' She said, 'Sit down.'

" 'This meeting is over,' he said, and walked out.

"Then Tenet stood up and said, 'This is bullshit. I'm leaving.'

"Rice told Tenet to sit down and he turned and walked out, too."

More than three years after KSM's capture, there remained no clear answers. Eventually, military prosecutors decided they needed DOJ help to reinvestigate the cases against KSM and other high-value detainees because everything that came from the CIA black sites, or even from leads that came from there, was poisonous.

The decision set off a vigorous shoving match between the

Pentagon's Defense Intelligence Agency (DIA) and the FBI, both of which wanted to run the new interviews. "You had all these DOD guys frothing at the mouth, saying, 'CIA didn't get shit out of them, but we will.' " There was a lot of head-butting to see who could have access to them," said a military lawyer familiar with the confrontations, which began immediately after KSM and the other high-value detainees landed on the island. "They figured, an hour with KSM and they'd find out where bin Laden is before dark."[14]

The DIA was held off while military prosecutors, the Justice Department, and the National Security Council staff worked out a compromise by which the FBI and the Criminal Investigation Task Force would share responsibility to reinterview all those who had been subjected to the "enhanced interrogation techniques," to build clean cases against them. They were asked, in effect, to reinvestigate the attacks, to remove the poisonous fruit from the tree, and to obtain confessions from men like KSM, who had endured all sorts of physical and psychological punishment. Some, like Ramzi bin al-Shibh, were prescribed strong psychotropic medications out of a belief that they had been driven at least partially crazy. No one knew if this would ever satisfy a court of law—"it was a crapshoot," one prosecutor said—but many viewed it as their only chance.

The clean teams sent down to Guantánamo interviewed dozens of the detainees. In an attempt to make the detainees comfortable and cooperative, they were catered to. One asked for steak and eggs, and an FBI agent from the New York JTTF cooked it for him. Another wanted a latte, and the head of the prosecution team drove all the way across Guantánamo to the base Starbucks to buy it. Many of the detainees talked uninhibitedly. KSM was especially loquacious, apparently relishing the human contact and the rapt attention. He also knew who held the power. When asked after one interview session if he would be ready to go at 8:00 a.m. the next day, he said he'd prefer to sleep in. "Let's start at ten," he said.[15]

For most within the FBI, this was a chance for bureaucratic

revenge. For Frank Pellegrino, it was far more than that. Being assigned to the clean team was a chance for redemption, a chance to at last absolve or mitigate the guilt and feelings of responsibility he had long carried.

In 2007, thirteen years after undertaking his pursuit of the elusive terrorist mastermind, Pellegrino was told he would finally get his chance to sit face-to-face across a table from KSM. He studied his voluminous case files. In a way, he didn't need to. Pellegrino was known for his encyclopedic knowledge of KSM, and it was all in his head. But he also needed to gain access to all the more recent files that had been compiled on KSM in order to get him to talk about what he had done after Pellegrino lost track of him—including the planning of 9/11.

On a sunny and bright afternoon in early 2007, Pellegrino met KSM across a gray metal government-issue table in a makeshift cell in Guantánamo. Pellegrino, now forty-six, was accompanied by Brian Antol, the analyst from FBI headquarters who had worked on the case nearly as long as Pellegrino, and by two agents from the CITF. Guantánamo was buzzing. Everyone had heard the stories by then of how the agent had chased the terrorist around the globe only to be kept out of the hunt for him after 9/11. They crowded into the small room housing the closed-circuit TVs so they could watch, expecting no one knew quite what. There was no great confrontation. It was in a strange way like a meeting of old combatants, soldiers from opposing sides meeting long after the war. When Pellegrino entered, he offered his hand, and KSM shook it. Pellegrino had prepared a lengthy opening, things he needed to say, in which he told the accused terrorist about why he was there, what he hoped to accomplish, and who he was. I was the guy who found out about your wiring money to New York for the first World Trade Center attack, he told him, and who was following you in Pakistan, and then in Manila. And I was the guy who went to Qatar to catch you, and who looked for you in the years after that, he said.

"Ah, so you're the one," KSM responded.

KSM told him that he had known when Pellegrino had arrived in Qatar to arrest him, and had also known the name of the hotel where he was staying. KSM thought that was funny; Pellegrino laughed, but after the session told a colleague that it had sent chills down his spine, as if he had suddenly realized that he had been the one who was being hunted.

KSM was relaxed, chatty. Pellegrino felt immediately that he knew KSM because of his eerie similarities to his nephew Abdul Basit Abdul Karim, whom the FBI agent had gotten to know well during his trial in New York. Pellegrino thought KSM might be the kind of guy you could sit down and have a beer with, if he hadn't been one of the worst mass murderers in American history.

Mohammed by then had a long, mostly gray beard. He had lost forty pounds and looked like nothing so much as a little old man. That first day, he wore a full-length white *dishdasha* for the interview, but normally wore the standard-issue prison jumpsuit. He was led into the room by guards and chained by the ankle to a metal clamp on the floor; his hands were free. They sat on opposing sides of the table, sometimes for as long as eight hours a day, for four days.

A government official who observed the interviews said everyone outside the room was amazed at how amiable the men were on the surface. They both cracked jokes, in part to ease the palpable tension. KSM talked freely from the outset, more so than many other detainees did.

Early on, KSM asked who had won the election. Thinking he must be referring to the 2004 presidential race, Pellegrino said that Bush had won. KSM said, Oh, no. I know that. I was asking about last fall's congressional elections. When told that the Democrats had won, he said, "Oh, that's very good for us." He apparently thought the Democrats would be more lenient.

By the time Pellegrino got "in the box" with him, KSM had been under near-constant interrogation for four years. He eventually tired of still more questions and told Pellegrino so. "I've already talked about that, Frank," he would say. Pellegrino persisted. Even given the fact that he found KSM a likable presence, he despised everything about the man and wanted finally to deliver him to justice. He pressed on; he changed the subject to the good old days in Manila, which nobody had ever cared enough to ask questions about. Almost like old friends at a high school reunion, they talked about Basit and Wali Khan and the fun times back in the Philippines—the bar girls, the karaoke joints, the good-looking dentists. Over the course of several days, mixed in with the nostalgia, Pellegrino coaxed new confessions from KSM that he hoped would one day form the basis for a trial in the old Sovereign District of New York.

There were a few dozen FBI and CITF agents swarming over the base conducting similar interviews with other inmates, all trying to make good on what they long maintained was their special ability to build rapport and coax secrets out of people without them even knowing it. The CIA didn't give up its turf easily. The agency kept agents in place at Guantánamo, and they appeared to be watching over everything, even the conversations between reporters and defense lawyers at the on-base restaurant and watering hole, O'Kelly's Irish Pub. At times they bumped other investigators from their chartered flights off the island and even parked a big yacht in Guantánamo Bay for its own agents. And after each day's questioning, the FBI and CITF agents trooped dutifully up a hill to the CIA compound to give a full briefing on that day's events. And the CIA officers would tell them what was permissible for them to use and what was, for security reasons, not permissible.

That ritual of constant observation and questioning of KSM had gone on for years as President Bush, then President Obama and his attorney general, Eric H. Holder Jr., deliberated about what kind of justice, if any, KSM would ultimately face.

Beginning in late 2006, Mohammed was allowed to write letters to his relatives. The letters and replies were delivered by the Red Cross. According to rules established by the American military, the correspondence had to fit on a six-by-six-inch portion of a preprinted form, and its content was restricted to the familial and personal; all else was stricken by censors. Mohammed mostly sent good wishes to his wife and children in southeastern Iran, and to other relatives.[16] He made repeated references to his Islamic faith and the beneficence of Allah and the Prophet. In photographs that accompanied one of the letters, Mohammed appeared shrunken from the man in the famous image taken the day of his capture. That image must have infuriated Mohammed, who was vain enough to have complained during a military court hearing that a sketch artist had made his nose look too big. In the jailhouse photographs, he looks frail but radiant. He stares directly at the camera, cloaked in long white robes, a headdress framing his small, still face, long beard, and piercing dark eyes. In one photo, a copy of the Koran lies open in his right hand. His ego was so large that military prosecutors contemplated charging all the 9/11 coconspirators *except* KSM with crimes that could bring the death penalty, "just to see how pissed off he would get," said one.

The Guantánamo letters were accompanied by identification forms in which the Red Cross asked that the correspondent provide basic biographical information. In the first of the letters, dated December 15, 2006, Mohammed dutifully filled in the details, writing out his full name and listing Guantánamo Bay as his place of residence. By 2009, he listed his residence as "Gitmo," using the military nickname. In the space for his own name, he wrote "KSM," adopting the intelligence community's name for him. Mohammed had spent almost his entire life as an outsider forced to live under other people's rules. When necessary, he had adapted. After six years in American custody, he seemed to have adapted again.

On June 25, 2009, Mohammed, writing in English to his brother, made what could be read as a surprising plea for absolution: "All praise is due to Allah. I praise Him and seek His aid and His forgiveness and I seek refuge in Allah from our evil in ourselves and from our bad deeds." Even if this were only a ritual expression of obeisance, it stood in contrast to his customarily belligerent behavior. Was he truly sorry? It appeared unlikely, given what he said during his court hearings.

The high-value detainees at Guantánamo live in a maximum-security prison, Camp 7, which is off-limits to almost everyone. They are held in isolation for up to twenty-two hours a day; as military prosecutors put it in arguing against allowing defense attorneys to visit the camp, each prisoner "has available to him outdoor recreation, socialization with a recreation partner, the ability to exercise, access to library books twice a week, the privilege of watching movies, and may meet with his attorneys upon request should he so choose. If the accused takes advantage of all the privileges offered to him, he would have a minimum of two hours a day outside his cell."

In formal military hearings—his arraignment, a tribunal to assess his status, and another session to argue points of law—KSM proved to be a forceful and at times vexing presence. He is a captive, of course, but in some ways he has controlled the legal proceedings against him, organizing his fellow captives to act as a group and then putting himself in charge. In 2007, he told his Combatant Status Review Tribunal that he often lied when he was tortured during interrogations and told the truth at other times. He lied when he needed to, he said.[17] He seemed almost gleeful about the prospect of American investigators chasing his lies around the world. In 2008, he wrote a memo to the judge, complaining about the incompetence of the military translators in court; he titled the memo "Better Translation."

He mocked the military courts, preached, instructed, or obstructed as the need arose. He apologized for killing children; it was an unavoidable consequence of waging war. He told his coconspirators to fall in line behind him and adopt a unified legal strategy. They did as he asked.

He compared himself to George Washington leading a valiant and morally righteous rebellion, and then went on to explain: "The way of the war, you know, very well, any country waging war against their enemy the language of the war are killing. If man and woman they be together as a marriage that is up to the kids, children. But if you and me, two nations, will be together in war the others are victims. This is the way of the language... You know forty million people were killed in World War I. Ten million kill in World War. You know that two million four hundred thousand be killed in the Korean War. So this language of the war. Any people who, when Osama bin Laden say I'm waging war because such and such reason, now he declared it. But when you said I'm terrorist, I think it is deceiving peoples. Terrorists, enemy combatant. All these definitions as CIA you can make whatever you want.... So finally it's your war but the problem is no definitions of many words. It would be widely definite that many people be oppressed. Because war, for sure, there will be victims."[18]

He chastised the government for its indiscriminate imprisonment of Afghan citizens who simply happened to be in Afghanistan when the United States invaded. "You have to be fair with people," he said. "There are many, many people which they have never been part of the Taliban. Afghanistan there have been many people arrested, for example, people who have been arrested after October 2001 after make attack against Afghanistan many of them just arrive after they don't what has happen."

In the Guantánamo hearing room, Mohammed and his four codefendants—Mustafa al-Hawsawi, Walid bin Attash, Ramzi bin al-Shibh, and Ali Abdul Aziz Ali—sat in separate rows at long tables, with Mohammed always in the front row. Seated with them were their translators, lawyers, and sometimes paralegals—as many as six people in a row. Mohammed did not always rely on a translator in court and fired his lawyers, so he was sometimes seated at his table with just one other person, a civilian lawyer who served as his personal representative but not his defense counsel.

When he was arraigned at Guantánamo in June of 2008, he asked that he be allowed to represent himself. The judge, Marine Colonel Ralph Kohlmann, asked KSM if he was certain he wanted to dismiss his attorneys, and whether he knew the proceedings could lead to his execution. Mohammed replied: "Yes. That is what I wish. I wish to be martyred. I will, God willing, have this by you."

His behavior in court has sometimes been bizarre. Once, he stood during the proceedings to sing Qur'anic verses aloud. After the judge repeatedly told him that he was out of order and had to stop, he suddenly shrugged, and in his disconcertingly high-pitched voice blurted, "Okay," and quit, provoking laughter throughout the courtroom. Commander Jeffrey D. Gordon, a former spokesman for the Department of Defense, witnessed nearly all Mohammed's court appearances. "At times, it's almost like theater," Gordon said. "He switches back and forth from very serious and devout to kind of a clown. I think he does that deliberately to draw people in, to charm them in some way, or to influence them. It's all calculated."

At his arraignment, his codefendants nervously looked to Mohammed for guidance. When he decided to defend himself, he attempted to have the others do the same. One, Hawsawi, chose to continue with his attorney. Mohammed turned to Hawsawi sternly and, according to Gordon, noted that his lawyer was in the American military, and then asked Hawsawi: "What, are you in the American army now?" Hawsawi appeared shaken and reversed his decision.

When another defendant, Ramzi bin al-Shibh, initially refused to appear before tribunals at all, it was not military prosecutors or lawyers who changed his mind but Mohammed. KSM organized what he called a Shura Council to coordinate his defense with those of his fellow accused. He dealt politely with his defense lawyers and was prone to giving lectures in court.

Mohammed seemed generally unbothered by prison life. He prayed and exercised[19] and at times appeared to be the most powerful person in the remote prison.

## *Washington, D.C., November 2009*

Eighteen months later, after years of secret imprisonment, after the clean teams spent almost another year reinvestigating the crimes of

9/11, and after more months of further internal deliberations, Attorney General Holder announced with much fanfare that the Obama administration would dismiss the military court charges and, following the rule of law, would try KSM, Hawsawi, bin Attash, Ali, and bin al-Shibh in civilian federal court in the Southern District of New York, in the shadow of where the World Trade Center once stood.

"For over two hundred years our nation has relied on a faithful adherence to the rule of law to bring criminals to justice and to provide accountability to victims. Once again we will ask our legal system in two venues to rise to that challenge. I am confident that it will answer the call with fairness and with justice," Holder said.

The decision was lauded by civil libertarians and lambasted by some politicians of both parties who said it would be impossible to secure the trial site and that New York would become a terrorist target. They had perhaps forgotten that the World Trade Center already had been attacked twice. Terrorists—including the embassy bombers, KSM's nephew, and two others on the Bojinka plot, which KSM helped mastermind—had previously been tried and convicted in lower Manhattan without incident.

To the FBI, bringing KSM back to New York was a restoration to the world as they thought it should be: first, somebody does something bad. Then we find them. Gather evidence. Indict and try them. Justice is served.

Matt Besheer, still a restless cop in a small Florida town haunted by the what-ifs of a decade earlier, missed a phone call from his old partner, Frank Pellegrino, after Holder made the announcement. Pellegrino's message went to Besheer's voice mail. In the years since then, Besheer has played the message over and over. Pellegrino, typically the stoic, had feelings he couldn't quite control that day. He was a man whose entire professional identity had been nearly undone by 9/11. Usually, he arrested guys; he didn't let them move on to commit other crimes. Except this once. Now maybe, finally, he could get some semblance of reconciliation, of peace.

The tape is scratchy. It is Pellegrino in rare, exposed form:

"Hey, Bash," it begins, Pellegrino using the term of affection he coined for Besheer long ago.

"Hey, Bash, I sent you an e-mail. It looks like they're bringing KSM back to New York where he should be, my friend." Pellegrino pauses; there is a brief silence, then a deep sigh, as if he is fighting to keep his composure. "I'm in Australia right now, and I'm a little overwhelmed at the whole thing. That's where the savage belongs, and where he'll get his time in court."

"Oh, man," he says, pausing for an even longer stretch. "Hopefully I can get to sleep one day. Just send me an e-mail and I'll see you when I get back to the States. It's two a.m. here. I was thinking about you, brother. I love you, man."

## *Washington, D.C., April 2011*

The decision on what to do with KSM and his coconspirators continued to plague the Obama administration and Congress. Politicians from both parties proclaimed loudly that it was impossible to bring a trial like this not just to New York but to anywhere in the United States. Former FBI director Louis Freeh suggested that Guantánamo be designated a satellite courtroom of the federal court. But no one had a solution that worked, or was politically palatable. Bills were introduced in Congress specifically to deal with the problems created by the unprecedented legal apparatus built up around the case, including a new law that would allow someone who pleads guilty in a military courtroom to be put to death. Many also objected to trying the case in Manhattan on principle, they said, because the terrorists didn't deserve the protections of American tradition and law. Others thought the trials would cost too much, or that the city simply could not be defended in the event of a trial, or that a trial, even if it were possible, would allow KSM a platform from which to distribute his propaganda. It was an odd consequence of the workings of justice that this little man—on occasion more Jackie Mason than Svengali—could by his mere presence upend the weight of Western jurisprudence. It was nonetheless a consequence that was broadly cited, if not necessarily believed.

Pellegrino and Besheer—and the FBI as a whole—didn't get to rejoice at the prospect of justice being served for long. The Congress, with votes from both Democrats and Republicans, banned the Obama administration from spending any money to transport prisoners from Guantánamo to the continental United States. The decision left Holder and Obama little choice. After more months of delay, Holder yielded. Outraged at the lack of support from the White House and Democrats in Congress, he was forced to reverse his decision. Military charges would be brought once again against KSM and his fellow defendants in preparation for a trial before a military court in Guantánamo. (Or perhaps not. In late 2011, President Obama signed into law legislation that would allow indefinite detention without trial of terror suspects.) Remarkably, KSM, the most prized captive in the War on Terror, had been in American custody for eight years and the American judicial system had not yet determined how to deal with him.

Events in the world beyond Washington continued apace. Publicly, CIA director Leon Panetta declared Al Qaeda all but vanquished as a fighting force. American drones and fighters kept picking off remnants of the group and killing them with startling efficiency. Al Qaeda seemed incapable of launching any kind of significant new attack on American soil, a continuing reminder of KSM's importance.

Privately, Panetta had dramatically escalated the hunt for bin Laden, focusing on the couriers that KSM and other detainees had been protecting. Then, in May of 2011, bin Laden was caught and killed by American commandos. He had been living and operating right under the noses of Pakistan's military establishment. After years of gradual accretion of evidence, then months of surveillance on the ground and from far above, teams of navy SEALs stormed a single-family compound in the city of Abbottabad in northern Pakistan and shot bin Laden dead. They then hauled his body onto a helicopter and flew themselves to safety and bin Laden to his end—a burial in the Arabian Sea.

The hunt for bin Laden had sprung from the hunt for KSM. The CIA was led to bin Laden's compound by a man whose movements, telephone calls, and e-mails they had been tracking for months. His name was Sheikh Abu Ahmed al-Kuwaiti, an ethnic Pakistani who, like KSM, was raised in Kuwait and came to Pakistan originally to fight in the jihad against the Soviet Union in Afghanistan. His name first surfaced when he was identified by captured Al Qaeda fighters as one of bin Laden's security guards. One of those fighters said al-Kuwaiti had died in the bombing barrage at Tora Bora. This seemed unremarkable at the time, but became a curiosity when others identified al-Kuwaiti as a man who worked closely with KSM—first in the Al Qaeda media house operated by KSM in Kandahar and later in Karachi—and then with KSM's successor, Abu Faraj al-Libi, more than a year after Tora Bora. Al-Kuwaiti was well known within Al Qaeda as a senior facilitator, courier, and subordinate of Mohammed. When Hambali and his wife left Kandahar for Karachi in November of 2001, they stayed at Abu Ahmed al-Kuwaiti's guesthouse for two weeks.

The CIA had realized soon after bin Laden escaped from Tora Bora that he had become invisible electronically. He had ceased to communicate by any means that could be intercepted by American satellites and other electronic equipment. He was in hiding. If he was to communicate at all with his followers, it would have to be by human couriers. So they had begun to look for who that might be. Al-Kuwaiti's name arose in the course of this search.[20] He was one of many courier candidates.

Then, in 2004, a man named Hassan Ghul was captured in Iraq. Under interrogation, he described al-Kuwaiti as a messenger for bin Laden, further intensifying the interest in him.[21] It took an additional three years to determine who al-Kuwaiti actually was and another two to locate him in Pakistan, then two more years to confirm the information and follow al-Kuwaiti to bin Laden.[22] KSM was asked about him repeatedly, but he gave the CIA nothing.

In a way, bin Laden's death, though celebrated, was inconsequential. He had been a remote, distant figure for years, so remote it was often rumored that he was already dead. His number two, Ayman al-Zawahiri, was seen as more of a propagandist than an operational force, and had been further marginalized during his own years of isolation.

By contrast, even years after his capture, KSM remained a threat. He couldn't be tried, some argued, lest whatever words he spoke during the trial would somehow incite others to attack. The network of cells he had painstakingly established was still out there—in Pakistan, of course, but also Southeast Asia, the Middle East, and possibly in the United States. Of particular concern to U.S. authorities were KSM's handpicked protégés, many of them computer experts who had spent years in the United States or Europe and were thought to be planning new attacks. There was also the very real fact of the attacks still being attempted. The 2009 attempt by Umar Farouk Abdulmutallab to hide a bomb in his underwear and blow up both himself and the airplane he was traveling on was a near replica of the KSM-directed odyssey of shoe bomber Richard Reid. The 2010 attempt to place a bomb in the cargo hold of a flight bound for the United States was eerily similar to ideas described by KSM and his nephew Abdul Basit Abdul Karim back in 1994.

Then there were the attacks that investigators thought were yet to come. KSM had dispatched no one knew how many agents from Karachi to hide in the West. Some were never known by their names. At least one of his protégés, Adnan el-Shukrijumah, had become famous years earlier for his invisibility and cunning. He was in many ways like KSM, with one foot in Arab culture and another in Asia. Shukrijumah was alleged to have been selected as José Padilla's partner in blowing up apartment buildings. They had, Padilla said, a falling-out, and Shukrijumah was then assigned by KSM to study targets throughout North and Central America. Several detainees identified him to be the most likely candidate to lead the next Al Qaeda attack against the United States. All this made him a target of investigators, none of whom have found a shred of evidence that would tell them where he is or what he might want to do.

Through his aura of invincibility, through ghosts such as Shukrijumah, KSM has retained his power, his ability to strike fear into the hearts of potential victims, which is the first goal of all terrorism. Caged within one of the highest-security prisons ever built—a prison within a prison within a military base on a remote island—he endured, through his network, his legacy, through ideas he had already given to others, as a threat. KSM, years after he was last able to issue a single order, remained, in some real sense, in command.

# ACKNOWLEDGMENTS AND SOURCES

Our first thank you must go to those men and women who participated in the events described in this book and who agreed to tell us their stories. For a variety of reasons, some professional—i.e., their employers would not allow them to speak publicly—and others personal, many of the people who were interviewed for this book have asked that their identities be kept confidential. We have in some cases been able to persuade them otherwise, but the book contains numerous passages attributed to unidentified sources, and others with no attribution at all. In all cases, nonattributed material is the product of our original research. We have endeavored to ensure the accuracy of the anonymously sourced material. In most cases the sources have been identified in the notes by their official positions at the time of the events. In other instances there is no identification, again according to the wishes of the interviewees.

There is a broad and rich literature on the events of September 11, ranging from immediate, in-the-moment accounts of the attacks themselves to reflective accountings of the underlying causes and long-term effects. We owe a debt to the authors of these deep resources and have relied on their work to some extent; we have attempted to correct the record where they might have erred and to clarify conflicting accounts. That said, most of the material in the book is the product of our own reporting over what is now a full decade. The reporting included hundreds of interviews across those ten years. These interviews occurred around the globe, in more than twenty countries. For the first seven of those years, both of us were reporters for the *Los Angeles Times,* which published the original stories based on that reporting. We thank the *Times.* In particular, we thank our editor, Dean Baquet, for supporting extensive coverage of terrorism even before the attacks of September 11. We were, in those post-9/11 years, often assisted by colleagues at the newspaper and have relied here once again on their reporting. In particular, we thank Patrick McDonnell for his reporting in Kuwait and North Carolina, Sebastian Rotella for his reporting in Europe, and Dirk Laabs for his reporting in Germany and Afghanistan. Additionally, some of the original research was undertaken for an earlier book, *Perfect Soldiers,* and for a profile of Khalid Sheikh Mohammed published by *The New Yorker* magazine. Thanks to David Hirshey at HarperCollins and Nick Trautwein and David Remnick at *The New Yorker.*

Much of the reporting for this book occurred abroad, and we would not have achieved any success whatsoever without the assistance of a small army of journalists, translators, drivers, friends, and fixers. We thank them all, especially Yaqoub al-Mansour in Kuwait; Ashraf Fouad Makkar in Abu Dhabi; Aamir Latif, Syed Sajid Aziz, Shamim-ur-Rahman, and the late Syed Saleem Shahzad in Pakistan; Abdulla Fardan in Bahrain; Baradan Kuppusamy in Malaysia; and Sol Vanzi in the Philippines.

We have obtained and examined tens of thousands of pages of documents, and they inform a substantial portion of the book. The individual documents are cited in reference notes throughout the text. We have attempted where possible to verify the origin of these documents. Most are investigative records of government agencies, foreign and domestic, and as such are not always reliable and almost never definitive. We have tried to vet the documents as we were able. Some of the documents were originally collected by the 9/11 Commission and obtained by us through Freedom of Information Act requests. Others were gathered by less obvious means. One unexpected source has been WikiLeaks, the online publisher of thousands of leaked official documents. We thank

WikiLeaks, especially for making available the documents detailing the histories of and allegations against hundreds of the prisoners held at Guantánamo Bay naval base at Guantánamo Bay, Cuba. These documents, known as Detainee Assessment Briefs, were compiled by Joint Task Force Guantánamo investigators and contain brief histories of the detainees' lives and alleged activities. Like most investigative records, they contain many inaccuracies, and we have attempted to verify the information contained in them.

We have also relied on and thank the American Civil Liberties Union, Human Rights Watch, and other nongovernmental organizations that have compiled a great deal of information and documentation about the War on Terror.

Other journalists and researchers have graciously shared information. These include Christina Lamb of the *Sunday Times* of London, Ira Rosen of *60 Minutes*, Adam Goldman of the Associated Press, Rohan Gunaratna, James Gordon Meek, John Berger, Bonnie Rollins, Maria Ressa, and Mark Danner. We thank them all. Three entrepreneurial enterprises, run largely by single individuals, have also collected and shared a great amount of information on 9/11. They are: Berger's Intelwire.com, at http://intelwire.egoplex.com/2006_11_21_exclusives.html; Andy Worthington's website, andyworthington.co.uk, at http://www.andyworthington.co.uk/category/2002-2011-the-complete-guantanamo-files-new/; and Paul Thompson's 9/11 time line, hosted at History Commons's website, http://www.historycommons.org/project.jsp?project=911_project. Berger and Worthington are both journalists, and their own research comprises much of the material on their sites. Thompson's effort is crowd-sourced to a significant degree, and suffers from accuracy concerns because of it, but is nonetheless an astonishing effort at aggregation.

We thank our editor, John Parsley, and his assistant, William Boggess, at Little, Brown for their enthusiasm for the project. We thank our agent, Paul Bresnick, for his intelligence and verve.

Last but not least, we thank our families for their support and forbearance.

# APPENDIX
# Verbatim Transcript of Combatant Status Review Tribunal Hearing for Khalid Sheikh Mohammed

## *Opening*

REPORTER: On the record.

RECORDER: All rise.

PRESIDENT: Remain seated and come to order. Go ahead, Recorder.

RECORDER: This Tribunal is being conducted at 13:28 March 10, 2007 on board U.S. Naval Base Guantánamo Bay, Cuba. The following personnel are present:

Captain _______ [names of all officials redacted by Department of Defense], United States Navy, President

Lieutenant Colonel _______, United States Air Force, Member

Lieutenant Colonel _______, United States Marine Corps, Member

Lieutenant Colonel _______, United States Air Force, Member

Lieutenant Colonel _______, United States Air Force, Personal Representative

Language Analysis _______

Gunnery Sergeant _______, United States Marine Corps, Reporter
Lieutenant Colonel _______, United States Army, Recorder
Captain _______ is the Judge Advocate member of the Tribunal.

## *Oath Session 1*

Recorder: All rise.

President: The Recorder will be sworn. Do you, Lieutenant Colonel _______, solemnly swear that you will faithfully perform the duties as Recorder assigned in this Tribunal so help you God?

Recorder: I do.

President: The Reporter will now be sworn. The Recorder will administer the oath.

Recorder: Do you, Gunnery Sergeant _______, swear or affirm that you will faithfully discharge your duties as Reporter assigned in this Tribunal so help you God?

Reporter: I do.

President: The Translator will be sworn.

Recorder: Do you swear or affirm that you will faithfully perform the duties of Translator in the case now in hearing so help you God?

Translator: I do.

President: We will take a brief recess now in order to bring Detainee into the room. Recorder note the date and time.

Recorder: The time is 1:30 pm hours on 10 March 2007. This Tribunal is now in recess. [The Tribunal recessed at 1330, 10 March 2007. The members withdrew from the hearing room.]

## *Convening Authority*

Recorder: All rise. [The Tribunal reconvened and the members entered the room at 1334, 10 March 2007.]

President: This hearing will come to order. Please be seated.

PRESIDENT: Before we begin, Khalid Sheikh Muhammad, I understand you speak and understand English. Is that correct?

DETAINEE: [Detainee nods his head in affirmative.]

PRESIDENT: All right. Are you comfortable in continuing in English or would you like everything translated in Arabic?

DETAINEE: Everything in English but if I have a problem the linguist will help me.

PRESIDENT: We will proceed in English. If you indicate to me that you would like something translated we will go ahead and do that. All right?

PRESIDENT: This Tribunal is convened by order of the Director, Combatant Status Review Tribunals under the provisions of his Order 22 February 2007.

PRESIDENT: This Tribunal will determine whether Khalid Sheikh Muhammad meets the criteria to be designated as an enemy combatant against the United States or its coalition partners or otherwise meets the criteria to be designated as an enemy combatant.

## *Oath Session 2*

PRESIDENT: The members of this tribunal shall now be sworn. All rise.

RECORDER: Do you swear or affirm that you will faithfully perform your duties as a member of this Tribunal; that you will impartially examine and inquire into the matter now before you according to your conscience, and the laws and regulations provided; that you will make such findings of fact and conclusions as are supported by the evidence presented; that in determining those facts, you will use your professional knowledge, best judgment, and common sense; and that you will make such findings as are appropriate according to the best of your understanding of the rules, regulations, and laws governing this proceeding, and guided by your concept of justice so help you God?

TRIBUNAL: I do.

President: The Recorder will now administer the oath to the Personal Representative.

Recorder: Do you swear or affirm that you will faithfully perform the duties of Personal Representative in this Tribunal so help you God?

Personal Representative: I do.

President: Please be seated.

President: The Recorder, Reporter, and Translator have previously been sworn.

## *Explanation of Proceedings*

President: Khalid Sheikh Muhammad, you are hereby advised that the following applies during this hearing:

President: You may be present at all open sessions of the Tribunal. However, if you become disorderly, you will be removed from the hearing, and the Tribunal will continue to hear evidence in your absence.

President: You may not be compelled to testify at this Tribunal. However, you may testify if you wish to do so. Your testimony can be under oath or unsworn.

President: You may have the assistance of a Personal Representative at the hearing. Your assigned Personal Representative is present.

President: You may present evidence to this Tribunal, including the testimony of witnesses who are reasonably available and whose testimony is relevant to this hearing. You may question witnesses testifying at the Tribunal.

President: You may examine documents or statements offered into evidence other than classified information. However, certain documents may be partially masked for security reasons.

President: Khalid Sheikh Muhammad, do you understand this process?

Detainee: Yes. If I have question can I ask you?

President: Yes, you may.

DETAINEE: About the testimony which I ask about the witnesses.

PRESIDENT: Yes, I'm going to address the witnesses shortly. So, if you will bear with us I will take that up in a few moments.

DETAINEE: Okay.

PRESIDENT: Do you have any questions concerning the Tribunal process?

DETAINEE: Okay by me.

## *Presentation of Unclassified Information*

PRESIDENT: Personal Representative, please provide the Tribunal with the Detainee Election Form.

PERSONAL REPRESENTATIVE: I am handing the Tribunal the Detainee Election Form, which was previously marked as Exhibit D.

PRESIDENT: All right, the Tribunal has received Exhibit D-a that indicates the Detainee wants to participate in the Tribunal and wants the assistance of the Personal Representative.

## *Recorder Presents Unclassified Information*

PRESIDENT: Recorder, please provide the Tribunal with the unclassified evidence.

RECORDER: I am handing the Tribunal what has previously been marked as Exhibit R, the unclassified summary of the evidence that relates to this Detainee's status as an enemy combatant. A translated copy of this exhibit was provided to the Personal Representative in advance of this hearing for presentation to the Detainee. In addition, I am handing to the Tribunal the following unclassified exhibits, marked as Exhibit R-2. Copies of these Exhibits have previously been provided to the Personal Representative. [Documents presented to Tribunal]

PRESIDENT: Recorder, please read the unclassified summary of evidence for the record. But before you proceed, Khalid Sheikh

Muhammad, let me remind you that you must not comment on this evidence at this time. You will be provided with an opportunity shortly to provide any comments that you would like. Recorder, please proceed.

RECORDER: The following facts support the determination that the Detainee is an enemy combatant:

Paragraph a. On the morning of 11 September 2001, four airliners traveling over the United States were hijacked. The flights hijacked were: American Airlines Flight 11, United Airlines Flight 175, American Airlines Flight 77, and United Airlines Flight 93. At approximately 8:46 a.m., American Airlines Flight 11 crashed into the North Tower of the World Trade Center, resulting in the collapse of the tower at approximately 10:25 a.m. At approximately 9:05 a.m., United Airlines Flight 175 crashed into the South Tower of the World Trade Center, resulting in the collapse of the tower at approximately 9:55 a.m. At approximately 9:37 a.m., American Airlines Flight 77 crashed into the southwest side of the Pentagon in Arlington, Virginia. At approximately 10:03 a.m., United Airlines Flight 93 crashed in Stoney Creek Township, Pennsylvania. These crashes and subsequent damage to the World Trade Center and the Pentagon resulted in the deaths of 2,972 persons in New York, Virginia, and Pennsylvania.

Paragraph b. The Detainee served as the head of the al Qaida military committee and was Usama bin Laden's principal al Qaida operative who directed the 11 September 2001 attacks in the United States.

Paragraph c. In an interview with an al Jazeera reporter in June 2002, the Detainee stated he was the head of the al Qaida military committee.

Paragraph d. A computer hard drive seized during the capture of the Detainee contained information about the four airplanes hijacked on 11 September 2001 including code names, airline company, flight number, target, pilot name and background information, and names of the hijackers.

Paragraph e. A computer hard drive seized during the capture of the Detainee contained photographs of 19 individuals identified as the 11 September 2001 hijackers.

Paragraph f. A computer hard drive seized during the capture of the Detainee contained a document that listed the pilot license fees for Mohammad Atta and biographies for some of the 11 September 2001 hijackers.

Paragraph g. A computer hard drive seized during the capture of the Detainee contained images of passports and an image of Mohammad Atta.

Paragraph h. A computer hard drive seized during the capture of the Detainee contained transcripts of chat sessions belonging to at least one of the 11 September 2001 hijackers.

Paragraph i. The Detainee directed an individual to travel to the United States to case targets for a second wave of attacks.

Paragraph j. A computer hard drive seized during the capture of the Detainee contained three letters from Usama bin Laden.

Paragraph k. A computer hard drive seized during the capture of the Detainee contained spreadsheets that describe money assistance to families of known al Qaida members.

Paragraph l. The Detainee's name was on a list in a computer seized in connection with a threat to United States airlines, United States embassies, and the Pope.

Paragraph m. The Detainee wrote the Bojinka plot, the airline bomb plot which was later found on his nephew Ramzi Yousef's computer.

Paragraph n. The Bojinka plot is also known as the Manila air investigation.

Paragraph o. The Manila air investigation uncovered the Detainee conspired with others to plant explosive devices aboard American jetliners while those aircraft were scheduled to be airborne and loaded with passengers on their way to the United States.

Paragraph p. The Detainee was in charge of and funded an attack against United States military vessels heading to the port of Djibouti.

Paragraph q. A computer hard drive seized during the capture of the Detainee contained a letter to the United Arab Emirates threatening attack if their government continued to help the United States.

Paragraph r. During the capture of the Detainee, information used exclusively by al Qaida operational managers to communicate with operatives was found.

Paragraph s. The Detainee received funds from Kuwaiti-based Islamic extremist groups and delivered the funds to al Qaida members.

Paragraph t. A computer hard drive seized during the capture of the Detainee contained a document that summarized operational procedures and training requirements of an al Qaida cell.

Paragraph u. A computer hard drive seized during the capture of the Detainee contained a list of killed and wounded al Qaida martyrs.

And lastly, Paragraph v. Passport photographs of al Qaida operatives were seized during the capture of the Detainee.

Recorder: Sir, this concludes the summary of unclassified evidence.

President: Very well.

President: Personal Representative, does the Detainee have any evidence to present to this Tribunal?

Personal Representative: Yes, sir. I am handing to the Tribunal the following unclassified exhibits marked as Exhibits D-b through D-d. Copies of these exhibits have been previously provided to the Recorder. [Documents presented to Tribunal]

President: Exhibit D-b appears to be a statement that the Detainee has provided.

Personal Representative: Yes, sir.

PRESIDENT: All right. And Exhibit D-c contains handwritten notes that appear to be Arabic and English as well as the typed version of that. Is that correct?

PERSONAL REPRESENTATIVE: Yes, sir.

PRESIDENT: All right. And D-d is a written statement regarding alleged abuse or treatment that the Detainee received.

PERSONAL REPRESENTATIVE: Yes, sir.

PRESIDENT: All right. We will go into those shortly.

PRESIDENT: Khalid Sheikh Muhammad, you may now make an oral statement to the Tribunal, and you have the assistance of your Personal Representative in doing so. Do you wish to make an oral statement to this Tribunal?

DETAINEE: He will start, the Personal Representative; PR will read then later I will comment.

PRESIDENT: Very well, you may proceed.

RECORDER: Sir, would you hold one moment?

PRESIDENT: Yes.

RECORDER: Ah, before the Detainee makes a statement, ah, I'd like to ah.

PRESIDENT: Question of the oath?

RECORDER: Ah, no sir.

RECORDER: Concerning classified evidence.

PRESIDENT: Very well.

PRESIDENT: Do you have any further evidence to present at this time, Recorder?

RECORDER: Mr. President, I have no further unclassified evidence for the Tribunal but I respectfully request a closed Tribunal session at an appropriate time to present classified evidence relevant to this Detainee's status as an enemy combatant.

PRESIDENT: Very well, your request for a closed session is granted and will be taken up in due course.

PRESIDENT: You may proceed, PR.

PERSONAL REPRESENTATIVE: The Detainee responds to the unclassified summary of evidence with the following key points.

Personal Representative: "Some paragraphs under paragraph number 3, lead sentence are not related to the context or meaning of the aforementioned lead sentence. For example, paragraph 3-a is only information from news or a historical account of events on 11 September 2001, and note with no specific linkage being made in this paragraph to me or the definition of Enemy Combatant. As another example, subparagraph 3-n makes no linkage to me or to the definition of Enemy Combatant."

Detainee: Are they following along?

Personal Representative: Ah, they have that in front of them for reference.

President: Yes.

Detainee: Okay.

Personal Representative: Second main point: "There are two false statements in the Summary of Evidence. Subparagraph 3-c is false. I never stated to the Al Jazeera reporter that I was the head of the al Qaida military committee. Also, Subparagraph 3-s is false. I did not receive any funds from Kuwait."

Personal Representative: Point number 3: "There is an unfair 'stacking of evidence' in the way the Summary of Evidence is structured. In other words, there are several subparagraphs under parent-paragraph 3 which should be combined into one subparagraph to avoid creating the false perception that there are more allegations or statements against me specifically than there actually are. For example, subparagraphs 3-m through 3-o, which pertain to the Bojinka plot should be combined into one paragraph, as should paragraphs 3-a through 3-h, which pertain to 9/11."

Personal Representative: Lastly, my name is misspelled in the Summary of Evidence. It should be S-h-a-i-k-h or S-h-e-i-k-h, but not S-h-a-y-k-h, as it is in the subject line.

President: Would you like to add anything to that, Khalid Sheikh Muhammad?

Personal Representative: Final statement.

Detainee: No, I just want to ask about witnesses.

President: Okay, ah, let's finish with these then I will get to the witnesses.

Detainee: Okay.

President: Try to keep it in order.

President: You want to continue, PR? Do you have another statement?

Personal Representative: That concludes this Detainee's response to the, ah, unclassified summary of evidence, sir.

President: Oh.

## *Calling of Witness*

President: We will now allow for the calling of witnesses. All witnesses called before this Tribunal may be questioned by the Detainee if present, the Personal Representative, the Recorder, and the Tribunal Members.

President: Does the Recorder have any witnesses to present?

Recorder: No, sir.

President: All right.

President: From the Detainee Election Form and I was informed earlier that the Detainee requested the presence of two witnesses to testify here today. Ramzi bin al-Shibh and Mustafa Hawsawi. The Detainee believes the witnesses can provide testimony related to the Detainee's actions specified in the unclassified summary of the evidence.

President: I have had the opportunity to review the request for witnesses and I have made some findings and I'm going to place them on the record now and when I conclude that, Khalid Sheikh Muhammad, you may respond to that if you'd like.

President: First the request for Ramzi bin al-Shibh, the proffer of the testimony from the Detainee was that Ramzi is alleged to have been present during the al Jazeera interview in June 2002 during which it is said the Detainee claimed to be head of al Qaida Military Committee. The Detainee claims he never stated that, to be the head of the Military Committee, during the Interview and states that Ramzi, if called, can confirm this.

President: This witness is not relevant in the President's view for the following reasons. In the totality of the circumstances and given the nature and quality of the other unclassified evidence, the Detainee's alleged statements as reported in al Jazeera are of limited value and negligible relevancy to the issue of combatant status. As such, any corroboration or contradiction by the proffered witness is not relevant. The creditability determinations with regard to R-2, which is the al Jazeera article, can be made by the Tribunal without the proffered testimony. As such, the Detainee's request for the production of that witness is denied.

President: As to the request for Mustafa Hawsawi, ah, it is proffered that Hawsawi, if called, could testify that the computer/hard drive referenced in the unclassified summary was not this Detainee's property and that the place of the Detainee's capture was not the house of the Detainee. In the President's view this testimony is not relevant to the issues regarding the Detainee's capture or his combatant status for the following reasons.

President: Whether the Detainee had actual legal title or ownership of the computer/hard drive or the house where the capture took place is irrelevant to the determination of the Detainee's status as an enemy combatant. Based on the proffer, if true, Hawsawi's testimony will not provide relevant information. The issue of ownership, while of some interest, is not relevant to status. What is relevant is possession, usage, connection, and presence. Hawsawi's testimony will not speak to any relevant information in regard to such points. As such, the request for the production of that witness is denied.

President: If you would like to respond to that, I'll hear you.

Detainee: Most of these facts which be written are related to this hard drive. And more than eleven of these facts are related to this computer. Other things are which is very old even nobody can bring any witnesses for that as you written here if it will be ah a value for you for the witness nearby you will do it. This computer is not for me. Is for Hawsawi himself. So I'm saying I need Hawsawi because me and him we both been arrested day. Same way. So this computer is from him long time. And also the problem we are not in court and we are not judge and he is not my lawyer but the procedure has been written reported and the way has mostly as certain charged against me; tell him, [Arabic phrase].

TRANSLATOR: [Translating] They are only accusations.

DETAINEE: So accusations. And the accusations, they are as you put for yourself ah definition for enemy combatant there are also many definitions for that accusation of fact or charges that has been written for any ah. [Arabic phrase]

TRANSLATOR: [Translating] Person is accused.

DETAINEE: So, if I been accused then if you want to put facts against me also the definition for these facts. If you now read number N now what is written the Bojinka plot. Is known many lead investigation it is not related to anything facts to be against me. So when I said computer hard drive/ hard disk, same thing. All these point only one witness he can say yes or not cause he is this computer is under his possession him computer. And also specifically if he said Mohammed Atta picture been this hard drive. I don't think this should accepted. There are many 100 thousand Americans who have a lot of picture on their computer. You cannot say I find Mohammed Atta on your computer then you use this fact against you. Or you find any files in your computer to be what about it's mine, it's not my computer. If this witness, he will state that this known and here that has been ninety percent of what is written is wrong. And for Ramzi, for reporter in Jazeera, he claimed that I state this one and you know the media man. How they are fashionable. What they mean in their own way in a whole different way. They just wrote it so he say I state. But I never stated and I don't have any witnesses and witness are available here at Guantánamo. He is Detainee. He was with me. Which he been mostly in all my interview with him. Me and them, there was three person, me and Ramzi and this reporter. So if you not believe me, not believe him, believe my witness Ramzi.

Then he's what he state the reporter most is false. I not denying that I'm not an enemy combatant about this war but I'm denying the report. It not being written in the proper way. Which is really facts and mostly just being gathered many information. General information that form in way of doing, to use in facts against me.

PRESIDENT: I have heard and understood your argument. In order for me to make my determinations regarding the production of witnesses I first have to believe that they are relevant for the reasons that I have stated. For the reasons I have stated, I do not believe they are relevant. Whether or not they may be available here on Guantanámo, is a second decision to be made, but only if I decide they are relevant. I have heard your arguments. I noted them. However, my ruling stands.

PRESIDENT: The Recorder has no witnesses, is that my understanding?

RECORDER: No, sir.

PRESIDENT: And there are no other approved witnesses to take up. Ah, we will take a brief moment to review the unclassified evidence that we received so far and then we will pick back up in the proceeding.

MEMBER: If I might ask a question real quick of the PR. This is the entire translation of the handwritten notes?

PERSONAL REPRESENTATIVE: Yeah. The handwritten notes are the Detainee is on yellow.

MEMBER: Yes.

PERSONAL REPRESENTATIVE: And, then the next set of notes, handwritten notes, are the Linguist's translation and then the final hard copy printed that's, ah, that...

MEMBER: Typewritten.

PERSONAL REPRESENTATIVE: Typed from Linguist's notes.

MEMBER: Typed from Linguist's translations. Okay.

PRESIDENT: Khalid Sheikh Muhammad, I did not offer you an oath early because I was informed by the Personal Representative that you would be making some statement later on in these proceedings relevant to the truthfulness of your comments. So, if you would like to take an oath I would administer one to you but I did understand that you going to make a statement.

Detainee: In the final statement, I will explain why then.

President: All right. Thank you. [Tribunal pauses to review D-a thru D-d]

Member: Seen those.

Translator: Sir.

President: Yes.

Translator: He wanted me to translate a Koranic verse on the spot.

President: I will permit it.

Translator: Thank you.

Translator: Can I ask him for clarification?

President: Yes.

President: Do you need a few more moments. Translator?

Translator: Yes, sir, about thirty seconds.

President: Go ahead and take your time.

Translator: Would you me to read the English translation after he read Arabic verse or would like him to read it?

President: You want to save that for later?

Translator: [Nods head]

President: All right.

President: Let me take up a few things that have come up as based on my review of these documents that have been provided to us so far. D-d appears to be a written statement regarding certain treatment that you claim to have received at the hands of agents of the United States government as you indicated from the time of your capture in 2003 up until before coming here to Guantánamo in September 2006.

President: Is that correct?

Detainee: Yes.

President: All right.

President: Now, I haven't seen any statements in the evidence we receive so far that claim to come from you other than acknowledging whether you were or not the head of the Military Committee. Were any statements that you made as the result of any of the treatment that you received during that time frame from 2003 to 2006? Did you make those statements because of the treatment you receive from these people?

DETAINEE: Statement for whom?

PRESIDENT: To any of these interrogators.

DETAINEE: CIA peoples. Yes. At the beginning when they transferred me ______. This is what I understand he told me: you are not American and you are not on American soil. So you cannot ask about the Constitution.

PRESIDENT: What I'm trying to get at is any statement that you made was it because of this treatment, to use your word, you claim torture. Do you make any statements because of that?

TRANSLATOR: Sir, for clarification.

PRESIDENT: Can you translate it?

TRANSLATOR: I will translate in Arabic.

PRESIDENT: Yes.

TRANSLATOR: [Translating above]

DETAINEE: I ah cannot remember now ______ be under questioning so many statement which been some of them I make up stories just location UBL. Where is he? I don't know. Then he torture me. Then I said yes, he is in this area or this is al Qaida which I don't know him. I said no, they torture me. Does he know you? I say don't know him but how come he know you. I told him I'm senior man. Many people they know me which I don't them. I ask him even if he knew George Bush. He said, yes I do. He don't know you that not means its false. ______ I said yes or not. This I said.

PRESIDENT: All right, I understand.

PRESIDENT: Is there anything you would like to correct, amend, modify, or explain to us from what you said back then?

DETAINEE: I want to just it is not related enemy combatant but I'm saying for you to be careful with people. That you have classified and unclassified facts. My opinion to be fair with people. Because when I say, I will not regret when I say I'm enemy combatant. I did or not I know there are other but there are many Detainees which you receive classified against them maybe, maybe not take away from me for many Detainees false witnesses. This only advice.

PRESIDENT: So you are aware that other...

DETAINEE: Yes.

PRESIDENT: People made false statement as a result of this?

DETAINEE: I did also.

PRESIDENT: Uh huh.

DETAINEE: I told him, I know him yes. There are and they are. Not even you show me. This I don't know him I never met him at all. So, unclassified which is both classified and unclassified so this is you know him you don't know him. You have to be fair with people. There are many, many people which they have never been part of the Taliban. Afghanistan there have been many people arrested for example people who have been arrested after October 2001 after make attack against Afghanistan many of them just arrive after they don't what has happen. When Russian came to Afghanistan they felt they went back but they did anything with Taliban and al Qaida then came after that. I don't know why it was younger people same thing for Afghanis people they show Afghanis people. I will give example one. His name is Sayed Habib. This I remember. Him they found his name in my notes and I told them this note is old note and have people which even before al Qaida I know. And he is not. He is one of my students and the Russian times and I don't know him. _________

PRESIDENT: All right.

PRESIDENT: Now what.

DETAINEE: For me nothing which was recorded. For which is written here is not related

PRESIDENT: I understand.

PRESIDENT: I do note that in one of the exhibits you indicate you are not under any pressure or duress today. Is that correct?

DETAINEE: That is about I'm hearing today. Yes.

President: So anything.

Detainee: Some of this information. I not state it to them.

President: The information that you are telling us today, so we are clear. You do not believe you are under any pressure or threat or duress to speak to us today, is that correct?

Detainee: Yes, that's correct.

President: All right.

President: Now what you have told us about your previous treatment is on the record of these proceedings now and will be reported for any investigation that may be appropriate. Also, we will consider what you have told us in making our determination regarding your enemy combatant status.

Detainee: I hope you will take care of other Detainees with what I said. It's up to you.

President: I will do as I've said. I'll see to it that it is reported.

President: All right. At this point, we are going to go into the final statement but I do want to give the opportunity to the Recorder, PR, and Tribunal member to ask questions if they would like. So, what we'll do is proceed then to the Detainee's final statement and then I'll have a question and answer session following that. All right just give me a moment.

President: All right.

President: Khalid Sheikh Muhammad, this concludes the presentation of unclassified information to the Tribunal. We are about to conclude the unclassified portion of the hearing. Do you wish to now make any final statement to the Tribunal? You have the assistance of your PR.

Detainee: I make a two part. Maybe he will read then I will go also.

President: Very well. You may continue.

Personal Representative: Mr. President, the Detainee has asked me to read his final statement to the Tribunal with the understanding he may interject or add statements if he needs to, to correct what I say. According to the Detainee:

"I hereby admit and affirm without duress to the following:

1. I swore Bay'aat (i.e., allegiance) to Sheikh Usama Bin Laden to conduct Jihad of self and money, and also Hijrah (i.e., expatriation to any location in the world where Jihad is required).
2. I was a member of the Al Qaida Council.
3. I was the Media Operations Director for Al-Sahab, or 'The Clouds,' under Dr. Ayman Al Zawahiri. Al-Sahab is the media outlet that provided Al-Qaida-sponsored information to Al Jazeera. Four."

Detainee: [speaking inaudibly to Personal Representative]
President: Please tell.
Personal Representative: In other channels or other media outlets.
President: Thank you.
Personal Representative: [continuing]

"4. I was the Operational Director for Sheikh Usama Bin Laden for the organizing, planning, follow-up, and execution of the 9/11 Operation under the Military Commander, Sheikh Abu Hafs Al-Masri Subhi Abu Sittah.
5. I was the Military Operational Commander for all foreign operations around the world under the direction of Sheikh Usama Bin Laden and Dr. Ayman Al-Zawahiri.
6. I was directly in charge, after the death of Sheikh Abu Hafs Al-Masri Subhi Abu Sittah, of managing and following up on the Cell for the Production of Biological Weapons, such as anthrax and others, and following up on Dirty Bomb Operations on American soil.
7. I was Emir (i.e., commander) of Beit Al Shuhada (i.e., the Martyrs' House) in the state of Kandahar, Afghanistan, which housed the 9/11 hijackers. There I was responsible for their training and readiness for the execution of the 9/11 Operation. Also, I hereby admit and affirm without duress that I was a responsible participant, principal planner, trainer,

financier (via the Military Council Treasury), executor, and/or a personal participant in the following:

1. I was responsible for the 1993 World Trade Center Operation.
2. I was responsible for the 9/11 Operation, from A to Z.
3. I decapitated with my blessed right hand the head of the American Jew, Daniel Pearl, in the city of Karachi, Pakistan. For those who would like to confirm, there are pictures of me on the Internet holding his head.
4. I was responsible for the Shoe Bomber Operation to down two American airplanes.
5. I was responsible for the Filka Island Operation in Kuwait that killed two American soldiers.
6. I was responsible for the bombing of a nightclub in Bali, Indonesia, which was frequented by British and Australian nationals.
7. I was responsible for planning, training, surveying, and financing the New (or Second) Wave attacks against the following skyscrapers after 9/11:
   a. Library Tower, California.
   b. Sears Tower, Chicago.
   c. Plaza Bank, Washington state.
   d. The Empire State Building, New York City.

8. I was responsible for planning, financing, & follow-up of Operations to destroy American military vessels and oil tankers in the Straits of Hormuz, the Straits of Gibraltar, and the Port of Singapore.
9. I was responsible for planning, training, surveying, and financing for the Operation to bomb and destroy the Panama Canal.
10. I was responsible for surveying and financing for the assassination of several former American Presidents, including President Carter.
11. I was responsible for surveying, planning, and financing for the bombing of suspension bridges in New York.

12. I was responsible for planning to destroy the Sears Tower by burning a few fuel or oil tanker trucks beneath it or around it.
13. I was responsible for planning, surveying, and financing for the operation to destroy Heathrow Airport, the Canary Wharf Building, and Big Ben on British soil.
14. I was responsible for planning, surveying, and financing for the destruction of many nightclubs frequented by American and British citizens on Thailand soil.
15. I was responsible for surveying and financing for the destruction of the New York Stock Exchange and other financial targets after 9/11.
16. I was responsible for planning, financing, and surveying for the destruction of buildings in the Israeli city of Elat by using airplanes leaving from Saudi Arabia.
17. I was responsible for planning, surveying, and financing for the destruction of American embassies in Indonesia, Australia, and Japan.
18. I was responsible for surveying and financing for the destruction of the Israeli embassy in India, Azerbaijan, the Philippines, and Australia.
19. I was responsible for surveying and financing for the destruction of an Israeli 'El-AP Airlines flight on Thailand soil departing from Bangkok Airport.
20. I was responsible for sending several Mujahadeen into Israel to conduct surveillance to hit several strategic targets deep in Israel.
21. I was responsible for the bombing of the hotel in Mombasa that is frequented by Jewish travelers via El-Al airlines.
22. I was responsible for launching a Russian-made SA-7 surface-to-air missile on El-Al or other Jewish airliner departing from Mombasa.
23. I was responsible for planning and surveying to hit American targets in South Korea, such as American military bases and a few nightclubs frequented by American soldiers.

24. I was responsible for financial, excuse me, I was responsible for providing financial support to hit American, Jewish, and British targets in Turkey.
25. I was responsible for surveillance needed to hit nuclear power plants that generate electricity in several U.S. states.
26. I was responsible for planning, surveying, and financing to hit NATO Headquarters in Europe.
27. I was responsible for the planning and surveying needed to execute the Bojinka Operation, which was designed to down twelve American airplanes full of passengers. I personally monitored a round-trip, Manila-to-Seoul, Pan Am flight.
28. I was responsible for the assassination attempt against President Clinton during his visit to the Philippines in 1994 or 1995.
29. I was responsible for the assassination attempt against Pope John Paul the Second while he was visiting the Philippines."

Detainee: I was not responsible, but share.

Personal Representative: I shared responsibility. I will restate number twenty-nine.

29. I shared responsibility for the assassination attempt against Pope John Paul the Second while he was visiting the Philippines.
30. I was responsible for the training and financing for the assassination of Pakistan's President Musharraf.
31. I was responsible for the attempt to destroy an American oil company owned by the Jewish former Secretary of State, Henry Kissinger, on the Island of Sumatra, Indonesia."

Personal Representative: Sir, that concludes the written portion of the Detainee's final statement and as he has alluded to earlier he has some additional comments he would like to make.

President: All right. Before you proceed, Khalid Sheikh Muhammad, the statement that was just read by the Personal Representative, were those your words?

## *Begin Detainee Oral Statement*

Detainee: Yes. And I want to add some of this one just for some verification. It like some operations before I join al Qaida. Before I remember al Qaida which is related to Bojinka Operation I went to destination involve to us in 94, 95. Some Operations which means out of al Qaida. It's like beheading Daniel Pearl. It's not related to al Qaida. It was shared in Pakistani. Other group, Mujahadeen. The story of Daniel Pearl, because he stated for the Pakistanis, group that he was working with the both. His mission was in Pakistan to track about Richard Reed trip to Israel. Richard Reed, do you have trip? You send it Israel to make set for targets in Israel. His mission in Pakistan from Israeli intelligence, Mosad, to make interview to ask about when he was there. Also, he mention to them he was both. He have relation with CIA people and were the Mosad. But he was not related to al Qaida at all or UBL. It is related to the Pakistan Mujahadeen group. Other operations mostly are some word I'm not accurate in saying. I'm responsible but if you read the heading history. The line there [indicating to Personal Representative a place or Exhibit D-c]."

Personal Representative: [Reading] "Also, hereby admit and affirm without duress that I was a responsible participant, principal planner, trainer, financier."

Detainee: For this is not necessary as I responsible, responsible. But within these things responsible participant in finances.

President: I understand. I want to be clear, though, is you that were the author of that document.

Detainee: That's right.

President: That it is true?

Detainee: That's true.

President: All right. You may continue with your statement.

Detainee: Okay. I start in Arabic.

President: Please.

Detainee: (through translator): In the name of God the most compassionate, the most merciful, and if any fail to retaliation by way of charity and I apologize. I will start again. And if any fail to judge by the light of Allah has revealed, they are no better than wrongdoers, unbelievers, and the unjust.

Detainee: For this verse, I not take the oath. Take an oath is a part of your Tribunal and I'll not accept it. To be or accept the Tribunal as to be, I'll accept it. That I'm accepting American Constitution, American law, or whatever you are doing here. This is why religiously I cannot accept anything you do. Just to explain for this one, does not mean I'm not saying that I'm lying. When I not take oath does not mean I'm lying. You know very well peoples take oath and they will lie. You know the President he did this before he just makes his oath and he lied. So sometimes when I'm not making oath does not mean I'm lying.

President: I understand.

Detainee: Second thing. When I wrote this thing, I mean, the PR he told me that President may stop you at any time and he don't like big mouth nor you to talk too much. To be within subject. So, I will try to be within the enemy combatant subject.

President: You can say whatever you'd like to say so long as it's relevant to what we are discussing here today.

Detainee: Okay, thanks.

Detainee: What I wrote here, is not I'm making myself hero, when I said I was responsible for this or that. But you are military man. You know very well there are language for any war. So, there are, we are when I admitting these things I'm not saying I'm not did it. I did it but this the language of any war. If America they want to invade Iraq they will not send for Saddam roses or kisses they send for a bombardment. This is the best way if I want. If I'm fighting for anybody admit to them I'm American enemies. For sure, I'm American enemies. Usama bin Laden, he did his best press conference in American media. Mr. John Miller he been there when he made declaration against Jihad, against America. And he said it is not no need for me now to make explanation of what he said but mostly he said about American military presence in Arabian peninsula and aiding Israel and many things. So when we made any war against America we are jackals fighting in the nights. I consider myself, for what you are doing, a religious thing as you consider us fundamentalist. So, we derive from religious leading that we consider we and George Washington doing same thing. As consider George Washington as hero. Muslims many of them are considering Usama bin Laden. He is doing same thing. He is just fighting. He needs his independence. Even we think that, or not me only. Many Muslims, that al Qaida or Taliban they are doing. They have been oppressed by America. This is the feeling of the prophet. So when we say we are enemy combatant, that right. We are.

But I'm asking you again to be fair with many Detainees which are not enemy combatant. Because many of them have been unjustly arrested. Many, not one or two or three. Cause the definition you which wrote even from my view it is not fair. Because if I was in the first Jihad times Russia. So I have to be Russian enemy. But America supported me in this because I'm their alliances when I was fighting Russia. Same job I'm doing. I'm fighting. I was fighting there Russia now I'm fighting America. So, many people who been in Afghanistan never leave. Afghanistan stay in but they not share Taliban or al Qaida. They been Russian time and they cannot go back to their home with their corrupted government. They stayed there and when America invaded Afghanistan parliament. They had been arrest. They never have been with Taliban or the others. So many people consider them as enemy but they are not. Because definitions are very wide definition so people they came after October of 2002, 2001. When America invaded Afghanistan, they just arrive in Afghanistan cause they hear there enemy. They don't know what it means al Qaida or Usama bin Laden or Taliban. They don't care about these things. They heard they were enemy in Afghanistan they just arrived. As they heard first time Russian invade Afghanistan. They arrive they fought when back than they came. They don't know what's going on and

Taliban they been head of government. You consider me even Taliban even the president of whole government. Many people they join Taliban because they are the government.

When Karzai they came they join Karzai when come they join whatever public they don't know what is going on. So, many Taliban fight even the be fighters because they just because public. The government is Taliban then until now CIA don't have exactly definition well who is Taliban, who is al Qaida. Your Tribunal now are discussing he is enemy or not and that is one of your jobs. So this is why you find many Afghanis people, Pakistanis people even, they don't know what going on they just hear they are fighting and they help Muslim in Afghanistan. Then what. There are some infidels which they came here and they have to help them. But then there weren't any intend to do anything against America. Taliban themselves between Taliban they said Afghanistan which they never again against 9/11 operation. The rejection between senior of Taliban of what al Qaida are doing. Many of Taliban rejected what they are doing. Even many Taliban, they not agree about why we are in Afghanistan. Some of them they have been with us. Taliban never in their life at all before America invade them the intend to do anything against America.

They never been with a Qaida. Does not mean we are here as American now. They gave political asylum for many countries. They gave for Chinese oppositions or a North Korean but that does not mean they are with them same thing many of Taliban. They harbor us as al Qaida does not mean we are together. So, this is why I'm asking you to be fair with Afghanis and Pakistanis and many Arabs which been in Afghanistan. Many of them been unjustly. The funny story they been Sunni government they sent some spies to assassinate UBL then we arrested them sent them to Afghanistan/Taliban. Taliban put them into prison. Americans they came and arrest them as enemy combatant. They brought them here. So, even if they are my enemy but not fair to be there with me. This is what I'm saying. The way of the war, you know, very well, any country waging war against their enemy the language of the war are killing. If man and woman they be together as a marriage that is up to the kids, children. But if you and me, two nations, will be together in war the others are victims. This is the way of the language. You know 40 million people were killed in World War One. Ten million kill in World War. You know that two million four hundred thousand be killed in the Korean War. So this language of the war.

Any people who, when Usama bin Laden say I'm waging war because such reason, now he declared it. But when you said I'm terrorist, I think it is deceiving peoples. Terrorists, enemy combatant. All these definitions as CIA you can make whatever you want. Now, you told me when I ask about the witnesses, I'm not convinced that this related to the matter. It is up to you. Maybe I'm convinced but your are head and he [gesturing to Personal Representative] is not responsible, the other, because you are head of the committee. So, finally it's your war but the problem is no definitions of many words. It would be widely definite that many people be oppressed. Because war, for sure, there will be victims. When I said I'm not happy that three thousand been killed in America. I feel sorry even. I don't like to kill children and the kids. Never Islam are, give me green light to kill peoples. Killing, as in the Christianity, Jews, and Islam, are prohibited. But there are exception of rule when you are killing people in Iraq. You said we have to do it. We don't like Saddam. But this is the way to deal with Saddam. Same thing you are saying. Same language you use, I use. When you are invading two-thirds of Mexican, you call your war manifest destiny. It up to you to call it what you want. But other side are calling you oppressors. If now George Washington. If now we were living in the Revolutionary War and George Washington he being arrested through Britain. For sure he, they would consider him enemy combatant. But American they consider him as hero. This right the any Revolutionary War they will be as George Washington or Britain. So we are considered American Army bases which we have from seventies in Iraq. Also, in the Saudi Arabian, Kuwait, Qatar, and Bahrain.

This is kind of invasion, but I'm not here to convince you. Is not or not but mostly speech is ask you to be fair with people. I'm don't have anything to say that I'm not enemy. This is why the language of any war is killing. I mean the language of the war is victims. I don't like to kill people. I feel very sorry they been killed kids in 9/11. What I will do? This is the language. Sometime I want to make great awakening between American to stop foreign policy in our land. I know American people are torturing us from seventies. _______ I know they talking about human rights. And I know it is against American Constitution, against American laws. But they said ever law, they have exceptions, this is your bad luck you have been part of the exception of our laws. They have something to convince me but we are doing same language. But we are saying we have Sharia law, but we have Koran. What is enemy combatant in my language?

DETAINEE: (through translator): Allah forbids you not with regards to those who fight you not for not for your faith nor drive you out of your homes from dealing kindly and justly with them. For Allah love those who are just. There is one more sentence. Allah only forbids you with regards to those who fight you for your faith and drive you out of your homes and support others in driving you out from turning to them for friendship and protection. It is as such to turn to them in these circumstances that do wrong.

DETAINEE: So we are driving from whatever deed we do we ask about Koran or Hadith. We are not making up for us laws. When we need Fatwa from the religious we have to go back to see what they said scholar. To see what they said yes or not. Killing is prohibited in all what you call the people of the book, Jews, Judaism, Christianity, and Islam. You know the Ten Commandments very well. The Ten Commandments are shared between all of us. We all are serving one God. Then now kill you know it very well. But war language also we have language for the war. You have to kill. But you have to care if unintentionally or intentionally target if I have if I'm not at the Pentagon. I consider it is okay. If I target now when we target in USA we choose them military target, economical, and political. So, war central victims mostly means economical target. So if now American they know UBL. He is in this house they don't care about his kids and his. They will just bombard it. They will kill all of them and they did it.

They kill wife of Dr. Ayman Zawahiri and his two daughters and his son in one bombardment. They receive a report that is his house be. He had not been there. They killed them. They arrested my kids intentionally. They are kids. They been arrested for four months they had been abused. So, for me I have patience. I know I'm not talk about what's come to me. The American have human right. So, enemy combatant itself, it flexible word. So I think God knows that many who been arrested, they been unjustly arrested. Otherwise, military throughout history know very well. They know war will never stop. War start from Adam when Cain he killed Abel until now. It's never gonna stop killing of people. This is the way of the language. American start the Revolutionary War then they starts the Mexican then Spanish War then World War One, World War Two. You read the history. You know never stopping war. This is life. But if who is enemy combatant and who is not? Finally, I finish statement. I'm asking you to be fair with other people.

President: Does that conclude your statement, Khalid Sheikh Muhammad?

Detainee: Yes.

President: All right.

## *Detainee Question & Answer*

President: Does the Personal Representative have any questions for the Detainee based on his statement?

Personal Representative: No, sir.

President: Does the Recorder have any questions for the Detainee?

RECORDER: No, sir.
PRESIDENT: Do either of the Tribunal members wish to question the Detainee?
MEMBERS: No, sir. Nothing further, sir.
PRESIDENT: All right.

## *Closing Unclassified Section*

PRESIDENT: All unclassified evidence having been provided to the Tribunal, this concludes the open tribunal session.
PRESIDENT: Khalid Sheikh Muhammad,* you shall be notified of the Tribunal decision upon completion of the review of these proceedings by the Combatant Status Review Tribunal convening authority in Washington, D.C. If the Tribunal determines that you shall not be classified as an enemy combatant, you will be released to your home country as soon as arrangements can be made. If, however, the Tribunal determines your classification as an enemy combatant, you may be eligible for an Administrative Review Board hearing at a future date.
PRESIDENT: The Administrative Review Board will make an assessment of whether there is continued reason to believe that you pose a threat to the United States or its coalition partners in the ongoing armed conflict against terrorist organizations such as al Qaeda and its affiliates and supporters or whether there are other factors bearing upon the need for continued detention.
PRESIDENT: You will have the opportunity to be heard and to present relevant information to the Administrative Review Board. You can present information from your family and friends that might help you at that Board. You are encouraged to contact them as soon as possible to begin to gather information that may help you.
PRESIDENT: A military officer will be assigned at a later date to assist you in the Administrative Review Board process.

*The U.S. government uses different spellings of many Arabic names.

## *Adjourn Open Session*

PRESIDENT: The open session of this Tribunal hearing is adjourned.

RECORDER: The time is 2:43 pm. The date is 10 March 2007.

RECORDER: All rise. [The Tribunal withdrew from the hearing room.]

## *Authentication*

I certify the material contained in this transcript is a true and accurate verbatim rendering of the testimony and English-language translation of Detainee's words given during the open session of the Combatant Status Review Tribunal of ISN 10024.

CAPT JAGC USN
Tribunal President

# NOTES

## Preface

1. Author interview with senior U.S. counterterrorism official, 2010.

## Chapter 1 — *Mukhtar*

1. Author interview, 2011.
2. Author interview, 2010.
3. The account of the raids is drawn from interviews with multiple intelligence and law enforcement officers. Former CIA case officer John Kiriakou has written about the raids in his book *The Reluctant Spy: My Secret Life in the CIA's War on Terror* and has been interviewed by other journalists. Elements of his account of his time in Pakistan, particularly his claimed knowledge of interrogations to which he was not witness, have been questioned and Kiriakou has acknowledged discrepancies in the details in his own recountings. This is hardly unique to Kiriakou. Time, memory, and conflicting ambitions have often created a less than clear historical record of events related to 9/11. We have tried here and throughout the book to reconcile conflicting accounts and, when unable to do so, have not included the material.
4. Kiriakou, *The Reluctant Spy: My Secret Life in the CIA's War on Terror* (New York: Bantam, 2010).
5. Jane Mayer, *The Dark Side: The Inside Story of How the War on Terror Turned into a War on American Ideals* (New York: Doubleday, 2008), 40.

6. Author interviews with multiple law enforcement officials, including former FBI special agent Ali Soufan.

## CHAPTER 2—*Those Without*

1. Mohammed family, author interview, 2010; passport copies, author collection.
2. Author copy of passport.
3. "Baluchistan During Persian Empires," accessed at http://www.balochrise.com/vb/showthread.php?t=507.
4. Central Intelligence Agency, "Khalid Shaykh Muhammad: Preeminent Source on Al-Qa'ida," July 13, 2004, author copy.
5. Author interview, June 2004.
6. Central Intelligence Agency, "Khalid Shaykh Muhammad."
7. Joint Task Force Guantánamo, Detainee Assessment Brief, December 8, 2006.
8. Enrollment records, Chowan University.
9. Author telephone interview, 2003.
10. Author telephone interview, 2003.
11. Author interview, 2003.
12. Central Intelligence Agency, "Khalid Shaykh Muhammad."
13. NGO records reviewed in Peshawar, 2003.
14. Author telephone interview, 2010.
15. Author telephone interview, 2003.
16. Joint Task Force Guantánamo, Detainee Assessment Brief, December 8, 2006.
17. Ibid.
18. Author interview, 2003.
19. Khalil A. Khalil, interviewed by the staff of the National Commission on Terrorist Attacks Upon the United States, and quoted in a memorandum prepared for the record, February 25, 2004, author copy.
20. Author interview, 2002.
21. Author interview, 2003.
22. Author interview, 2002.

## CHAPTER 3—*Jihad*

1. The account of Basit's time in New York is drawn primarily from transcripts of the trials United States v. Ramzi Ahmed Yousef, et al.; United States v. Mohammed A. Salameh, et al.; United States v. Usama bin Laden; and United States v. Ismoil, et al.

2. Much of the information about Murad and his relationship with Yousef comes from transcripts of Murad's interrogations by Philippine intelligence during the period from January through March of 1995, and from summaries of his interrogation by the FBI in April of 1995 (author copies).
3. Graff, Garrett M., *The Threat Matrix: The FBI at War in the Age of Global Terror* (New York: Little, Brown, 2011), 167.

## CHAPTER 4—*Bojinka*

1. Internal FBI memos, 1998, author copies. Details of Basit's and Mohammed's activities in Manila are drawn from these memos, from Murad's interrogations, and from Basit's interrogations and trial transcripts.
2. Khalid Sheikh Mohammed, interrogation report, author copy.
3. "The Islamic Fundamentalist/Extremist Movements in the Philippines and Their Links with International Terrorist Organizations," unpublished special report by the Philippine National Police Intelligence Group, Special Investigations Command, December 1994, author copy.
4. Murad interrogation reports.
5. Internal FBI memos, 1998.

## CHAPTER 5—*Making a Case*

1. Author interview, October 2011.
2. The arrest of Basit has been described numerous times. One of the first accounts, and still one of the best and most comprehensive, is contained in Simon Reeve's *The New Jackals* (Boston: Northeastern University Press, 1999). Reeve's book was prescient in its description of the dangers posed by radical Islamist terror.
3. United States v. Ramzi Ahmed Yousef, et al.

## CHAPTER 6—*Sorting It Out*

1. FBI FD-302 on the interrogation of Murad, April 1995, author copy.
2. FBI internal report, 1996.
3. Presidential Decision Directive 39, June 21, 1995, accessed at http://www.fas.org/irp/offdocs/pdd39.htm.
4. George Tenet, "Written Statement for the Record of the Director of Central Intelligence before the National Commission on Terrorist Attacks Upon the United States," March 24, 2004, author copy.

5. As quoted in John Kiriakou, *The Reluctant Spy: My Secret Life in the CIA's War on Terror* (New York: Bantam Books, 2010), 170.
6. Author interview, 2010.
7. Author interview, 2002.
8. Interview with Balkan journalist Esad Hecimovic, 2011, and review of documents.
9. Accessed at http://intelfiles.egoplex.com/cia-ngos-1996.pdf.
10. National Commission on Terrorist Attacks Upon the United States, Final Report, 488.

## Chapter 7—*A Near Miss*

1. Author interview, 2010.
2. Author interview, 2003. The account of this meeting derives from interviews with several of its participants; there was broad agreement over its general tone and outcome.
3. Author interview with senior NSC official.
4. Author interviews, 2002, 2010.
5. Melissa Mahle, author interview, 2011.
6. Author copy.
7. FBI internal memorandum, author copy.
8. Author interview with senior Justice Department official, 2011.
9. Author interview, 2011.
10. Author interview, 2010.
11. Internal 1997 FBI memorandum, author copy. The same memo indicated that KSM might have had more contacts with al-Gama'a al-Islamiyya. When authorities raided an al-Gama'a al-Islamiyya cell in Milan, Italy, they found an address book that contained KSM's Doha telephone number.
12. National Commission on Terrorist Attacks Upon the United States (the 9/11 Commission), Staff Statement 16 (Twelfth Public Hearing), June 16, 2004. The Congressional Joint Inquiry final report, December 2003, page 30, contained the first official confirmation of the sequence of events that brought Khalid Sheikh Mohammed and the airliner plot to Al Qaeda. The 9/11 Commission elaborated on this in much greater detail.

## Chapter 8—*Thin Air*

1. Mike Garcia, author interview, 2011.

2. George Tenet, "Written Statement for the Record of the Director of Central Intelligence before the National Commission on Terrorist Attacks Upon the United States," March 24, 2004, author copy.

## CHAPTER 9—*The Plot*

1. FBI internal memorandum, 1999, quoting CIA reporting.
2. Central Intelligence Agency, "Khalid Shaykh Muhammad: Preeminent Source on Al-Qa'ida," July 13, 2004, author copy.
3. Author interview, 2001.
4. CIA, "Khalid Sheikh Mohammad Revelations," undated analysis, author copy.
5. Jack Roche, author telephone interview, 2011.
6. Author interview, 2002.
7. Author interview, 2010.
8. Author copy.
9. National Commission on Terrorist Attacks Upon the United States (the 9/11 Commission), Staff Statement 16 (Twelfth Public Hearing), June 16, 2004.
10. Author interview, 2011.

## CHAPTER 10—*September 11*

1. George Tenet, "Written Statement for the Record of the Director of Central Intelligence before the National Commission on Terrorist Attacks Upon the United States," March 24, 2004, author copy.
2. Pervez Musharraf, *In the Line of Fire* (New York: Free Press, 2006), 240.
3. Yosri Fouda and Nick Fielding, *Masterminds of Terror: The Truth Behind the Most Devastating Terrorist Attack the World Has Ever Seen* (London: Arcade Publishing, 2003), 159.

## CHAPTER 11—*Panic*

1. Flight manifest, United Airlines flight 93, FBI investigative record, author copy. The manifests for all four doomed flights were later offered in evidence in United States v. Zacarias Moussaoui, 2006. There has been considerable debate among 9/11 conspiracy theorists as to whether the hijackers were actually on board that day. The manifests, which were obtained independently, are evidence that they were.

2. FBI investigative record, author copy. Atta's rental car was caught on camera entering the parking garage just fifteen minutes before the scheduled departure of the commuter flight. The trip to Maine beggars explanation; Atta nearly wrecked the whole plot by going. The best explanation law enforcement has been able to devise for the trip was that Atta somehow thought it would lessen his exposure to airport security. In fact, he doubled his exposure because he had to go through a separate security check upon arrival and transfer at Logan.
3. Author interview, 2011.
4. Author copy, obtained from John Berger at Intelwire: http://intelwire.egoplex.com/2006_11_21_exclusives.html.
5. Pickard had been acting director of the Bureau before Mueller was appointed. He was everything Mueller was not—a known quantity, a career FBI man, a one-time undercover agent on the ABSCAM sting. For more on the insularity of FBI culture, see Garrett M. Graff's *The Threat Matrix: The FBI at War in the Age of Global Terror* (New York: Little, Brown, 2011), which is an excellent guide to the history and administrative workings of the contemporary FBI.
6. Dennis Lormel, author interview, 2011.
7. Ron Suskind, *The One Percent Doctrine: Deep Inside America's Pursuit of Its Enemies Since 9/11* (New York: Simon & Schuster, 2006). Suskind's book is excellent throughout.
8. Suskind, *The One Percent Doctrine*. Jane Mayer also includes a detailed description of Black's proposals in *The Dark Side* (28–43).
9. E-mail from Moussaoui to Pan Am International Flight Academy, May 23, 2001, offered as evidence in *Moussaoui*.
10. Author interview, 2011.
11. Testimony before the National Commission on Terrorism Attacks Upon the United States, April 13, 2004.

## Chapter 12—*KSM Ascendant*

1. KSM's role in organizing the retreat from Afghanistan was detailed by captured jihadis. These accounts are memorialized in various Joint Task Force Guantánamo Detainee Assessment Briefs (author copies).
2. For more on the history of these sorts of groups, see Stephen Tankel, "Lashkar-e-Taiba: Past Operations and Future Prospects" (Washington, D.C.: New America Foundation, April 2011). Lashkar-e-Taiba later became infamous for staging the deadly attacks in Mumbai, India, in 2008. Tankel's book, *Storming the World Stage: The Story of Lashkar-e-Taiba* (New York:

Columbia University Press, 2011), incorporates this paper and provides a definitive account of Lashkar-e-Taiba's founding, growth, and operations.

3. KSM family members, author interviews, 2002, 2003, 2010.
4. The Pearl Project, *The Truth Left Behind: Inside the Kidnapping and Murder of Daniel Pearl* (Washington, D.C.: The Center for Public Integrity, 2011).
5. Department of Defense, "Summary of José Padilla's Activities with Al Qaeda," contained in correspondence with the Department of Justice, May 28, 2004, author copy.
6. Joint Task Force Guantánamo, Detainee Assessment Brief, December 8, 2006.
7. http://www.9-11commission.gov/report/911Report_Ch5.htm.
8. Transcripts of the interrogation of Mohammed Jabarah.
9. Jack Roche, author telephone interview, 2011.
10. Joint Task Force Guantánamo Combatant Status Review Tribunal for Saifullah Paracha, December 24, 2004, author copy.
11. Senior Sindh provincial police official, author interview.
12. Knowledgeable American intelligence source, author interview. This account is different from some others, notably in identifying KSM's accomplices, but rings true given the more general descriptions offered otherwise and KSM's heavy reliance on his relatives for sensitive work. The Pearl Project, for example, identifies the accomplices as Baluchi—the ethnicity of KSM's nephews.
13. Pearl Project, *The Truth Left Behind.*

## Chapter 13—*In Plain Sight*

1. Memo sent to all FBI offices by the New York bin Laden unit, April 13, 2001, author copy.
2. Ty Fairman, author interview, 2011.
3. Hussain Baloch, KSM's uncle, author interview.
4. Don Van Natta, Jr., and Desmond Butler, "How Tiny Swiss Cellphone Chips Helped Track Global Terror Web," *New York Times*, March 4, 2004. The *Times* originally broke this story. It has been elaborated upon since then, and details of the surveillance were revealed in European courts.
5. Participants in the interrogation and Department of Justice documents, author copies.
6. Joint Task Force Guantánamo, Detainee Assessment Briefs.
7. Author interview, 2002.
8. Yosri Fouda and Nick Fielding, *Masterminds of Terror: The Truth Behind the Most Devastating Terrorist Attack the World Has Ever Seen* (New York: Arcade Publishing, 2003), 22–27; 105–10.

9. Fouda and Fielding, *Masterminds of Terror*, 114.
10. Suskind, *The One Percent Doctrine*, 139.
11. Senior Sindh provincial police official, author interview.
12. Joint Task Force Guantánamo, Combatant Status Review Tribunal, summary of evidence.

## Chapter 14—*Betrayal*

1. Author interview, Pakistan, November 2002.
2. Senior intelligence operative, author interview, Washington, D.C., 2011.
3. The *Limburg* was saved by its modern, double-hull design. A tanker with a capacity of more than 500,000 barrels, the ship stayed afloat and leaked just 90,000 barrels of oil as a result of the attack by bomb-laden speedboats. Al-Nashiri, at his tribunal at Guantánamo, said almost comically that he knew the men involved in both attacks and might have given them money that originated with Osama bin Laden, but he thought he was investing in fishing boats—or perhaps it was a wedding gift; Joint Task Force Guantánamo Combatant Status Review Tribunal, March 14, 2007, author copy.
4. Senior UAE official, 2003, author interview.
5. Author copy.
6. Abdul Aziz Ali (Ali Abdul Aziz Ali's father), author interviews, Kuwait, 2002, 2010.
7. Most of the account of Ali's activities is drawn from his 2006 Detainee Assessment Brief and his 2008 Combatant Status Review Tribunal, both conducted by the Joint Task Force Guantánamo. Corroborating details were obtained from other Detainee Assessment Briefs.
8. Except for small amounts provided by the families of the hijackers, virtually all the money spent by the hijackers in preparation for the 9/11 plot was funneled to them by electronic transfers from Ali and al-Hawsawi in the United Arab Emirates. The total was less than $300,000, according to the financial investigation conducted by the FBI. Almost all that was spent on flight training and living expenses.
9. Joint Task Force Guantánamo Combatant Status Review Tribunal, November 26, 2004. Paracha said later that the money was an investment in a proposed production deal that was never realized.
10. FBI FD-302s on the interview with Abdul Hakim Murad, May 1995, author copy. The housing was usually for the associates, not Basit, who preferred to stay at hotels. He told his Manila Air accomplice, Abdul Hakim Murad, that he didn't get along with Abdul Karim and preferred not to

spend time with him. Another brother, a schoolteacher who lived in Quetta, also provided lodging for Basit's associates upon request.

11. A senior ISI officer said that almost everyone they arrested seemed to know Mukhtar, even though most of them didn't know one another; author interview, November 2002.
12. Senior U.S. government official, author interview, August 2011.
13. Author interviews, Pakistan, 2002.
14. Joint Task Force Guantánamo Detainee Assessment Brief, 2006. A letter he had written advising others on preparations for bombing hotels in Karachi was found at the safe house where his children had been taken into custody. No one had a clear idea what it said until he translated his personal code after he was captured.
15. Senior intelligence operative, author interview, Washington, D.C., 2011.
16. Author interview, Pakistan, 2002.
17. The name of and other details about the informant have been withheld at the CIA's request. The agency says that he has been targeted by Al Qaeda and that if his real name was revealed he and his family would be put at risk and they would have to be relocated again.

    This account is drawn from multiple author interviews with KSM's relatives during 2010 and 2011, and from interviews with a senior American intelligence officer and an American intelligence operative, both during 2011. Key aspects of this account were further corroborated by author interviews with senior government officials.
18. Senior CIA official, author interview, 2011.
19. George Tenet, *At the Center of the Storm: My Years at the CIA* (New York: HarperCollins, 2007), 251.
20. Senior government official, author interview, August 2011.
21. Joint Task Force Guantánamo Combatant Status Review Tribunal for Mustafa al-Hawsawi, March 21, 2007.
22. Ibid.
23. Senior Pakistani government official, author interview, May 2011.
24. Tenet, *At the Center of the Storm*, 252.

## Chapter 15—*In Captivity*

1. Christina Lamb, "Was Khalid Arrested Where the FBI Said He Was?" *Sunday Times* (London), March 9, 2003.
2. The man, Adil Qadoos, was later court-martialed and sentenced to ten years in prison.
3. CIA senior official, background briefing, July 21, 2004.

4. Author copy.
5. Author interview, 2003.
6. Author interview, Washington, D.C., 2010.
7. Department of Justice, Office of the Inspector General, "A Review of the FBI's Involvement in and Observations of Detainee Interrogations in Guantánamo Bay, Afghanistan, and Iraq," May 2008.
8. A copy of the video was later obtained by *60 Minutes* producer Ira Rosen, who graciously shared it with us.
9. Central Intelligence Agency, "Detainee Reporting Pivotal for the War Against Al-Qa'ida," June 2005, author copy.
10. Department of Defense, Detainee Biographies, accessed at http://www.defense.gov/pdf/detaineebiographies1.pdf.
11. Senior FBI official, author interview, 2011.
12. Author interview, 2010.
13. Ibid.

## CHAPTER 16—*The Black Sites and Beyond*

1. An exquisitely detailed set of memos from the Department of Justice, Office of Legal Counsel, authorized the use of the specific methods as well as the conditions under which they could be employed. The first memo, signed by Jay S. Bybee, an assistant attorney general, was written in August of 2002. It specifically cites the origin of the interrogation procedures in army torture-resistance manuals.
2. Author interview, 2011.
3. International Committee of the Red Cross, "ICRC Report on the Treatment of Fourteen 'High Value Detainees' in CIA Custody," February 2007. This remarkable document, first brought to light by Mark Danner writing in the *New York Review of Books*, is based on interviews conducted with the fourteen residents of the black sites who were sent to Guantánamo in 2006. In summary, the ICRC said: "The ICRC wishes to underscore that the consistency of the detailed allegations provided separately by each of the fourteen adds particular weight to the information provided below. The general term 'ill-treatment' has been used throughout the following section; however, it should in no way be understood as minimizing the severity of the conditions and treatment to which the detainees were subjected. Indeed...the ICRC clearly considers that the allegations of the fourteen include descriptions of treatment and interrogation techniques—singly or in combination—that amounted to torture and/or cruel, inhuman or degrading treatment."

4. Central Intelligence Agency, "Detainee Reporting Pivotal for the War Against Al-Qa'ida," June 2005, author copy.
5. Ibid.
6. Forty seconds, according to the Office of Legal Counsel memos.
7. Two senior intelligence operatives, author interviews, 2011. The female officer routinely visited the black sites. She was not well liked by many of those who worked with her.
8. Senior intelligence operative, author interview, 2011.
9. International Committee of the Red Cross, "ICRC Report."
10. Author interview, 2011.
11. Joint Task Force Guantánamo Combatant Status Review Tribunal for Khalid Sheikh Mohammed, March 10, 2007, author copy. A verbatim transcript of the tribunal is included in the appendix.
12. Author copy.
13. Author interview, 2006.
14. Author interview, 2011.
15. Senior Department of Defense prosecutor, author interview, 2011.
16. Author copies.
17. Joint Task Force Guantánamo Combatant Status Review Tribunal for Khalid Sheikh Mohammed, March 10, 2007, author copy.
18. Ibid.
19. Former attorney general Michael Mukasey complained in a 2011 speech that the exercise room next door to KSM's cell had the same elliptical machine as did his gym when he was attorney general.
20. Michael Isikoff, "How Profile of bin Laden Courier Led CIA to Its Target," MSNBC.com, May 4, 2011. There are numerous accounts of the CIA's interest in al-Kuwaiti that were confirmed by author interviews. Isikoff's is among the best.
21. Scott Shane and Charlie Savage, "Bin Laden Raid Revives Debate on Value of Torture," *New York Times*, May 3, 2011.
22. Isikoff, "How Profile of bin Laden Courier Led CIA."

# SELECTED BIBLIOGRAPHY

Bergen, Peter L. *The Longest War: The Enduring Conflict Between America and Al-Qaeda*. New York: Free Press, 2011.

Coll, Steve. *Ghost Wars: The Secret History of the CIA, Afghanistan, and bin Laden, from the Soviet Invasion to September 10, 2001*. New York: Penguin Press, 2004.

Fouda, Yosri, and Nick Fielding. *Masterminds of Terror: The Truth Behind the Most Devastating Terrorist Attack the World Has Ever Seen*. New York: Arcade Publishing, 2003.

Graff, Garrett M. *The Threat Matrix: The FBI at War in the Age of Global Terror*. New York: Little, Brown, 2011.

Gunaratna, Rohan, and Khuram Iqbal. *Pakistan: Terrorism Ground Zero*. London: Reaktion Books, 2011.

Kessler, Ronald. *The Terrorist Watch: Inside the Desperate Race to Stop the Next Attack*. New York: Three Rivers Press, 2008.

Kiriakou, John, with Michael Ruby. *The Reluctant Spy: My Secret Life in the CIA's War on Terror*. New York: Bantam Books, 2010.

Lance, Peter. *Triple Cross: How bin Laden's Master Spy Penetrated the CIA, the Green Berets, and the FBI—and Why Patrick Fitzgerald Failed to Stop Him*. New York: Regan Books, 2006.

Lieven, Anatol. *Pakistan: A Hard Country*. New York: Public Affairs, 2011.

Mayer, Jane. *The Dark Side: The Inside Story of How the War on Terror Turned into a War on American Ideals*. New York: Doubleday, 2008.

McDermott, Terry. *Perfect Soldiers: The Hijackers—Who They Were, Why They Did It*. New York: HarperCollins, 2005.

Al-Mdaires, Falah Abdullah. *Islamic Extremism in Kuwait: From the Muslim Brotherhood to al-Qaeda and Other Islamist Political Groups.* London: Routledge, 2010.

Reeve, Simon. *The New Jackals: Ramzi Yousef, Osama bin Laden, and the Future of Terrorism.* Boston: Northeastern University Press, 1999.

Ressa, Maria A. *Seeds of Terror: An Eyewitness Account of Al-Qaeda's Newest Center of Operations in Southeast Asia.* New York: Free Press, 2004.

Scheuer, Michael. *Through Our Enemies' Eyes: Osama bin Laden, Radical Islam, and the Future of America.* Dulles, Va.: Potomac Books, 2002.

Shahzad, Syed Saleem. *Inside Al-Qaeda and the Taliban: Beyond bin Laden and 9/11.* Sydney: Palgrave Macmillan, 2011.

Shenon, Philip. *The Commission: The Uncensored History of the 9/11 Investigation.* New York: Twelve, 2008.

Soufan, Ali H., with Daniel Freedman. *The Black Banners: The Inside Story of 9/11 and the War Against al-Qaeda.* New York: W. W. Norton, 2011.

Suskind, Ron. *The One Percent Doctrine: Deep Inside America's Pursuit of Its Enemies Since 9/11.* New York: Simon & Schuster, 2006.

Tenet, George. *At the Center of the Storm: My Years at the CIA.* New York: HarperCollins, 2007.

Wright, Lawrence. *The Looming Tower: Al-Qaeda and the Road to 9/11.* New York: Alfred A. Knopf, 2006.

# INDEX

# ABOUT THE AUTHORS

Josh Meyer is the former chief terrorism reporter for the *Los Angeles Times* and has reported on international terrorism for more than a decade. His work, including contributions to the *Times*'s "Inside Al Qaeda" series, won numerous awards and was nominated for a Pulitzer Prize, and he has twice been part of teams at the newspaper that have won the Pulitzer Prize. Meyer is also a screenwriter and television producer who cocreated, wrote, and produced the network TV crime drama *Level 9*. He spent a total of twenty years at the *Times*, and currently is on the faculty of the Medill School of Journalism, where he is director of education and outreach for the groundbreaking Medill National Security Journalism Initiative, based in Washington, D.C.

Terry McDermott is the author of *Perfect Soldiers* (2005) and *101 Theory Drive* (2010). His work has appeared in *The New Yorker, The Wilson Quarterly, Columbia Journalism Review*, the *Los Angeles Times Magazine*, and *Pacific Magazine*. McDermott has worked at eight newspapers, most recently at the *Los Angeles Times*, where he was a national correspondent for ten years.